The Only Self-Help Book You'll Ever Need

— FROM —
ANXIETY
— TO —
AWAKENING

11 INSIGHTS THAT TRANSFORM WORRY INTO WISDOM AND FEAR INTO FREEDOM

JAKE YANITZ RUBIN

From Anxiety to Awakening
© 2025 Jake Yanitz Rubin

First edition published by Inner Path Press

Disclaimer:
This book is not intended to replace professional medical advice, diagnosis, or treatment. If you are experiencing severe anxiety or other mental health issues, please consult a licensed healthcare provider.

For Irin, Eden, and Mia

You are my heart, my inspiration, and my greatest teachers.
I love you endlessly. Now, forever, and more each day.

For Paula and Silviu

Your love and support gave me the freedom to find my own
way. Thank you for being exactly who I needed you to be.

YOU ARE HERE TO DISCOVER
THE DEEPEST TRUTH ABOUT YOURSELF.

WHAT IF EVERYTHING YOU'VE BEEN TOLD ABOUT ANXIETY IS WRONG?

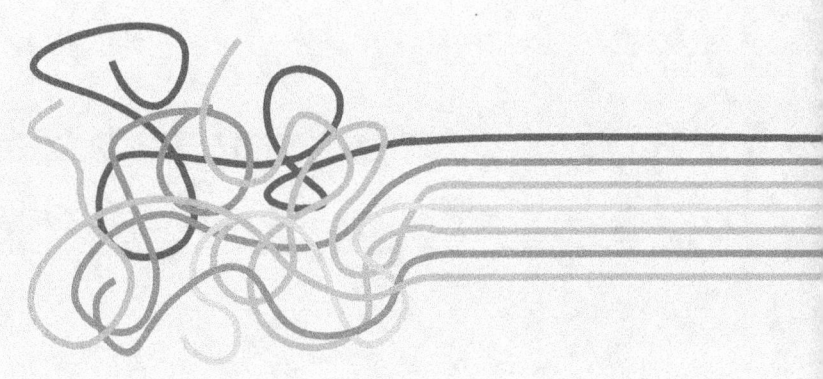

SPOILER ALERT: IT IS.

WHY THIS BOOK IS DIFFERENT

This isn't your typical self-help book.

What you're about to discover in this book is the natural antidote to anxiety.

The truths within these pages have the power to dissolve anxiety completely, like sunlight melting away the morning fog, awakening you to the truth of who you truly are.

I know that might sound like a bold claim.

Maybe even impossible.

If you're skeptical, I get it.

If I were reading this years ago, I would've thought the same thing.

Most of my life, I was deeply skeptical. If something wasn't backed by science, I didn't believe it. I needed proof. I needed logic. And if you feel the same way, I understand. Skepticism is healthy. In fact, I encourage it.

But here's the thing: science is now confirming what ancient traditions have known for thousands of years. And more importantly, you can verify this for yourself.

This book is not about sugarcoating things or regurgitating tired old advice you would find in the thousands of other anxiety self-help books out there.

Instead, it's about challenging your longest-held beliefs and reconnecting you with the deepest essence of who you are.

Unlike most self-help books, this book has no exercises.

Zero exercises.

There are no checklists, tools, or techniques you need to master.

Why?

Because you're not the problem.

Because transforming anxiety isn't about doing more.

It's not about fixing or improving yourself.

It's not a task or a skill.

Transforming anxiety is about being.

It's recognizing a place within you, untouched by the anxiety itself.

True transformation doesn't come from doing more, it comes from seeing more clearly.

This book helps you realize the truths already within you, requiring only your openness and willingness to explore new perspectives.

All that's required is that you read the book and allow yourself to reflect on it.

By the end of this book, you'll not only understand anxiety, you'll see it as your greatest ally in becoming free.

This book isn't about curing anxiety, because anxiety doesn't need to be cured.

It's about understanding it, transforming your relationship with it, and learning to use it as fuel for your awakening.

Note: This book is designed to be read from cover to cover during your first experience.

Instead of exercises, this book is centered around eleven Insights, each one guiding you progressively from anxiety to awakening.

After each Insight, you'll find a series of Reflections designed to deepen your understanding and make the concepts more applicable to your daily life.

As you move through the book, the Insights and Reflections build on one another, creating a powerful transformation.

Once you've completed the book, feel free to revisit the Reflections that resonate most strongly with you—they will continue to deepen your understanding over time.

Throughout this book, you'll notice I use various terms: Source, Infinite Awareness, Supreme Intelligence, and Life, to describe the indescribable.

Each one points to the same unnameable presence, the boundless energy underlying all existence.

Choose any word that feels most meaningful to you, or none at all.

Take your time with this book.

Let each Reflection meet you where you are and carry you forward, one step at a time.

As you do, know that this journey is not new.

Through my direct work with my clients, I've seen firsthand how they've released anxiety and embraced a completely new way of being, grounded in lasting inner peace.

I didn't write this book for me.

It was written *through* me, for you.

And I'm confident that what I'm about to share with you will absolutely transform your life.

If you've been fighting anxiety, it's time to stop.

Not because you're giving up, but because you're stepping into a deeper truth:

Anxiety isn't here to destroy you.

It's here to wake you up.

It's no accident that you're reading these words right now.

Something brought you here, whether it was curiosity, synchronicity, or a quiet nudge from within.

Trust that pull.

Trust that this is your journey.

You're about to uncover a transformation that has always been waiting for you.

Your transformation isn't coming someday. It starts right now.

In fact, it's already happening.

CONTENTS

INSIGHT #3: WHEN YOU STOP FIGHTING LIFE AND YOURSELF, YOU START LIVING

INSIGHT #4: FREEDOM BEGINS WHERE CONTROL ENDS

INSIGHT #5: THE EGO IS A CAGE—AND YOU'RE HOLDING THE KEY

INSIGHT #6: THE WAY YOU LOVE YOURSELF IS THE WAY YOU LOVE YOUR LIFE

INSIGHT #7: LIFE IS HAPPENING FOR YOU, NOT TO YOU

INSIGHT #8: YOU ARE EVERYTHING AND NO-THING

INSIGHT #9: WHAT YOU ARE CAN NEVER DIE

INSIGHT #10: EVERYTHING IS INTERCONNECTED

INSIGHT #11: YOU'VE NEVER SEEN REALITY—NOT EVEN ONCE

YOUR JOURNEY STARTS HERE:

ANXIETY IS NOT
WHAT YOU THINK IT IS

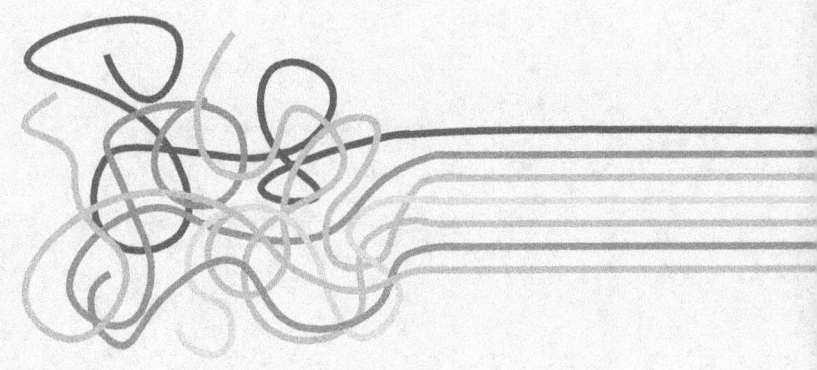

ANXIETY IS NOT THE ENEMY—
IT'S YOUR TEACHER

If you're feeling overwhelmed, stuck, or even hopeless, you're not alone.

I was there too, for *decades* on end.

For years, I saw anxiety as my enemy. It pushed me, controlled me, drained me. But over time, I began to see and understand the truth: anxiety wasn't a problem. It was trying to show me something.

For so many of us, anxiety feels like an inescapable storm, a relentless pressure that tightens its grip no matter how hard we try to break free.

It's exhausting, disorienting, and at times, unbearable.

But what if I told you that anxiety isn't the enemy you think it is?

What if it's not a flaw in your mind or a problem in your life that needs fixing?

What if anxiety is something else entirely?

This may be surprising or even refreshing to hear, but it's the truth:

Anxiety is *not* a mental disorder.

It's not an illness, a weakness, or a failure.

It's not some defect for a doctor to diagnose and medicate out of existence.

Anxiety is a signal—a natural and universal part of the human condition.

As a clinical hypnotherapist, I've worked with countless clients over the years, and one thing has become strikingly clear: almost every issue they bring to me—whether it's stress, fear, self-doubt, or even physical symptoms like chronic pain or insomnia—has anxiety at its root. It doesn't matter where they're from, what they do, or how their life looks on the outside— anxiety is the force that keeps them stuck. But this isn't because anxiety is some rare defect.

It's because anxiety is universal.

You've probably heard it before:

"Anxiety runs in my family."

Maybe you've even said it yourself, or had someone say it to you. And yes, growing up in an anxious household or around anxious parents can make anxiety feel more pronounced. Environmental factors, family dynamics, and learned behaviors certainly shape how anxiety shows up in your life.

But here's the deeper truth: anxiety doesn't "run in families" because of some rare genetic flaw.

It "runs in families" because *it runs in humanity*.

Anxiety is woven into the fabric of being human.

It is a natural part of the mind's attempt to grasp for control in a world that is inherently uncertain. Whether your family is highly anxious or seemingly carefree, anxiety is something we all experience.

It's not a rare defect—it's a shared part of being human.

And yet, the system we trust to help us treats it as a problem to be fixed.

Here's the truth: your doctor is trained to categorize you and give you a prescription.

That's the framework they've been taught, and it's designed to treat symptoms, not address the root cause.

But it goes deeper than that.

The health system as we know it isn't designed to help you heal—it's designed to keep you dependent.

There's a monetary interest in managing your symptoms, labeling you, and keeping you on medication and in treatment for as long as possible.

That's the business model.

For some, medication provides temporary relief, and that's okay. But real freedom comes from seeing anxiety clearly, not just numbing it.

So, let me ask you this: if any of these solutions truly worked, why are we more anxious than ever?

Why do millions—if not billions—of people all around the world still feel stuck despite endless medications, treatments, and therapies?

It's because anxiety isn't a problem to be eradicated—it's a message.

Anxiety is the alarm clock of the soul, jolting you out of autopilot and into the clarity of awakening.

It's important to understand that anxiety is not the same as fear. Fear is an instinctual response to an immediate threat—a necessary survival mechanism that helps us escape danger in the moment.

Anxiety, however, is anticipatory.

It's not about what's happening right now; it's about the mind's projections of what might go wrong.

Anxiety arises when the mind clings to control and certainty in a world that is inherently uncertain. It's the friction created when the truth of who you are comes into conflict with the stories, fears, and illusions of the mind.

For too long, we've been taught to view anxiety as a problem to be solved, a defect to be hidden, or a battle to be fought. But none of these approaches truly work, do they?

That's because anxiety is not a problem—*it's an invitation.*

It's life calling you to pause, to question, and to see beyond the limitations of the mind into the truth of your being. Without anxiety, many of us would never stop long enough to examine the beliefs and attachments that keep us stuck. Anxiety is not here to harm you—it's here to guide you.

This doesn't mean the discomfort of anxiety isn't real. It doesn't mean your experience of it is invalid.

But it does mean that anxiety is not a mistake.

In fact, it's the very friction that will lead to your transformation.

Transformation is inherent in the friction—like pressure creating a diamond, or soil nourishing a seed.

It's not just a possibility; it's the natural outcome when you embrace the process.

When you stop resisting it, suppressing it, or running from it, you begin to see anxiety for what it truly is: the gateway to awakening.

Anxiety isn't the enemy. It's your teacher.

It's not a flaw. It's the beginning of freedom.

ANXIETY IS NOT YOURS TO OWN

Let's clear one thing up right away: you don't *have* anxiety.

Anxiety is not something you own, it's not something you *are,* and it's definitely not something you need to carry like some badge of honor.

I hear it from new clients all the time:

> » *"I've had anxiety my whole life."*

> » *"My anxiety won't let me do that."*

> » *"I have anxiety."*

> » *"I'm an anxious person."*

No, you don't. And no, you're not.

Anxiety is not *yours.* It doesn't belong to you. And it's not a defining feature of who you are.

Here's where you start:

Stop saying "my anxiety."

From now on, let's *completely* drop that phrase.

Every time you say "my," you're claiming something that doesn't belong to you.

You're identifying with it and reinforcing the false idea that it's a permanent part of who you are.

I understand how deeply this identity may have shaped you up until now. But don't worry, I'm here to guide you through this shift.

Now, let's take the next step:

Call it what it really is: nervous energy.

Or simply, *the* anxiety.

This subtle change matters more than you think.

Words carry *tremendous* power.

By shifting how you speak about it, you begin to loosen its grip and change how you see yourself.

Here's the truth: anxiety isn't some rare disorder or personal defect. It's not a badge of honor or a scarlet letter. It's not a personality trait.

Anxiety is not your identity.

It's energy.

It's temporary, and it's passing through you. It's not yours to possess.

Imagine if you treated hunger the same way people treat anxiety.

You wouldn't say, "I have a hunger disorder" every time your stomach growled. You'd feel the signal, recognize the need, and eat. Hunger is a survival mechanism that lets you know your body needs fuel.

Anxiety works the same way. It's a signal, a natural response designed to alert you that something in your life needs attention or alignment. It's not here to punish you; it's here to guide you.

Anxiety isn't a personality trait. It's not your identity. It's not your shadow, your label, or some permanent part of who you are.

Let me say it again: anxiety is simply energy.

It's an innate part of life's system, existing to direct your attention to beliefs that are not in alignment with your deepest truth.

It comes.

And it goes.

But here's the problem: somewhere along the way, society turned anxiety into something it's not.

We labeled it, pathologized it, and started handing out pills for it like candy.

We made it a "condition," and millions of people bought into the lie.

For decades, I bought into it too.

We were taught to treat anxiety like an illness, a defect, something broken that needs fixing.

It's not.

Anxiety is no different than hunger.

Hunger, like anxiety, is a signal. It tells you something needs attention.
When you're hungry, you don't label it as a defect, or panic that something is wrong with you.

You don't sit around thinking, "Why do I have this hunger? How can I make it stop forever?" You don't try to medicate it out of existence.

You simply meet the need, and then you move on.

And like hunger, anxiety is influenced by what you feed it. Just as processed foods and empty calories can distort your hunger cues, past conditioning, constant negativity, fear-based media, and toxic environments can amplify and distort your anxiety signals.

The good news is that just as you can nourish your body with wholesome food to restore balance, you can nourish your mind in ways that calm anxiety and bring clarity. We'll explore this more in future chapters, but for now, know this: the anxiety you feel isn't who you are.

It's not something to own or identify with. Anxiety is not a flaw in who you are. It's a natural part of your humanity, calling for your attention. Instead of fearing it or fighting it, you can begin to understand it as a signal pointing to something deeper.

Remember, anxiety is just energy, sending you a signal. But instead of listening to that signal and addressing the root cause, we've been taught to fear it, fight it, and slap a label on it.

Why? Because we've been *conditioned*.

Society, culture, and family shaped the way you think, and the doctors we often trust to help us have been conditioned in much the same way.

They go to medical school and are taught to see anxiety as a defect, something to diagnose and medicate away. That's just what they've been trained to do.

But let me tell you a secret: some of the most anxious people I've ever met are doctors themselves.

In fact, a systematic review published in *The British Medical Journal* (BMJ) found that doctors experience anxiety at rates up to three times higher than the general public.

Let me say that again:

Doctors experience anxiety at rates *three hundred percent higher* than most people.

Think about that for a second.

The very people diagnosing you with anxiety, telling you it's a disorder, and prescribing you pills are often drowning in their own anxiety.

They're stuck in the same mental traps you are, but they've been trained to see anxiety as a "problem" because that's what the system teaches them, and most of them don't question that.

And let's be honest: the system doesn't want you free from anxiety. There's no profit in that.

The truth is, anxiety isn't a problem. *It's your relationship with anxiety that's the problem.*

You've been taught to resist it, to suppress it, to try to escape it.

None of that works.

The more you resist anxiety, the stronger it gets.

The more you suppress it, the more it builds.

But here's the good news: you can change your relationship with anxiety.

When you stop seeing anxiety as a defect and start seeing it as a signal, everything begins to transform. Anxiety isn't here to harm you. It's here to guide you. It's here to point out the stories, beliefs, and attachments that are no longer serving you. It's here to show you where you're out of alignment with the truth of who you are.

Let me be clear: anxiety doesn't feel good. It's uncomfortable, intense, and overwhelming.

But just like hunger, that doesn't mean it's wrong. It doesn't mean it's a flaw.

Anxiety is the friction that sparks transformation.

Anxiety is the catalyst that pushes you to grow. Without it, you'd stay exactly where you are.

Anxiety isn't your enemy, it's your greatest teacher.

But you'll never understand that if you keep labeling it as a disorder.

If you keep wearing it like an identity,

If you keep saying, *"I have anxiety," "My anxiety,"* or *"I'm an anxious person,"* like it's something you'll carry forever.

Anxiety is *not* you.

It doesn't belong to you.

And it's not permanent.

What it is is temporary passing energy.

And when you learn to listen to it, instead of resisting it, it becomes one of your greatest teachers.

Here's the truth: anxiety arises when your mind tries to control what it can't. It's a survival mechanism designed to protect you, but it goes haywire when you let it run unchecked. The more your mind fights to control the uncontrollable, the stronger anxiety becomes.

But when you stop trying to control everything, when you surrender to the present moment, anxiety starts to dissolve.

Anxiety is not here to harm you. It's here to show you where your life is out of alignment.

It's not a defect.

It's a call to pay attention, to let go of control, and to embrace what's unfolding.

What if, instead of resisting it, you chose to listen?

YOU'RE NOT THE PROBLEM

But you are the solution.

You've been hypnotized—not by a therapist, but by the world around you.

From the moment you were born, your parents, your culture, and your education all programmed you. They handed you beliefs, fears, and expectations, layer by layer, until you couldn't tell where they ended and you began.

You didn't choose this conditioning, but it became your reality—*until now.*

It's not your fault.

It's simply the world we're born into.

But there comes a point when this programming no longer fits.

You start to feel trapped or restless, as if life is happening *to* you instead of through you.

That feeling shows up as anxiety. A quiet tension you can't shake. A loud and overwhelming fear that something is fundamentally wrong.

I know how that feels.

For decades, I lived with an invisible weight I couldn't quite name.

On the surface, everything seemed fine.

But underneath, I was always bracing for impact, like a storm was on the horizon and I had to be ready.

I tried the usual prescription medications, spent years in talk therapy, and read countless self-help books on anxiety. Nothing truly made a difference.

Anxiety became a constant companion, fueled by the endless hum of a fight-or-flight response that never switched off.

But what most people don't realize about anxiety is this: it's not a flaw.

It's not a sign of weakness or failure.

Anxiety is the body's attempt to protect you, even when there's nothing immediate to protect you from. It's an overreaction to a threat that isn't real, or to a future you can't control.

But when your mind and body are stuck in this cycle, it takes over everything. The tension builds, the worry grows, and it feels like you're trapped in a loop you can't escape.

One night, that cycle overwhelmed me completely.

My heart raced, my chest tightened, and I could barely breathe.

It felt like the walls were closing in.

I thought, *This is it. Something's wrong. I'm not going to make it.*

That night ended in the emergency room.

As I lay there, surrounded by the relentless beeping of machines monitoring my irregular heartbeat and dangerously high blood pressure, I realized something: *If I don't take control of my mind, this will kill me.*

That was the breaking point.

What followed wasn't just a search for relief, it was a search for understanding.

I wanted to know why this was happening and how I could stop it.

What I found was something I never expected: the realization that the way I saw myself and the world was completely skewed.

Anxiety isn't just pointing to a problem, it's inviting you to awaken to a deeper truth.

Imagine a bird sitting in a cage.

She feels trapped, staring at the bars, convinced there's no way out.

But what she doesn't realize is that *the cage has no back.*

She is free to fly the moment she turns herself around and looks in a new direction.

Even more than that, the cage itself is an illusion.

She has always been free.

The cage feels real because she's spent her whole life staring at it, believing it's solid, unbreakable, and all there is.

But it's not.

That's what anxiety is like.

It keeps you focused on the bars, on the fears, the doubts, and the what-ifs, so you can't see the freedom that's been there all along.

Awakening to that freedom takes more than just looking.

It takes letting go of all the old programming.

It takes pulling yourself out of the autopilot you've been on most of your life.

Because freedom and clarity don't happen while you're still soaking in the false beliefs and programming you've carried for years.

It's like trying to light a match that's wet.

It doesn't matter how much friction you apply.

The spark is there, but it won't ignite.

You were born with the spark.

The fire of awakening has always been inside of you.

But like the match, you need two things for it to light: resistance and readiness.

Resistance comes from the friction of life's challenges.

Pain, struggle, and suffering.

These aren't punishments.

They're the striking motion, the friction that creates the conditions for the fire of your awakening.

But readiness?

Readiness is up to you.

It's about drying out the dampness of the old programming: the fears, the doubts, the false identities and narratives you've been holding onto.

The fire can't ignite when you're still soaked in those stories.

Letting go of them clears the way for the spark to catch.

Awakening isn't about achieving something new.

It's about peeling back the layers of what isn't true.

It's about stepping out of the loop of fight-or-flight, fear, and limitation.

It's about seeing clearly for the first time.

This is why I wrote this book.

Because I know firsthand how heavy life can feel when you're stuck in that anxiety loop, and I know how liberating it is to step outside of it.

And I want that for you.

I want you to know that the freedom you're searching for isn't something you have to create.

It's already within you.

Right now, anxiety might make you feel like that bird, staring at the bars and wondering if you'll ever be free.

Or maybe you feel like the match, waiting for the moment you'll finally catch fire.

But here's the truth: the cage was never real, and the fire has always been inside of you.

This book is here to help you turn around and see the truth.

It's here to help you dry out the dampness of that old programming, understand the signal anxiety is sending, and begin looking in a new direction.

You don't need to have all the answers right now.

You don't need to know exactly how things will change.

All you need is a willingness to consider that there's more to this thing called life than you've understood so far.

So let me ask you this:

Are you ready to see things differently?

Are you ready to stop fighting and start waking up?

FEAR IS THE OLDEST
HYPNOSIS IN THE WORLD

By now, you've started to see it.

The way beliefs are handed to you.

The way fear is planted, reinforced, repeated—until it feels like it's yours.

But what if it's not?

What if fear was just another hypnotic suggestion—one you never chose?

For millennia, organized religion has relied on fear as its foundation.

Concepts like hell, sin, and eternal punishment weren't created to free people—they were created to control them.

They instill a deep, insidious fear of the unknown: fear of death, fear of judgment, and perhaps most damaging, fear of not being good enough.

And once fear takes hold, it doesn't just shape your beliefs—it shapes you.

It tells you how to live. What to say. What to think.

These systems place themselves as the gatekeepers to salvation, making fear the dominant motivator for behavior.

And when something is repeated enough times, it doesn't feel like control—it feels like truth.

But here's what no one tells you: fear is not truth.

Fear is a script—one you may have been following without realizing it.

And that script runs deep.

When fear is the foundation, it builds a life that is small, reactive, and obedient.

It convinces you that questioning is dangerous. That obedience is safety. That stepping outside of the system means stepping into the unknown—and that the unknown is something to fear.

But fear doesn't liberate. It confines.

And like any hypnotic suggestion, it only works as long as you believe it.

If you've found comfort, community, or meaning in your faith, that's real.

Spirituality in any form can be a powerful source of connection.

But it's important to separate the essence of spirituality—the love, the peace, the stillness—from the fear-based structures that have been used to control and divide.

The systems that have told you to fear were not designed to awaken you.

They were designed to keep you dependent—on doctrines, rituals, and intermediaries that claim to stand between you and the truth.

But here's the thing:

You don't need an intermediary to be connected to the divine.

You don't need permission to think for yourself.

You don't need fear to keep you safe.

And most importantly—you don't have to believe everything you were taught.

Because fear only has power as long as you feed it.

So, ask yourself:

"Who benefits from my fear?"

"Who gains something from keeping me small, afraid, and compliant?"

And now, consider this:

What might your life feel like if you saw that fear for what it truly is—conditioning, not truth?

Because you were not born afraid.

Fear is learned. And what is learned can be unlearned.

The next time fear whispers in your ear, pause.

Ask yourself, "Is this my fear, or was it given to me?"

Because the moment you see the script, you are no longer controlled by it.

And that is how de-hypnosis begins.

ANXIETY CANNOT
EXIST WITHIN THE TRUTH

This book is about sharing the truth with you.

Not *my* truth.

Not a subjective truth or a perspective rooted in my experience.

But *the* truth—the truth that is universal, unwavering, and timeless.

You may have spent much of your life hearing different "truths"—beliefs passed down through culture, society, or the opinions of others.

Perhaps you've even held onto ideas that seemed true because they were comforting or made sense in the moment. But believing in something is very different from *knowing* it.

The truth I speak of is not up for debate.

It is not a matter of opinion, nor can it be owned or controlled by any one person or entity. It is not something that changes with time, perspective, or circumstance.

It simply *is*.

Knowing this truth does not rely on external validation or proof, because it is not outside of you; it is something you *experience* as undeniable.

Belief is fragile. It can be shaken, questioned, or discarded in the face of life's challenges. Belief relies on words, on ideas, on faith that what you are told *might* be true.

But knowing?

Knowing is unshakable. Knowing does not come from your mind. It is not dependent on external proof or validation.

Knowing comes from within, from an inner recognition that transcends thought. It is the moment you no longer need to believe, because you *experience* it as truth.

The truth does not need to be learned.

It simply needs to be revealed.

Learning is what we do when we acquire something new—a skill, a fact, a concept. But the truth is not something you acquire, because it has always been there. It is not hidden somewhere outside of you, waiting to be found. Instead, it lies quietly beneath the noise of the mind, like the clear sky behind the clouds. To reveal it, you do not need to add anything; you need only to *see through* what is in the way.

The truth is what remains when all else falls away.

This is what I want for you as you move through this book. My intention is not to present you with concepts to debate or philosophies to memorize.

I'm not asking you to believe *me* or to accept my words at face value. Instead, I want you to experience these truths for yourself—to move beyond belief into a space where you *know* them.

Each chapter in this book guides you toward that direct experience.

This is not a theoretical journey.

It is a deeply experiential one.

You will not be asked to *think* your way to awakening, but to recognize it—to see it, feel it, and know it as the truth that has always been within you.

The structure of this book reflects that intention. While it can and should be read in order the first time, it is not a linear process.

Awakening is not about climbing steps toward some distant goal. It is about realizing what is already here—in this moment. At times, a single sentence may stop you in your tracks, revealing something you had always known, but never seen. Other times, you may need to return to a Reflection again and again, each time peeling back another layer of illusion.

I encourage you to take your time.

Let the words settle within you.

Allow space for stillness, and for recognition to arise.

Do not rush to understand with your mind.

Instead, tune into the part of you that already *knows*—the awareness behind the thoughts, the presence that never changes.

This book is not about finding answers outside of yourself. It is about realizing the truth that has always been within you.

My role is not to give you something you don't already have, but simply to open your eyes— to guide you to a place where belief falls away, and all that remains is the truth—unshakable, undeniable, and yours to know forever.

And once your eyes are open, you can never unsee the truth.

YOU ARE NOT YOUR MIND, THOUGHTS, OR EMOTIONS

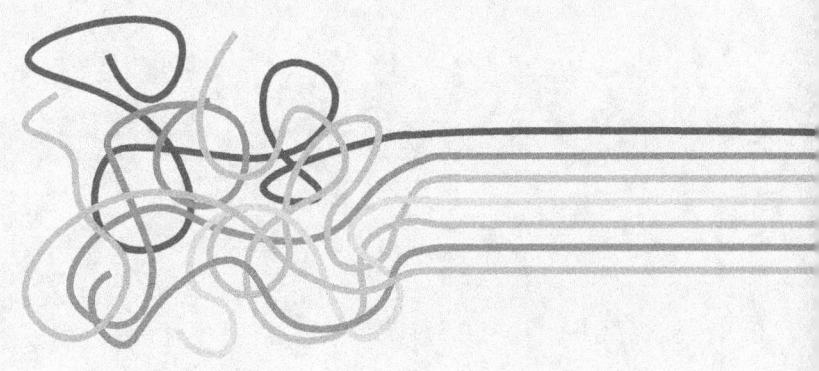

YOU THINK WAY TOO MUCH

You know what I know about you for sure? You're an overthinker. You think way too much, and you think all the time.

You spend your life lost in thought.

How do I know? Because I used to live like that too. Before my awakening, my mind was going nonstop, all the time.

And every single client I've ever helped overcome anxiety has struggled with overthinking as well.

Here's the thing: an overactive mind is the perfect breeding ground for anxiety.

Your mind is like a wild horse.

And up until now, it's been running your life.

It's pulling you in a hundred directions, reacting to every trigger, bolting into fears that aren't real, and dragging you into distractions that don't serve you. The wild horse doesn't stop to ask where it's going or whether its panic is justified.

It just moves, fast and unrestrained.

Most of the time, you don't even realize you're just along for the ride, whether you want to be or not.

It takes off before you even have a say.

This is the nature of an untamed mind: impulsive, restless, and chaotic.

But here's what changes everything:

You are not the horse.

You are its owner, trainer, and rider.

The horse works for you. Not the other way around.

This is the shift that begins to change your relationship with your mind. The mind is a force of incredible energy, but that energy is not who you are.

As you begin to watch, you might start to notice something strange: there's a part of you that isn't caught up in the thinking.

A part that is simply observing.

The more you watch, the more you sense a distance between you and your thoughts.

At first, the wild horse will resist being watched.

The mind will buck, try to pull you into its chaos, insist that you identify with it, and want to take you along for the ride.

It will tell you its fears are urgent, its worries are necessary, and its stories are true. But here's the key: You don't have to fight it. You don't need to wrestle the horse into submission. Your job at this point is simply to observe it.

Step off the horse, and let it run. Watch it bolt, wander, and drift. Don't judge it. Don't chase it. Just notice it. Like watching the current of a river, observe the thoughts that come and go, the feelings that rise and fall, and the impulses that fade as quickly as they appear.

This is how anxiety works. When the mind runs wild and unchecked, it drags you into fears and worries that feel overwhelming and all-consuming. But the moment you step back and watch, you begin to see anxiety for what it is: movement in the mind, not the truth of who you are. This separation is where your power begins.

When you begin to watch your mind, you start to see that your thoughts are just passing by, not who you are. This is where the journey begins—not by trying to control or tame the mind, but by learning to watch it.

Take this moment right now.

Notice the thoughts appearing in your mind. Watch how one thought leads to another. Watch how they try to pull your attention or create a sense of urgency. Don't react. Don't follow them. Just observe.

And then ask yourself, if I can watch these thoughts, who is the one watching?

That question takes you to a place deeper than the mind—a place of stillness and clarity where the wild horse begins to calm on its own. It's a place where you start to sense something beyond the movement of thought—something steady and unchanging.

You'll start to notice something extraordinary.

You are not the horse. You are not the current of the river.

You are the stillness on the bank, the observer watching it all unfold.

That stillness has always been there, waiting for you to notice.

Your only task for now is to observe. Let the horse run. Let the river flow. Watch without judgment, and see what happens.

This is the beginning of your freedom.

STOP BUYING WHAT
YOUR MIND IS SELLING

You've been watching the wild horse of your mind. Observing it. Noticing how it runs—how it reacts, pulls, and tries to take off in every direction.

But now, it's time to do more than just watch.

It's time to train it.

Because here's the thing: you don't have to follow it.

Your mind will keep trying to pull you into fear, doubt, and endless thinking. It will insist that every anxious thought needs your full attention. It will act like everything is urgent, demanding that you engage with every worst-case scenario it throws at you.

But you don't have to buy what your mind is selling.

Have you ever walked into a store and had a pushy salesperson latch onto you? Before you even know what you're looking for, they're in your face.

"Can I help you? What about this? This would be great for you. Here, try this one…"

Maybe at first, you engage. You explain that you're just looking.

But they don't stop. They keep pushing, keep insisting.

And eventually, you realize that reasoning with them is pointless.

So, what do you do?

You shut it down.

You look them in the eyes and say:

"No, thank you. I'm *not interested*."

And then you walk away.

This is exactly how you have to treat your mind sometimes.

Not every thought deserves your attention. Not every fear is worth engaging with. The mind will always try to pull you into its chaos, but you get to decide whether you follow.

When an anxious thought shows up—when your mind starts spiraling into *What if this goes wrong? What if I fail? What if something bad happens?*—you don't have to fight it.

Or maybe it's not just doubts—it's that familiar voice in your head, questioning you.

Who do you think you are to do this? You're not good enough. You're going to embarrass yourself. Just stay where it's safe.

You don't have to argue with it.

You don't have to explain yourself.

You don't even have to acknowledge it beyond a simple, firm response.

"No, thank you. I'm not interested. We're not going there."

Tell your mind: *I decide what I'm buying, and I'm not buying your bullshit right now.*

And then, you move forward.

This isn't about suppressing emotions or pretending thoughts don't exist. It's about realizing that not every thought is worth following.

Some thoughts are just noise. Some are old patterns trying to convince you that they're important. Some are just automatic scripts, playing on a loop, hoping you'll react.

But you don't have to.

You are the rider. You are the one holding the reins.

Remember, your horse works *for you*. Not the other way around.

And when you stop following every anxious thought, when you refuse to get pulled into every mental spiral, your wild horse starts to slow down.

It learns that you're in control. It stops reacting to every little thing.

And little by little, the noise in your mind begins to quiet.

So, take a moment now.

What anxious thoughts does your mind keep trying to sell you?

What stories does it keep spinning, hoping you'll take the bait?

And what would happen if, just for today, you didn't let go of the reins?

Because here's the truth: your mind may try to sell you, but *you* are the one who decides whether you're buying.

And the moment you see that … you're free.

YOU'RE NOT WHO
YOU'VE BEEN TOLD YOU ARE

One of the most liberating truths you can realize is this: the self-limiting beliefs you hold about yourself don't actually exist.

They are not real. They are illusions—constructs that you've been conditioned to accept as true. And yet, they shape your life. They shape your thoughts. They shape the way you hesitate, overthink, and hold yourself back.

Limitation creates fear. It creates anxiety. It wires the brain into hesitation, doubt, and avoidance. But what if none of it was ever true? What if the limits that seem so real were never real at all?

Think about it. If you were born without exposure to judgment, criticism, or societal conditioning, would you carry these beliefs? Would you inherently believe that you are not good enough? That you are incapable? Of course not. These beliefs were learned. And because they were learned, they can be *unlearned.*

You didn't come into this world thinking you weren't smart enough, strong enough, or capable of doing great things. Someone or something planted that thought in you. Maybe it was a teacher who dismissed you, a parent who was too hard on you, a moment where you were laughed at for trying. Maybe you heard it once, or maybe you heard it over and over until it became part of how you see yourself.

But here's the truth: those beliefs were never about you.

They were never a reflection of your potential. They were a reflection of the *people you got them from.*

And without realizing it, you were hypnotized into believing them.

Not in some dramatic, swinging-pocket-watch kind of way, but in the way all beliefs are formed—through repetition, emotion, and authority.

A child who raises their hand in class and gets laughed at might never raise their hand again. Not because they aren't smart, but because that *one* moment planted a belief: *If I speak up, I'll be humiliated.* A kid who is constantly criticized might stop trying altogether—not because they aren't capable, but because they've been conditioned to believe *nothing I do is ever good enough.*

And so the cycle continues. A belief becomes a habit. A habit becomes an identity.

But *none of it was ever actually true.*

And now, it's time to break that spell.

Right now, take a moment and ask yourself:

What belief about yourself have you been carrying that isn't actually yours?

What have you been repeating in your head for years that came from someone else's limitations, fears, or judgments?

Because that's all self-limiting beliefs are: echoes of other people's fears, projected onto you.

And here's the thing: just because someone told you something, or made you feel something, doesn't mean it was ever true.

The only reason those beliefs have stuck around is because you've *kept reinforcing them.* The mind accepts what it hears repeatedly. But if a belief can be installed, it can be *uninstalled* just the same.

So now, challenge it.

Ask yourself:

Is this actually true?

Who told me this? Where did this come from?

What happens if I stop believing it?

Because the moment you question it, the illusion starts to break. The belief that once felt so solid, so unquestionable, starts to fall apart. You start to see it for what it really is.

Just a thought.

Just conditioning.

Just a voice that was never yours to begin with.

The only limits that exist are the ones you choose to believe in.

And the moment you stop believing in them, they lose their power.

So, right now, make a choice.

Decide to let go of the beliefs that were never yours to begin with.

Because you are not limited. You never were.

MEDITATION ISN'T
ENOUGH TO END ANXIETY

Meditation is overrated.

I know, I know—that's not what you're supposed to say in an anxiety book. But let's be real: if sitting quietly and observing your breath was the answer, anxiety wouldn't be a global epidemic. You've heard it everywhere: "Just meditate, and you'll find peace."

But here's the thing: if you don't understand the deeper purpose of meditation, it can feel like a losing battle.

Because if you're trying to force your mind to be still without knowing *why*, you're missing the real point.

For many people, meditation doesn't quiet the mind.

It turns the volume up.

I first tried meditating at nineteen, during my sophomore year at UCLA, in the first-ever group at the university's newly launched Mindful Awareness Research Center. I was eager to quiet my overthinking mind and find the stillness everyone was talking about.

But let me tell you something: what was happening in my mind during those meditation sessions was anything but peaceful.

I sat there, eyes closed, trying to focus on my breath or the present moment, but my mind had other plans. Thoughts came rushing in—thoughts about my thoughts.

Why am I thinking so much? Isn't this supposed to feel relaxing? Am I even doing this right?

Then there was the frustration: *Why can't I just stop thinking?*

And the distractions: *Why is that guy coughing so much? Am I supposed to pay attention to that?*

And don't even get me started on the breath. I'd focus on it for a moment, but then it would start to feel weird, like I was forcing it. I'd catch myself taking these unnatural, overly deep breaths, and suddenly, I was too aware of my own breathing—on the verge of hyperventilating—which only made it worse.

My mind felt like a noisy, chaotic carnival—the complete opposite of stillness.

Apparently, I wasn't alone.

Neuroscientist Willoughby Britton has found that for people with high anxiety, meditation can sometimes increase distress rather than reduce it. In some cases, focusing on the breath or trying to "quiet the mind" doesn't create peace—it amplifies self-focus, making thoughts feel even louder instead of quieter.

Does this sound familiar?

If you've ever tried to meditate, chances are you've experienced something similar, some if not most of the time. And if so, I want to tell you something important: it's not your fault.

For decades, I kept trying to quiet my mind by attempting to sit and meditate, convinced that this was the path to peace. But what I've come to realize is that I was going about it all wrong. I was trying to force stillness, to "do" something that couldn't be done.

What no one really explains about meditation is that *it's not about effort*—it's about allowing.

And for me, the key to allowing wasn't my breath or my thoughts—it was sound.

Unlike the breath, which can easily become something you try to control, sound is effortless. You don't create it or manipulate it—it simply happens.

You hear the hum of the air conditioner, the distant bark of a dog, or the faint murmur of voices outside, and these sounds enter your awareness without effort. You don't have to "do" anything.

Try it right now. Just listen.

Not with the goal of hearing something specific, but simply noticing.

There's a sound happening somewhere around you. Maybe it's near, maybe it's far. Maybe it's steady, maybe it comes and goes. It doesn't matter what it is—don't label it. Just hear it.

Then listen beyond it.

Notice the space between sounds.

Notice the silence underneath it all.

That silence is always there. It's not something you have to create—it's something you tune into. And the more you notice it, the more you realize that it's not just in the world around you—it's also within you.

For some, this alone is enough. Simply listening—*really* listening—can bring you into a state of stillness more naturally than trying to force focus on the breath. It's meditation without meditating.

If this works for you, consider making it a daily practice—even just a few moments of listening, with no effort, no technique, just awareness.

But for others, even this can feel difficult. When your mind is used to running nonstop, when anxiety has wired you to stay on high alert, sitting in stillness—even just to listen—can feel impossible.

The mind fights against it, constantly pulling you back into thoughts, emotions, and mental noise. And when that happens, frustration sets in, making the whole process feel pointless.

If that's you, I want you to know something: It's not because you're incapable of finding stillness. It's because your mind has been trained to keep moving, and expecting it to stop on command is like asking a rushing river to go still in an instant.

This is why meditation often doesn't work for anxiety. It tries to calm the surface instead of dissolving the storm underneath.

But here's where people get stuck: they think meditation is the only way to awakening.

Many people believe they need to sit cross-legged for hours or follow some rigid practice to break free from anxiety or to wake up to reality. And sure, meditation can help—it's a powerful tool for some people. But you don't need it.

The reason anxiety exists is because you're trapped in a false understanding of reality. You think you're your thoughts. You think you're your mind. You believe the story your brain is telling you about the past and the future.

But once you see through that illusion, anxiety dissolves.

It can't survive in the presence of truth.

And you don't have to wait for a meditation session to see that truth.

When you awaken, *life itself becomes your meditation.*

Anxiety depends on resistance, on fighting what is.

But when you realize that everything is exactly as it's meant to be—that there's nothing to fix or control—resistance fades. And without resistance, anxiety has nothing to hold onto.

When I began my studies in clinical hypnotherapy, I realized that sound could do more than bring me into stillness—it could transform me.

Some people call hypnotherapy a form of guided meditation, and on the surface, they might seem similar. Both involve listening to a calm voice guiding you toward relaxation.

But hypnotherapy, when done correctly, goes far beyond meditation. It's not just about stillness—it's about lasting change to your inner beliefs.

After years of working in hypnotherapy, I realized I wasn't hypnotizing people.

I was *de-hypnotizing* them.

People think change requires going into a trance, but they're already in one—trapped by false beliefs and mental noise.

Real transformation isn't about putting you under—it's about waking you up.

From this understanding, I developed what I call MindPower Sessions.

These are not meditations in the traditional sense. They're guided experiences that first calm your mind in a way that feels natural, then combine deep relaxation, subconscious work, and proven psychological techniques to help you release the patterns and programming that hold you back, creating the space for real change.

MindPower Sessions don't ask you to fight your thoughts or force your mind to be quiet.

Instead, they guide you on an inner path to stillness—a place where your mind can finally let go, where the noise fades, and where transformation happens.

If you've struggled with meditation or felt like you just can't quiet your mind, it's not your fault.

Maybe you weren't failing. Maybe you just needed a different tool.

If simply listening doesn't click for you right away, that's okay.

Sometimes the mind needs a little guidance to get there.

If you're ready to experience this for yourself, I've put together a free MindPower Session designed to help you access that deeper shift.

Not by forcing your mind to be quiet, but by working with it—guiding it into a state where calm happens naturally.

You'll find it in the resources section of my website at AnxietyToAwakening.com

No techniques to master. No forcing. Just a direct experience of the peace that's already inside you.

Because stillness isn't something you chase.

It's something you uncover.

And once you hear it ... you can't unhear it.

STOP FEEDING YOUR MIND
THE CHAOS THAT KEEPS IT WILD

Your mind—your wild horse—doesn't run wild on its own. You feed it. And for most people, the diet is toxic: constant hits of speed. Mental amphetamines. Breaking news, fear-driven headlines, doomscrolling, and buzzing notifications.

For years, I let the world decide what my mind consumed. I didn't think twice about it. News websites. Social media. Notifications that interrupted my day with every headline, every "breaking" update. And TV news? It was often on in the background, filling the room—and my mind—with noise and fear. I thought I was staying informed. I thought it was responsible.

But it wasn't helping me. It wasn't serving me.

Here's what you need to understand: The news cycle isn't designed to inform you. It's designed to hook you. Fear drives clicks, and clicks drive revenue. More fear equals more clicks. More clicks equal more revenue. And more revenue means more money for the media outlets. That's all they care about. Their job isn't to keep you calm, clear, or informed—it's to keep you anxious, reactive, and hooked, bringing them billions of dollars in advertising revenue.

And here's the truth: Knowing all of this "news" doesn't change anything. It doesn't benefit you. It doesn't make your life better. It only steals your focus, your peace, and your mental energy.

It keeps your mind restless, anxious, overstimulated—like a wild horse pumped full of amphetamines, running in endless circles.

I was tired of the constant anxiety-inducing headlines and stories. So, I stopped. I took back control.

I deleted every news app from my phone.

I turned off every single notification—the dings, the buzzes, the red badges that pulled me in.

I turned off TV news altogether. I stopped watching it. It's not harmless background noise—it's a steady stream of fear, chaos, and negativity you don't need.

I stopped visiting news websites.

But here's the critical part: I didn't just stop. I replaced the habit.

The urge to check didn't go away immediately. I'd feel it creep in—when I was in between clients or projects, while waiting in line at the supermarket, or during a quiet moment when I didn't know what else to do. My hand would instinctively reach for my phone or computer, and my mind would say, *Let's see what's happening in the world.*

But I stopped myself. I redirected the urge. Instead of feeding the chaos, I chose something nourishing.

Over and over again, day after day, week after week, I just kept pulling myself away and redirected myself to nourishing food for my beautiful wild horse.

I opened YouTube and searched for a video by someone who inspires me—thinkers, philosophers, or leaders whose words make me feel calm, expansive, and alive.

I started following people who add value to my mind, not drain it—visionaries, teachers, and creators who focus on growth, not outrage.

I read books or listened to audiobooks that challenged my thinking, expanded my perspective, and filled me with energy instead of anxiety.

When I redirected the habit, the transformation was incredible.

Every time I chose something positive, my mind got a little clearer. I felt a little calmer. I started to look forward to those moments—not as a chance to feed my mind noise, but as an opportunity to feed it something that lifted me up.

Here's what happens when you redirect the urge:

Instead of spiraling into fear, you start expanding into clarity.

Instead of feeling small, you feel inspired.

Instead of wasting energy on things you can't change, you focus on what you can.

Over time, the pull to check the news weakened. It no longer had a hold on me. Because I'd given my mind something better. And as a result, my wild horse began to be much calmer.

All that noise coming into your mind isn't harmless. It's not "just background." It's a product, and you're the customer. If you let the world decide what your mind consumes, it will flood you with fear and noise—not to inform you, but to keep you hooked.

Like I mentioned before, more fear equals more clicks. More clicks equal more revenue. That's the game. But you don't have to play it.

If you want to calm your wild horse, you have to stop feeding it speed. And more importantly, you have to redirect the habit, replacing the chaos with nourishment.

Here's where to start:

Delete the news apps. Every single one.

Take the news out of your social media feed by removing or muting those posts.

Unfollow and unsubscribe from accounts that thrive on outrage and fear.

Turn off notifications. No exceptions. Your mental space is worth more than a random buzz.

Turn off the TV news. It's not serving you. Let it go.

Redirect the habit.

Open YouTube and search for an inspiring speaker.

Follow thinkers and leaders who help you grow.

Pick up a book that challenges and expands your mind.

Listen to an uplifting podcast, or take a moment to sit in silence and breathe.

When you feel the urge to check the chaos, ask yourself, *Does this serve me?* Then choose something that does.

Imagine waking up and feeling light. No phone buzzing. No flood of anxiety pulling you under. No endless scrolling to "catch up" on a world you can't control.

Your thoughts are clear.

Your focus is sharp.

And instead of reacting to the world's chaos, you're creating your own calm, your own vision for your life.

When you take back control, you'll see what your mind is capable of when it's no longer weighed down by the noise.

You'll feel it—the space, the stillness, the clarity.

YOUR MIND CAN'T BE
CALM IF THE RIDER IS WEAK

If you've started to calm your wild horse—your mind—by cutting out the noise, you're already on the path. You're beginning to see what happens when you stop feeding it chaos, stop letting the media keep it overstimulated, anxious, and hooked.

But here's the next question you need to ask:

What about the rider?

Your wild horse doesn't run alone. It has a rider: you. And if the rider isn't strong, steady, and clear, the horse will never calm down.

Right now, the rider is being fed garbage. Not by accident. Not by coincidence. By design.

The food industry has turned nourishment into addiction. They've taken what was supposed to fuel your body and turned it into a drug.

Food scientists—people paid well for this—are engineering flavors, textures, and combinations that hook you. Sugar, chemical flavor enhancers, artificial oils, dyes—all of it crafted to hijack your brain and make you crave more.

They've perfected what's called "the bliss point," a term the food industry itself coined. The exact balance of sugar, fat, and salt designed to light up your brain's reward system without ever fully satisfying you.

It's not about nourishment.

It's about addiction.

They've put sugar where sugar doesn't belong. Salad dressings, sauces, soups, bread. Foods that don't need it. They hide MSG behind names like "natural flavor" or "yeast extract." They fill boxes, bags, and bottles with ingredients you can't pronounce.

None of this is an accident. It's calculated.

And why? Because the more you eat, the more you crave. The more you crave, the more you buy. And the more you buy, the richer they get.

Your cravings are their currency.

If you've ever felt foggy, sluggish, or out of control—like you can't think clearly, like you're always reaching for something to eat to make you feel better—that's part of it. What you're feeding yourself affects your mind just as much as it affects your body.

And yet, they're feeding you poison and calling it food.

I honestly don't know how these people sleep at night.

But you don't have to play along. You don't have to let their business model rob you of your clarity, your energy, and your strength.

The next time you walk into a grocery store, pay attention.

The real food—the food your body was made for—is on the perimeter. That's where you find vegetables, fruits, eggs, dairy, meat, fish, nuts. Food that is the ingredient.

Everything in the middle? That's the trap. That's where the brightly colored boxes and bags live, stacked high, filled with sugar, oils, flavor enhancers, and chemicals designed to keep you coming back.

Flip the package over and look at the label. If you can't pronounce it, your body can't process it. If it's full of artificial flavors, artificial colors, refined sugars, or hidden chemicals, it's not food. It's a synthetic product.

It's simple, really: eat the foods your great-grandmother would recognize.

Eggs, vegetables, fruits, meats, nuts—simple, whole foods that have nourished generations.

But deception isn't just in the food industry... The alcohol industry has done the exact same thing.

They've taken something undeniably destructive and disguised it as "relaxation." They've packaged it as fun, as sophistication, as a social norm.

But what it really does is strip you of control—over your body, your mind, and your emotions.

Alcohol is a poison. A toxin. And it has no place in your body.

We've been sold a lie—that it relaxes you, that it helps you unwind. The truth? It does the exact opposite. It destroys your ability to regulate your emotions. It hijacks your brain and weakens your ability to think clearly.

Alcohol lowers your vibration, dulls your energy, and disconnects you from your highest self.

It reduces the rider's control and aggravates the wild horse.

It disrupts sleep.

It spikes stress hormones.

It leaves you more out of sync with yourself.

It tricks you into thinking it helps, but the reality is, it magnifies the very thing you're trying to escape.

It doesn't calm anxiety—it fuels it.

It overstimulates your nervous system and leaves you even more on edge than before.

It doesn't relieve anxiety. It makes it worse.

It keeps you stuck in a cycle—one where you drink to "relax," only to wake up feeling even worse.

Stop lying to yourself.

If you drink, the best thing you can do for your mind, your body, and your clarity is eliminate it completely.

Not cut back.

Not drink "mindfully."

Eliminate it.

It's not helping you. It's hurting you. And the sooner you stop, the sooner everything in your life begins to shift.

I used to drink occasionally, thinking nothing of it. It was normal, after all—a socially acceptable way to relax, celebrate, or take the edge off.

But since I eliminated it completely, I don't miss it at all. Not even a little. In fact, I can't believe I ever saw it as something worth putting in my body. My mind is clearer. My energy is higher. I feel stronger, clearer, and more alive.

And here's the truth most people don't want to admit:

Alcohol is a socially accepted delusion.

We look back at the days when people smoked cigarettes on airplanes and in hospitals, and we shake our heads. We think, *How could they not see how insane that was?*

That's exactly how history will view alcohol.

One day, we'll look back at bars, clubs, and weddings filled with people drinking a literal poison—waking up foggy, inflamed, and out of sync with themselves—and wonder, *What the hell were we thinking?*

But you don't have to wait for history to catch up.

You can see it clearly now. You can step outside of the trap. You can make the choice to stop poisoning yourself—whether it's with toxic food, toxic habits, or the toxic media and influences you've been consuming.

And when you do, you start to feel it.

Here's what happens when the rider gets stronger:

Your mind begins to trust you.

Your wild horse—the one that was running in every direction—sees you, the rider, holding the reins and starts to calm.

Because here's the connection you need to see:

What you feed yourself isn't just about your body—it's about your mind.

It's time to take back control.

When the rider is strong, and the wild horse is calm, everything stabilizes.

HOW TO STOP MISUSING YOUR MIND

For years, I lived in a state of constant unrest.

My thoughts were like a relentless machine, always spinning, trying to figure out how things were going to go.

Would my plans succeed?

Would things fall apart?

What if this? What if that?!

My mind would race ahead, running scenario after scenario, convinced that if I could just think hard enough, I'd be able to control what happened.

It didn't stop there. I'd also look back—replaying mistakes, second-guessing decisions, and wishing I could rewrite the past. It felt like I was carrying the weight of both the future and the past on my shoulders, and it was crushing me.

Anxiety kept me tethered to an imagined future filled with worst-case scenarios, while regret dragged me into a past I couldn't change. The harder I tried to think my way out of it, the worse it got. I couldn't sleep well, couldn't focus, and couldn't shake the feeling that no matter what I did, I'd never get it right.

Then one day, it hit me: The problem wasn't my mind. It was how I was using it.

Imagine if I handed you a flashlight and said, "This is a powerful tool. It will help you navigate the dark." You'd turn it on and point it ahead, expecting it to light up the path in front of you. And that's exactly what it's designed to do—give you clarity in the moment, one step at a time.

But what if you decided to use it differently? What if you pointed it at a wall, expecting it to reveal what's on the other side?

Or you aimed it far down the path, demanding that it illuminate not just the next few steps, but the entire road six months or two years ahead?

No matter how long or hard you tried, the flashlight wouldn't work that way. You'd get frustrated. You'd shake it, adjust the beam, and maybe even start blaming yourself—or the flashlight—for not working.

But the truth is, the flashlight isn't broken. It's just not designed to do that.

This is exactly what happens when we try to use our minds to predict the future.

The mind is an incredible tool, but it's built to light up the present moment, helping us solve problems and take action right here, right now. It wasn't built to see around corners, to guarantee what's coming, or to make sure nothing will go wrong.

I spent years trying to force my mind to illuminate the entire path ahead. I wanted to know how every decision would play out, how every plan would unfold, and whether the future would go the way I wanted it to. But no matter how much energy I poured into trying to "figure it all out," I always came up short.

The flashlight simply can't light up a road that doesn't yet exist.

And that's where anxiety comes from. It's the tension and frustration of demanding certainty about the future when it's impossible to have it.

The harder you push, the more anxious you feel, because the future isn't something you can control, predict, or plan perfectly.

The flashlight also doesn't work if you turn it backward and try to fix the road you've already walked. It can show you the path behind you, but no matter how much you focus on it, you can't rearrange the steps you've already taken. That's where regret lives, and if you keep shining the light on the past, trying to change it, you'll find yourself stuck in a loop of frustration and sadness.

The truth is, anxiety happens when we misuse the mind by forcing it to predict the future.

Depression takes hold when we stay trapped in the past. Neither of these is what the mind was built for.

But here's the shift: the flashlight is at its best when it's focused on the steps directly in front of you.

It's not meant to reveal the entire path or rewrite what's behind you. It's meant to guide you in the present moment, one step at a time. And when you let it do just that, the weight of trying to control everything else begins to lift.

Now, take a moment and ask yourself: how are you using your flashlight?

Are you trying to see too far ahead, demanding that it show you the future?

Are you trying to use it to see through walls?

Or are you pointing it backward, reliving what you can't change?

What would happen if you let it light up just this moment?

What if, just for today, you stopped fighting your mind and let it guide you step by step?

Trust your flashlight.

Let it simply illuminate what is in front of you right now.

The clarity and peace you've been searching for have been here all along, waiting for you to see them.

YOUR EMOTIONS ARE GUESTS—LET THEM VISIT, BUT DON'T LET THEM UNPACK

For most of my life, I felt like my emotions were in control of me.

When a wave of sadness, anger, or frustration hit, I resisted.

If I felt sadness, I'd become sad about being sad. If I felt anger, I'd get angry about being angry.

I layered judgment on top of my emotions, convinced that, as someone who has spent decades studying psychology and the mind, as a clinical hypnotherapist, I shouldn't be feeling this way. I thought, *I should know better. I should be better than this.*

Perhaps you've experienced this too.

Maybe you get frustrated about being frustrated, angry about being angry, or sad about being sad. It's a common cycle—one that seems logical on the surface, but in reality, it keeps us stuck.

Through my awakening, I've come to understand these experiences in a completely different way.

I've realized that I'm not my emotions; I'm the awareness in which they arise.

This wasn't a sudden revelation, but a gradual, deepening understanding—a clarity that emerged as I became more aligned with the truth of who I am. And on a recent morning, I was reminded of just how powerful this awareness can be.

When I woke up, I felt a wave of sadness. I don't know where it came from—maybe a dream, maybe something unspoken deep within me.

Nothing at all had changed in my life. I had no "reason" to be sad.

But instead of resisting it or questioning why it was happening, I simply let it in.

I welcomed the sadness like a guest, its own little being, its own character, dropping into my inner world. I gave it space to exist without trying to push it away.

And as I did, I noticed something profound: I wasn't sad. I was *aware* of sadness. That energy wasn't me. I was the space in which it landed. And the moment I allowed it to just be, it began to soften and transform.

It moved through me like a wave, leaving me lighter and more centered.

This ability to create space for emotions is life-changing, and I think it's captured beautifully in certain languages. For example, in Irish, they don't say, "I am sad." Instead, they say, "*Tá brón orm,*" which means, "Sadness is upon me."

Sadness isn't who they are—it's something external, something temporary. It comes. It stays for a while. And then it goes.

Compare that to English, where we say, "I am sad," "I am angry," "I am frustrated."

These phrases trap emotions in our identity, making us believe that what we feel is who we are. But that's not the truth.

Emotions are not who you are—they are simply experiences.

They are energies in motion: E-motion.

Now imagine what would change for you if instead of saying, "I am sad," you thought, *Sadness is here?*

Instead of "I am angry," you said, "Anger has landed on me"?

How much lighter would you feel knowing that emotions are just visitors? They come to be felt. And when you allow them that space, they naturally begin to shift and transform.

Perhaps you've heard the phrase, "What you resist persists." And it's true: whatever you push against pushes back.

But the moment you stop fighting and start allowing, something shifts. Their grip on you loosens.

You're no longer ruled by your emotions. You no longer drown in them.

You recognize them, allow them, and let them pass—because they always do.

And as they move, something remarkable happens.

What remains isn't sadness.

What remains isn't anger.

What remains is you.

The awareness.

The steady, calm, and unshakable presence beneath it all.

YOU DON'T HAVE TO
FEEL EVERYTHING YOU FEEL

One of the most liberating truths you can realize is that many of your emotions are a choice.

While frustration, annoyance, anger, worry, or guilt may feel like they just happen to you, on a deeper level, they are choices. And those choices don't change the situation—they only add layers of suffering that only you experience.

You alone.

Even if those emotions feel justified, and they often are, ask yourself, "Why would I add unnecessary suffering to my life?"

This realization can be profoundly empowering. Because if you're choosing to feel frustrated, annoyed, or angry, then you can also choose something different. You can choose peace, calm, or clarity. Once you understand that the emotions you hold onto are within your control, you begin to see that holding onto frustration, anger, or disappointment serves no purpose other than to create more suffering for you.

It doesn't improve the situation; it just weighs you down.

Take a common scenario:

You've been working hard on a project, and suddenly, something goes wrong—a system crashes, a colleague drops the ball, or another unexpected problem arises. Immediately, frustration bubbles up. You feel the tension building as your expectations for how things should go are shattered.

It's natural to have this initial reaction, but here's the truth: whether or not you stay in that frustration is up to you.

Frustration occurs when you resist reality—when you believe things should be different than they are. But clinging to frustration doesn't fix the situation; it just makes it harder for you to think clearly and move forward.

Ask yourself, *Why do I need this frustration?*

What is it adding to the situation?

Is it solving the problem, or just adding more weight to my mind?

By holding onto it, you're *only* creating more suffering for yourself.

You can choose to let go.

You can choose to say, "I refuse to let this frustration control me. I accept what is, and I choose peace."

By releasing the frustration, you free yourself from the emotional suffering it creates. The situation hasn't changed, but *you* have. Now you're in a space where you can approach the problem with calm and clarity, without the fog of frustration.

The key to all of this is understanding that allowing these challenging emotions—frustration, annoyance, anger, outrage, disappointment, guilt, or worry—to take over is a choice, and they don't change the situation you're in. They only add layers of unnecessary suffering to your reality. Even when these emotions feel justified, holding onto them only deepens your suffering.

Again, ask yourself: "Why do I need this? What is this emotion doing for me?"

If the answer is that it's only adding pain, then let it go.

You don't need to hold onto these emotions. They don't serve you. They don't make the situation better. They only create more suffering in your internal world.

The beautiful truth is that you always have the power to choose how you respond. In any moment, you can choose to hold onto emotions that create suffering, or you can choose to let them go. You can choose peace, clarity, and calm.

When you make the choice to let go, you create space for something else: peace, acceptance, or even gratitude. These are also choices, and they are always available to you.

Recognizing that emotions are choices allows you to reclaim your power. You are no longer a victim of your emotional responses; you are in control of them. By choosing not to hold onto these emotions, you free yourself from the unnecessary suffering they create.

Emotions are temporary, fleeting clouds passing through the sky of your consciousness. In any moment, you have the power to return to that place of peace. You have the power to choose a response that doesn't add more suffering to your journey.

Choosing peace over frustration, calm over anger, and clarity over worry is a practice. It requires awareness and conscious effort, especially at first. But the more you practice letting go, the more natural it becomes. You start to recognize the signs of suffering and make a deliberate choice to release it.

This allows you to live with a greater sense of ease, no matter what external challenges arise. It reminds you that you are the master of your inner world, and no situation or person has the power to take that from you unless you allow it.

Realize that nothing outside of you can make you feel a certain way unless you give it permission.

Your inner world is your domain—your kingdom.

The emotions that seem to grip you so tightly are only as real and powerful as you allow them to be.

They don't serve to fix the situation or make you feel better. In fact, they only add unnecessary layers of suffering to your existence.

But the moment you see them for what they are—choices—you reclaim your freedom.

The choice is always yours.

Choose wisely, and choose freedom.

NOT EVERY SITUATION
DESERVES YOUR ENERGY

For much of my life, I attached emotion to almost everything I encountered.

As an empath, I've always felt things deeply.

If there was something I didn't want to do—a task, a responsibility, even something as mundane as washing the dishes—I'd feel an emotion about it.

I'd feel resistance, annoyance, frustration, or even guilt.

And for so long, I thought that was just part of being human, part of being me.

But here's the truth I've come to realize: most situations in life don't actually require an emotional reaction.

Think about it.

How many times have you felt annoyed at a chore, overwhelmed by an obligation, or frustrated by something like a cluttered room or a messy countertop?

How often have you allowed emotion to hijack your experience, draining your energy before you even acted?

The reality is, most of these situations are neutral. It's our emotions—our attachment to how we think things should be—that make them feel so heavy.

Here's an example:

Let's say you have to do the dishes. It's a simple task, really. There's no inherent meaning in it beyond cleaning up and restoring order. But if you're like I was, you might resist it, thinking, *Why should I have to do this right now?* That resistance creates tension, turning a neutral task into something unnecessarily heavy.

I used to feel this way about a lot of things, but one that stood out was my bedtime routine. It's a little extensive: flossing, brushing my teeth, using a tongue scraper, and then mouthwash. After that, showering, shaving my face, and applying face lotion. Then, going to the kitchen to fill up a big glass of water for the morning and setting it on the nightstand. And finally, taking our dog, Buster, out one last time before bed.

Night after night, it felt like an endless series of chores. I'd get frustrated, thinking, *This is so annoying! Why does this take so long? I'm tired… I just want to go to sleep!*

But one evening, I paused and asked myself a different question:

How lucky am I to even have this routine?

A warm, relaxing shower. Running water. An electric toothbrush. Really nice products to care for myself. Clean, filtered water to drink—luxuries that so many people in the world don't have.

And how lucky am I to have a sweet dog who depends on me, who looks up at me with those loving, trusting eyes, waiting for our last little walk of the night?

Suddenly, it didn't feel like a series of chores anymore. It felt like a privilege.

I don't have to do this, *I get to do this.*

That realization changed everything from that day forward.

My frustration turned into gratitude.

I now actually look forward to this time of day, and what once felt like a burden has become a time of self-care, mindfulness, and appreciation.

The truth is, life requires us to do things we don't want to do.
That's just part of being human.
You don't need to feel something about brushing your teeth or flossing.
You don't need to get frustrated about doing laundry, paying bills, or tidying a cluttered room.
These are simply things that need to get done.

And when you take a step back, you might realize—you're actually fortunate to be able to do them at all.

When you attach emotion to these tasks, ask yourself, does anything change?

Does the task become easier or faster?

Of course not.

The only thing that changes is you.

You suffer.

Instead, why not approach these tasks differently? Why not fully accept them for what they are—just a necessary part of human life? Or what if you might actually find peace or joy in them?

Washing the dishes, for example, can become grounding when you notice the sensation of warm water on your hands, the sound of the sponge gliding over the plate, or the satisfaction of rinsing it clean.

Brushing your teeth can be a ritual of self-care when you focus on the soothing rhythm of the bristles, the cool freshness of the toothpaste, or the simple act of caring for your body.

And beyond that, what if you reminded yourself that there are people who wish they could do these things?

Some people don't have the physical ability to stand at a sink and wash their own dishes.
Some people don't have access to clean, running water.
Some people don't have a home, a routine, or even the smallest luxuries that you take for granted.

You don't have to clean up your space—you *get* to clean up a space that you're fortunate to have.

You don't have to exercise—you *get* to move your body, something many people only wish they could do.

You don't have to do laundry—you *get* to wash and wear clean clothes, something many people don't have the luxury of.

See how different that feels?

These small moments, done mindfully, can anchor you in the present and bring a surprising sense of peace.

When you stop attaching emotion to everything, you create space. You conserve energy. And you free yourself from the stories that weigh you down.

At the very least, if you truly can't enjoy what you're doing, then accept it.
Accept that this is what needs to be done right now.
That this is what the moment requires.
And just do it.

Otherwise, you're adding pointless suffering to your experience.

It changes absolutely nothing.

And the only person it affects is *you*.

I'm not saying to suppress your emotions or avoid feeling what's real.
There are moments in life when emotions are absolutely appropriate and necessary.
But not every situation requires them. Some moments simply ask for your presence, your awareness, and your action.

So, the next time you feel resistance, guilt, annoyance, or frustration about something small, pause.

Ask yourself, "Does this situation truly need emotion, or can I let it be what it is?"

"Can I approach it with neutrality and simply decide how I want to respond?"

What if, instead of seeing a task as something being forced upon you, you saw it as a privilege?

What if you replaced "I have to do this" with "I *get* to do this"—and meant it?

When you do this, something shifts.

You move through life with greater ease, clarity, and freedom.

You stop wasting energy on stories and start finding peace in even the smallest moments.

And that's the difference between struggling through life and truly living it.

ONE DAY, THIS WILL BE THE MOMENT YOU MISS THE MOST

Stop.

Wherever you are. Whatever is happening. Just stop.

Feel the breath moving in and out of your body.

Notice that you are here. Alive. Awake. Reading these words.

And right now, your mind is carrying something.

Maybe it's stress.

Maybe it's uncertainty.

Maybe it's the weight of everything you think is missing.

The mind is always searching, scanning for what's wrong, for what's lacking, for what needs to be fixed. It's always reaching forward, into the next problem, the next worry, the next thing to solve.

And if you let it, it will keep searching forever.

Right now, as I write this, I could do the same.

There are real-world demands that don't always go the way I want them to.

There are things happening in the world that I can't control.

There are people I love who are struggling.

But even as I notice those things, something else is true.

I get to wake up in a bed that's warm.

I get to see my children laughing, healthy, full of life.

I get to open my eyes and witness another day.

And if I lost any of it—if I woke up tomorrow and it was gone—

I would give *anything* to have it back.

So, why do you wait?

Why wait until something is taken from you to realize how much you had?

Why let gratitude be something you only feel in hindsight?

Because right now, in this moment, you are living in the middle of things you would ache for if they were gone.

The voice of someone who loves you.

The ability to move, to breathe, to see, to hear.

The ordinary, beautiful moments that slip by unnoticed.

Right now, there are things you're taking for granted. Not because you're ungrateful, but because that's what the mind does: it normalizes what is constant.

But if they were gone tomorrow, how much of what you're stressing about today would even matter?

How much of what feels urgent right now would fade in the face of what you lost?

Pause for a moment.

Really think about it.

If the things you take for granted today were gone tomorrow ... how would you feel?

Would the things you're stressing over still matter?

Let that sink in.

And not just you.

There are people in the world who would give anything to have what you have right now.

To sleep in a safe place. To drink clean water. To know that the people they love are okay.

To have even a *fraction* of the choices, the comforts, the opportunities that you wake up with every day.

You don't have to lose them to notice them.

You don't have to wait until they're gone to appreciate what's already here.

Gratitude isn't about pretending that life is perfect.

It's not about forcing yourself to be positive.

It's about seeing clearly.

Anxiety lives in what's missing.

It pulls you into the future, into what-ifs, into everything that could go wrong.

But gratitude brings you back.

Back to what's here.

Back to what's real.

Back to the life that is still yours.

And when you feel it—not just as an idea, but as something real—your whole perspective changes.

So, take a breath.

Let gratitude in.

Because life is happening now.

And you are already standing in the middle of so much more than you realize.

THE PRESENT MOMENT IS ALL THERE IS

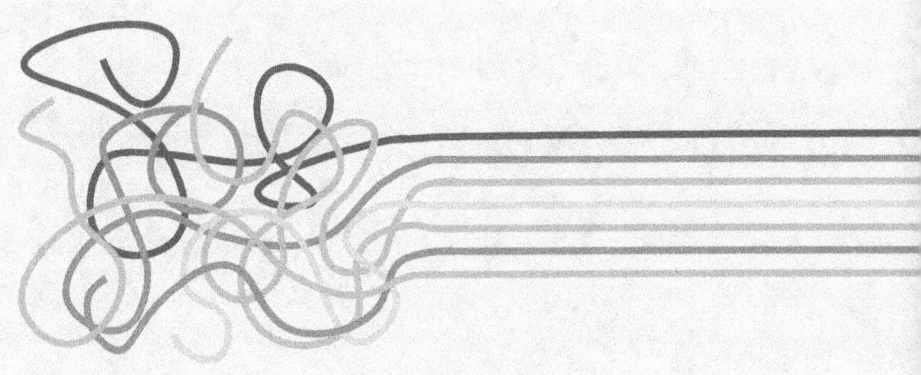

RIGHT NOW IS ALL YOU HAVE

The only moment you ever need to take care of, and the only moment you *can* take care of, is the one you're in right now.

That's it.

Right now.

This moment is the only reality you have access to. Everything else? Doesn't exist.

The past is done.

It's like the wake of a boat.

It's behind you, churned up and fading, with zero influence on the direction the boat is heading right now. You can look at it, sure, but it doesn't have any power to steer you unless you hand it the wheel. Why would you do that? You're driving the boat.

And the future?

The future is a mirage.

It exists only in your imagination. You're projecting, guessing, worrying, but none of it exists anywhere except in your mind right now.

Think about that for a second. When you're thinking about tomorrow, or next week, or ten years from now, you're doing it now. Every moment you spend tangled up in what-ifs or what-might-be's, you're missing the one moment you actually have: the present.

Let me make this even clearer.

Imagine the present moment as the only room you have access to in a series of rooms connected by doors. The past is the room with a locked door behind you, and the future is a door to a room you can't open yet.

You're standing in the only room that's real.

The room of *now*.

It's the *only room* you have access to.

No matter how much you want to leave it, you can't. So, why not make yourself at home?

Get comfy.

Look around, settle in, and focus on what you can do here.

This room is all there is, and everything else is just imagination.

This understanding of the power of now owes much to the groundbreaking work of Eckhart Tolle, whose insights into presence have transformed millions of lives, including my own. His teachings laid the foundation for this realization: the present moment is where your power lies.

Living in the now doesn't just free you from anxiety. It opens the door to peace, creativity, and a profound sense of aliveness.

Awakening is not about escaping your life.

It's about fully stepping into it.

The present moment is waiting for you, and it's the only place where life is actually happening.

And here's another important truth to reflect on:

The same intelligence, the same intellect, the same resourcefulness you have right now is the same intelligence, intellect, and resourcefulness you'll have if or when a challenge arises in the future.

Think about all the mental energy you waste trying to predict every possible "what if," worrying about how things might unfold. The truth? Most of what you're worried about—if not all—never happens.

So, why not save your energy?

Why not stop exhausting yourself over imagined scenarios that will likely never come to pass?

Trust that when or if something happens, you'll have the intelligence and strength to respond in the best way you can. After all, isn't that what you've always done?

Consider this:

You have overcome *every single challenge and obstacle* that has ever come your way.

One hundred percent of them.

Because you're still here.

Anxiety thrives on the illusion that you have to solve everything ahead of time, but you don't.

And you can't.

You only have to handle what's in front of you—in the *room of now*—and you already have everything you need to do that.

Recognizing this is a huge shift. It's a release of unnecessary mental clutter and a return to the clarity and simplicity of the present.

Pause for a moment and reflect on this…

The past and the future literally do not exist.

If the past existed, I'd ask you to go there right now.

Can you?

No. You can only think about the past, and when you do, you're thinking about it in this present moment.

Now try the future.

Fast-forward to it.

Can you?

No. You can imagine it, plan for it, worry about it, but you can't actually go there. You can only think about the future right now.

So, what does that mean?

It means that the only moment you ever need to take care of is this one right now.

There's no other moment you need to take care of, and there's no other moment *you can* take care of.

And what happens to anxiety when you realize this?

Anxiety falls apart.

It can't survive in the present moment. It's like a shadow. It needs something to project onto, some imagined future or unresolved past. But the now doesn't give it anything to hold onto.

And yet, the mind is tricky. Even when we know this, thoughts try to pull us away, back into worries and distractions. But presence is always accessible.

And here's something else to consider: most people have an adversarial relationship with the present moment.

Think about it. How often do you resist what's happening right now?

How often do you find yourself wishing this moment were different, fighting with reality, or waiting for the next moment to bring relief?

But when you recognize that the present moment is all there is, you also recognize that if you're fighting with it, you're fighting with life itself. And that's exhausting.

What if, instead of resisting, you could make friends with the present moment?

What if you could extend a hand of friendship to it, like you would to someone you deeply care about?

When you do this, something profound happens.

The moment softens.
Life softens.
You stop fighting, and instead, you start flowing. You become aligned with life as it's happening.

Here's the beauty of living this way:

When you take good care of the now, your future takes care of itself.

If you make the best choices you can in this moment, in the *room of now*, and do your best with what's in front of you, you'll find that the future unfolds naturally.

All of the mental energy you've been wasting trying to control what hasn't happened yet becomes unnecessary, because everything you need to create a better future exists in the present moment.

Right now is the moment to begin. Not tomorrow, not later, but now.

This is where your life is happening.

This is where you are free.

THE SOUND THAT DISSOLVES ANXIETY

The mind is restless. Even when you recognize the power of the present moment, it pulls you away—into worries, distractions, and noise.

But presence is always within reach.

And sound is a powerful doorway to it.

Sound exists only in the now—it cannot be heard in the past or future.

When you listen—*really listen*—everything else falls away. The mind quiets. Thoughts slow. Awareness sharpens.

In sound, you are *here*.

Music has always been a doorway for me.

When I put on earbuds and listen, everything else falls away. The sound becomes more than sound—it becomes the moment itself. There's no effort, no thinking, no need to do anything.

The music simply moves through me, alive and complete. It reminds me, in the simplest way, of what it means to just *be*.

Music has a unique power to bring you into the present. Unlike the mind, which pulls you into thoughts of what was or what might be, music exists only in the now.

It unfolds moment by moment, effortlessly drawing you with it.

When you're fully here, anxiety has no space to exist. Anxiety is the mind's creation. It arises from resistance, from trying to control or escape. But music doesn't demand anything from you.

It invites you to let go.

You don't need to analyze music. You don't need to make sense of it or try to control it. All you have to do is listen.

The sound flows, and as it does, you surrender to it—not because you try to, but because it happens naturally.

The music carries you, and in that space, the noise of the mind fades.

What's left is stillness, clarity, and a quiet joy that feels as though it's always been there, waiting for you to notice it.

Think about your own experience with music.

Have you ever been so moved by a song or a melody that everything else disappeared? A moment where the music wasn't just something you heard, but something you *felt*—as if it were meeting you exactly where you were?

How did that feel?

What might happen if you allowed music to become a tool, not just for entertainment, but for presence?

What would it feel like to simply let the sound carry you, without resistance, without effort, and notice where it takes you?

Music doesn't just distract you from anxiety. It dissolves it.

Not by fixing or changing anything, but by bringing you back to the truth of this moment.

The stillness isn't something you need to create. It's already here, waiting for you to notice.

All it takes is listening.

THE FIRE THAT LEAVES YOU WHOLE

Not long ago, I had a session with a client in Los Angeles.

She was living through the devastating fires sweeping through her hometown. More than ten thousand structures had already been destroyed, and people had lost not just their homes, but everything they owned.

Earlier, she had already evacuated once, and now she was back in her home, watching the flames creep steadily closer to her neighborhood, unsure if she would need to evacuate again.

As we spoke, I could sense a profound shift in her.

"I feel really present," she said.

I paused, curious. "Present?" I asked.

"Yes," she replied. "I'm not thinking about what's going to happen, because I just don't know. And I'm not thinking about the past, because it doesn't matter."

She paused and seemed momentarily perplexed.

"My mind is just quiet. It's weird… I'm not thinking."

In that moment, I couldn't help but smile. She had unknowingly stumbled upon something profound.

"Disasters like this," I told her, "as awful as they are, tend to pull us into the present moment. They strip away the distractions and force us to be here, now. And in that, there's something liberating."

She agreed. "It's strange. I'm not used to having no thoughts. But it feels peaceful."

She stopped for a moment and looked around her home.

"The fire could burn everything here," she said quietly.

"But it can't take what actually matters."

I waited, sensing that something deeper was coming.

She looked at me, her eyes calm yet certain. "It can't take my creativity. My talent. My energy. That's what's important, and it's not tied to anything outside of me."

Her realization is a reminder to all of us.

The things we cling to—our possessions, our titles, even our plans—aren't what truly define us.

What matters most is already within you.

This is the essence of awakening. It's not about some grand spiritual experience or mystical event. It's about stepping out of the relentless activity of the mind and into the stillness of the present. It's about realizing that who you are is not tied to your possessions, your achievements, or even your circumstances.

Most of us spend our lives lost in thought, believing that the voice in our head is who we are. We think we are the constant chatter, the worries, the regrets, the plans.

But that voice is not you.

It's just mental activity.

You are the one aware of the thoughts.

You are the observer, the presence behind the noise.

The mind pulls us into the past, replaying old memories, or projects us into the future, spinning stories about what might happen. Anxiety thrives in these moments because the mind is trying to control what it cannot.

But what if you didn't need to control everything?

What if you didn't need to think all the time?

My client's experience during the fires revealed something powerful.

When the mind stops, even for a moment, you discover peace.

She wasn't thinking about the future, because she couldn't predict it. She wasn't dwelling on the past, because it didn't matter.

All that remained was the eternal now.

And in that stillness, she saw that what truly mattered was untouchable.

And here's the beauty of it: you don't need a disaster to experience this.

Right now, as you're reading this, take a moment to notice your thoughts. Don't judge them. Don't try to stop them. Just observe them.

Now notice something deeper: the part of you that is aware of those thoughts. That quiet, still presence.

That is you.

The more you practice this awareness, the more you'll realize that you are not the storm of your thoughts.

You are the sky, vast and unchanging, in which the storm appears.

Overthinking is the mind's way of trying to solve problems that don't exist in the present. It's a futile attempt to gain control. But life isn't meant to be controlled.

It's meant to be experienced.

When you step out of the mind's activity and into the present, you awaken to the truth that this moment is all there ever is.

The past is gone.

The future is just an idea.

But right here, right now, is real.

Even when the fire rages, even when the mind storms, there is a part of you that remains untouched.

That is the essence of who you are.

And it's always here, waiting for you in the stillness of this moment.

So, ask yourself, if you're not your thoughts, who are you?

Sit with that question.

In the quiet space between the asking and the mind's attempt to answer, you'll find something deeper—what you've been seeking all along.

HOW TO FULLY LIVE
THE MOMENT YOU'RE IN

Let me ask you a question: how many times today were you truly *there* in what you were doing?

I mean *fully* there.

Not half-scrolling on your phone while eating breakfast, not lost in your head during a conversation, not rushing through a task while your mind jumped ahead to what's next.

Most of us live in a constant state of *half being*.

We're physically present, but mentally elsewhere, planning, replaying, worrying.

It's like we're standing with one foot in the present moment and the other in some imagined future or past. And while we might feel productive or busy, this state of divided attention leaves us empty, and prone to anxiety.

There's no depth to half being; when we're in this place, we're missing the beauty, the peace, and the joy that's available to us in the *now*.

Some might call this mindfulness, but I think of it as something simpler: immersive focus. It's not about trying to meditate through your day or forcing yourself to be present. It's just doing one thing, completely.

It's not about trying to make every moment profound or forcing yourself to savor every detail. That's just more mental clutter. Immersive focus is simple: when you're in something, be *in it*.

When you tie your shoelaces, just tie your shoelaces.

When you make coffee, just make coffee.

It sounds almost absurdly simple, but there's a hidden depth to it. When you immerse yourself fully, the simplest actions become rich.

Mundane moments reveal themselves as opportunities for peace and joy.

Immersive focus grounds you. It's the fastest way to pull yourself out of anxiety and back into reality. Not the version of reality in your head, but the one unfolding *right now*.

Let's bring this to life with a few simple moments.

Most of us make coffee on autopilot.

A means to an end.

But what if you turned it into a small ceremony?

Listen to the sound of the beans grinding.

Notice the texture of them.

Pay attention as the aroma fills the air.

Watch the steam rising, and feel the warmth of the cup.

This isn't about dragging the process out; it's about allowing yourself to *be there* for it. For those few minutes, nothing else exists but you and this cup of coffee.

Most of us walk to get somewhere, to burn calories, or to check a box.

But what if the walk was the point?

Feel your feet on the ground.

Feel the breeze as it hits your face.

Notice the rhythm of your breath and the subtle sounds around you—leaves rustling, a distant hum of life.

When you walk like this, you're not *getting somewhere*; you're *being there*. And suddenly, that quick walk becomes a moment of freedom.

How often do we "listen" to people while multitasking or thinking about what we're going to say next?

Instead, try *just listening*.

Let every word sink in.

Watch their facial expressions.

Be fully there for the other person.

It doesn't just transform how you experience the moment, it transforms the connection itself.

When you approach life with immersive focus, something incredible happens: you start *living*.

Anxiety fades because your attention isn't tangled in thoughts about tomorrow or yesterday.

Fulfillment increases because you're no longer rushing past your life.

You're in it.

Sitting quietly becomes a moment of peace.

It's not the world that changes—it's how you meet it.

The art of fully being is more than just a technique. It's a way of life.

When you start practicing immersive focus in small daily actions, you build a foundation of presence. You start to quiet the mental noise that keeps you anxious and disconnected. And over time, this presence becomes your natural state.

You awaken to the richness of your life, moment by moment.

So, start small. Tie your shoelaces. Make a cup of coffee. Take a walk. And let yourself *be there*. Because this moment, as simple as it seems, is your life. It's happening *now*.

As someone in my favorite movie once said, life moves pretty fast. If you don't stop and look around once in a while … you could miss it.

YOUR LIFE ISN'T MEANT
TO BE FIGURED OUT

Every now and then, I'll pause to taste honey—not as something I stir into tea or drizzle over toast, but just as it is. A spoonful of pure, golden honey. One of nature's many miraculous creations. I'll let it rest on my taste buds, noticing its texture—thick, smooth, almost alive. The sweetness unfolds slowly, rich and layered, carrying the essence of wildflowers and sunlight.

It's a moment I allow myself to simply experience.

Honey isn't just sweet. It's beyond words. You can try to describe it, call it "smooth" or "golden" or "floral," but none of that comes close. Honey is something you have to taste to understand.

And as I let the honey linger, I always come back to the same realization:

This is life.

You can't explain it.

You can't think your way into it.

You can only live it.

You weren't put on this earth to think about life. You weren't designed to spend your days worrying, planning, or overanalyzing every detail. That's not why you're here.

You are here to *experience* life.

You are here not just for the grand moments, but for the small ones too—the quiet, fleeting experiences that make up the fabric of life.

But somewhere along the way, we got lost. We started living in our heads, turning life into a mental exercise. We overthink the past, rehearse the future, and narrate every moment instead of living it.

Think about it. How often are you truly present? How often do you let yourself just be, without trying to control, fix, or plan what's next?

When you live in your head, you miss the point. Life isn't happening in your mind. It's happening here.

The mind is a powerful tool, but that's all it is: a tool. It's not your master, and it's not where life happens.

The mind can describe honey, but it can't taste it.

It can tell you all about love, but it can never feel it.

It can analyze joy, but it can't live it.

When you let the mind take over, life becomes something to think about, not something to experience. The problem isn't your mind itself—it's forgetting what the mind is for. It's meant to serve you, not control you.

Look at the body you've been given. Your senses aren't random. They are your connection to life itself.

Your eyes aren't meant to stare at a screen all day and skim over the world.

They're here to drink in the colors of a sunset, the glint of light on water, the details you rush past every day.

Your ears aren't meant to absorb endless noise.

They're here to enjoy music, to catch the laughter of a child or the silence of the morning.

Your tongue isn't just for eating. It's for tasting. For savoring. For letting you feel the richness of the moment through something as simple as a spoonful of honey.

Your senses are your gateway to the present moment. Through them, life opens itself to you. But when you're trapped in your thoughts, you slam the door shut.

A few years ago, I made a rule for myself: no phones or distractions during meals. Whether I'm eating alone or with family, I sit down, and I eat. I look at the food. I notice the colors, the textures, the way it's been prepared. I take a bite, close my eyes, and let myself taste it—really taste it.

At first, it felt strange. I kept reaching for my phone and then reminding myself of this new rule. As this new way of being became more natural, I realized how much of my life I'd spent eating mindlessly, distracted by a screen or my own thoughts. But as I kept at it, I started to feel something shift.

Meals became more than a habit. They became a moment of connection. Not just to the people I may be eating with, but to the food, to the nature that created it, to the effort that went into preparing it, and to life itself.

This simple practice taught me something profound: life is not something you think about. *Life is something you live.*

The beauty of life is that it's always here, waiting for you. You don't need to wait for some grand event or a perfect moment to experience it.

It's in the ordinary.

It's in the spoonful of honey.

The feeling of sunlight on your face.

The sound of the breeze moving through the trees.

It's in every bite of food, every breath, every moment you let yourself be present.

When you take the time to notice these things, something amazing happens. You stop feeling like life is something you need to chase or fix. You realize it's already here, and it's enough.

Let me be clear: you are not here to figure life out.

You are not here to constantly strive for something better.

You are not here to live in your head.

You are here to *experience life.*

You are here to feel the sweetness and the struggle, the light and the shadow, the extraordinary and the ordinary. You are here to taste the honey, not just describe it.

So, start now.

I challenge you to set your phone down.

Look at the world around you. Taste your food. Let the sunlight warm your skin. Listen to the sound of your own breath.

Not because it's what you're supposed to do, but because it's why you're here.

To experience. To feel. To live.

THE TIME YOU ENJOY
WASTING IS NOT WASTED TIME

There are days when I step away from work—not because I need to, but because I choose to.

I'll walk outside, feel the warmth of the sun, or watch funny shorts that leave me laughing until my stomach hurts.

In those moments, I'm not thinking about what needs to be done or what time I'm "wasting."

I'm simply alive.

And that's enough.

For most of my life, before my awakening, anytime I stepped away from work it always carried this tinge of guilt.

No matter how much I tried to relax or enjoy myself, there was always this subtle voice in the back of my mind, whispering that I was wasting time—that instead, I should be "productive."

That guilt hung over everything, robbing me of the joy I was trying to experience.

Through my awakening, I finally saw how absurd that was.

I realized this time isn't just a part of life—it *is* life.

"Time you enjoy wasting is not wasted time."

This quote stays with me because it cuts through the noise of our productivity-obsessed culture. Somewhere along the way, we started believing that every second must be justified—that if you aren't grinding, you're falling behind.

But what are you falling behind on, really?

The chance to live your life in the only moment that matters—the one you're in right now?

This isn't about numbing out with endless scrolling or feeding your mind comparisons that make you feel small. That's not joy. That's avoidance.

I'm talking about the time you *choose* to spend on what truly makes you feel good.

The kind of moments that remind you that there's more to life than what you accomplish.

Here's the truth:

You are not a machine.

Life isn't meant to be squeezed into a series of to-do lists or measured by the amount you produce.

Some of the most meaningful experiences have no outcome at all.

The sound of your laughter.

The peace of a quiet walk.

Gazing at a breathtaking sunset.

The release of losing yourself in a moment for no reason other than that it feels good.

You don't owe the world an explanation for how you spend your time.

The joy you feel is reason enough.

For years, I couldn't see that. I couldn't give myself permission to stop, to step away, to just *be*.

But now I know:

Stepping away isn't wasted.

It's living.

So, ask yourself:

When was the last time you gave yourself permission to enjoy a moment for its own sake?

What would it feel like to let go of the guilt, to stop measuring your worth by how much you do?

Can you allow yourself to believe that joy, in and of itself, is productive?

And if not now, then when?

The choice is yours, and it always has been.

LIVE TODAY LIKE
IT'S THE WHOLE STORY

We often hear people talk about "designing their life," this grand idea of creating a vision for the future, achieving goals, and building something extraordinary over time.

But what if I told you that *you don't need to design your entire life*?

Instead, the real magic happens when you focus on making each day your masterpiece. When you start approaching every day with the intention of making it the best it can be, you begin to create an extraordinary life, one day at a time.

The truth is, all you ever have is today.

Tomorrow is unknown, and yesterday is already gone.

What you do have control over is how you spend this very day. And when you intentionally design your day, focusing on what matters most to you, you begin to live a life that aligns with your values, your passions, and your deeper sense of purpose.

You don't need to figure everything out.

You don't need a five-year plan or a meticulously mapped-out life path.

Instead, ask yourself, *What would it look like if today were a masterpiece?*

Designing your day doesn't mean you need to fill every moment with productivity or achieve massive goals every twenty-four hours. It's about intentionally creating space for what is important to you. Whether you work for someone else or yourself, it's less about what you *do* and more about how you *choose* to approach your day.

Think about what truly matters to you.

Maybe it's your health, your relationships, your creative pursuits, or simply finding moments of peace in the chaos. Whatever it is, *design your day* around those priorities. You can work a job that may not completely align with your ultimate dreams, but still carve out time for what nourishes your soul. You can dedicate an hour to writing, taking care of your body, enjoying a hobby, or being fully present with loved ones.

When you focus on the day ahead and ask yourself, *How can I make today meaningful?*, you're not burdening yourself with the pressure of creating a perfect life all at once. Instead, you're taking small, meaningful steps toward a life that feels rich, fulfilling, and intentional.

One of the key aspects of making each day your masterpiece is knowing that it's not about grinding endlessly or being productive every minute. It's about choosing quality over quantity. It's about asking yourself, *What can I do today that would bring fulfillment, joy, or peace?*

Instead of focusing on getting more done, focus on getting the *right things* done.

The things that need to get done.

The things that matter to you.

The things that light you up.

Every day is an opportunity to create something beautiful, even if it's small.

You are the artist of your life, and each day is a fresh canvas.

You don't have to paint the whole picture all at once. Instead, focus on each brushstroke—each decision, each moment, each interaction. These small strokes, when made with intention, will eventually come together to create a masterpiece that reflects your deepest values, passions, and purpose.

One day, your life will be a collection of days.

So, make this one count.

Make today your masterpiece.

WHEN YOU STOP FIGHTING LIFE AND YOURSELF, YOU START LIVING

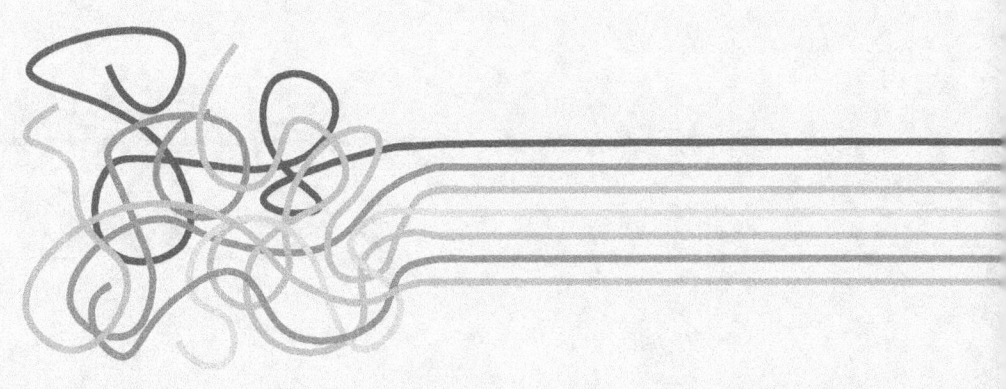

YOU ARE NOT BURIED,
YOU ARE BEING PLANTED

Your transformation is not a choice.

It's a law of nature.

Nature holds a mirror to our journey, showing us again and again that transformation is not just possible, it's inevitable.

It's woven into the very fabric of life.

Everywhere we look, the world around us whispers the same truth: growth and becoming require discomfort, pressure, and surrender.

A seed, when buried in the soil, might seem to be lost in darkness, pressed down and covered.

But it isn't buried—it's planted.

The weight of the soil, the darkness, the pressure—it's all part of the process.

And just when the little seed might think it can't take any more, a bull walks by and drops its waste right on top.

At first, it feels like too much, like adding insult to injury. But that bullshit is actually a gift to the little seed. It enriches the soil, giving the seed even *more* strength and nourishment to break through the surface and grow into something extraordinary.

Without the darkness, the weight, and even the bullshit, the seed would never reach its full potential.

It's just like the struggles you've faced. Heartbreak, failure, uncertainty… They're not burying you. They're planting you.

A diamond, dazzling and brilliant, begins as a lump of coal.

Only through intense pressure, heat, and time does the coal transform.

That pressure doesn't just change its shape; it pushes out impurities, leaving behind something pure, clear, and extraordinary.

The challenges pressing down on you now—the weight of anxiety, fear, or self-doubt—are not breaking you.

They're refining you, revealing the brilliance within.

The caterpillar enters the cocoon, not knowing what lies ahead. But what looks like confinement is actually transformation.

The cocoon is tight, dark, and unyielding.

It feels as though every option has closed, every path is blocked.

It's as if the whole world is pressing in, leaving nowhere to turn.

But that restriction makes the transformation possible.

Inside, the caterpillar dissolves entirely, breaking down so it can become something unrecognizable: a butterfly, dazzling and free.

Those moments in your life where it feels like everything is closing in, where you've tried everything and nothing works—those are your cocoon. They are not the end.

They are the beginning.

Even fire, which seems destructive, is a catalyst for renewal.

A forest fire clears away the old, the dead, and the stagnant, making space for new growth.

The ashes enrich the soil, creating the conditions for life to flourish.

What looks like destruction is often regeneration.

The losses you've experienced, the endings you never wanted—they're clearing space for something new to grow.

Here's the truth:

The discomfort and challenge you are feeling are not signs that something is wrong—they are part of your transformation.

You are not separate from these processes—you are them.

You are the seed, buried, but pushing toward the light.

You are the coal, enduring the pressure that reveals the diamond inside.

You are the caterpillar, dissolving and rebuilding, becoming something entirely new.

You are the forest, burning and regrowing, constantly renewing.

I know it's hard.

I know it feels like too much.

I've been there.

Before my awakening, I can't even tell you how many times I looked at all the bullshit and challenges coming my way and thought, "This isn't fair." I felt like life was piling on, refusing to let me catch a break. I questioned why it had to be so hard, why I had to go through so much.

But now, when I look back, I see it differently. Every single one of those struggles—every heartbreak, every failure, every moment of doubt—was an essential ingredient in my awakening. What felt like punishment then was actually preparation. It was life giving me exactly what I needed to transform.

And just like me, you need time.

These transformations don't happen overnight.

The seed doesn't sprout the moment it's planted.

The coal doesn't become a diamond in a single instant.

The caterpillar doesn't enter the cocoon in the morning and emerge as a butterfly by nightfall.

Transformation takes time, and that time is essential. Give yourself the space and grace to evolve at your own pace.

Nature doesn't avoid transformation—it embraces it.

It teaches us that growth isn't comfortable, but it is essential.

It reminds us that what feels like darkness or pressure is not the end—it's the beginning.

So, the next time you feel the weight and bullshit of life pressing down, remember the seed. The next time you feel crushed by pressure, remember the coal. The next time you feel stuck, remember the caterpillar. The next time you feel like everything is falling apart, remember the fire.

You are part of this same cycle.

Just as nature transforms itself over and over, so do you. It's not happening to you—it's happening *for* you. And just like the seed, the diamond, the butterfly, and the forest, you will emerge stronger, brighter, and more alive than ever before.

WHY EVERY TIME YOU FALL IS A STEP FORWARD

Transformation doesn't just happen—it happens through struggle. And I know that firsthand.

In my younger years, I was far from healthy.

At my heaviest, I was more than 50 pounds overweight and classified as obese. I carried that weight not just on my body, but in my mind and emotions.

I felt trapped, heavy in every sense of the word.

But even back then, I knew deep down that the overweight version of me wasn't who I was meant to be. I had visions of myself as I am now—lean, strong, and muscular. I could see it so clearly, but it felt so far out of reach.

Literally for *decades*, I cycled through failed attempts to change.

I'd start a workout plan or a diet, throw myself into it for a couple of weeks, and then quit— over and over again. I'd tell myself, "This time, I'll stick with it," only to lose momentum and fall back into old habits. I must have started and stopped a hundred different diets and workouts. And every time, at the beginning of each attempt, there was a little voice in the back of my mind whispering, *What makes you think you're going to stick with it this time? You've failed so many times before.*

That voice was relentless, and I believed it more times than I'd like to admit.

But here's the thing. Even with that voice taunting me, I kept showing up. I kept moving forward. And eventually, something shifted.

For me, it started with a panic attack—one that landed me in the hospital with dangerously high blood pressure and an irregular heartbeat. It was a rock-bottom moment, a wake-up call I couldn't ignore. I knew I couldn't keep living the way I was, and that realization finally pushed me to change. I started, and this time, I didn't stop. I kept showing up, kept doing the work, and step by step, I transformed.

As I look back now, I realize it doesn't matter how many times I failed before, because ultimately, I succeeded.

And the same is true for you.

A setback doesn't mean you've failed. It just means you need to get back up and do it again.

Persistence is the key.

Every time you rise after a fall, you're moving closer to where you want to be. It's not about never stumbling.

It's about refusing to give up. As long as you keep getting back up, failure never wins.

Looking back, I'm grateful for every failed attempt. At the time, it felt like I was getting nowhere, but those moments taught me something vital.

Transformation doesn't happen in a straight line.

Every misstep was part of the process, giving me the lessons and resolve I needed to eventually succeed. That version of me who struggled yet kept pushing forward wasn't a failure. He was building the foundation for the person I am today.

The struggle itself became the springboard.

If I'd been naturally lean or athletic, I wouldn't have had the chance to experience the deep satisfaction of transforming my body and my life. That journey taught me that transformation isn't just about the destination. It's about the resistance along the way. Without the weight I carried, both literally and figuratively, I wouldn't have had the opportunity to create something extraordinary.

Here's the truth about transformation: it begins in the tension.

Every setback, every moment of discomfort, has shaped you into someone more powerful than before. The resistance doesn't weaken you. It transforms you.

This idea changed the way I see not only my own journey, but life itself. The discomfort you feel in the moment isn't a punishment. It's propulsion. It's the energy that will carry you forward if you let it.

Your starting point doesn't define you.

It launches you.

No matter how far life has pulled you back, remember this: just like an arrow drawn deep into the bow, the greater the tension, the more powerful the release. Every setback, every struggle, every moment of resistance is building potential energy—preparing you to launch forward with even greater strength, speed, and purpose.

To this day, I still show up. I live a healthy lifestyle—not perfectly, but consistently—and I plan to keep showing up for the rest of my life.

That's the real lesson.

Persistence is everything.

Transformation doesn't end. It's not a one-time event.

It's a way of being.

So, if you're in the middle of your own resistance right now, whatever that looks like, embrace it.

You don't have to like it, but you can trust it.

The struggle you're feeling isn't the end. It's the beginning.

One day, you'll look back and see it for what it was: the gift that helped you become everything you were always meant to be.

PEACE COMES WHEN YOU FINALLY STOP FIGHTING REALITY

So much of life is spent dealing with things we don't want—things we'd never choose if given the option.

Living in Florida means hurricanes are a reality—just like earthquakes and wildfires in California. Maybe it's an election outcome that didn't go your way, or a parking ticket you never saw coming. Life brings unexpected disruptions, big and small.

It's sitting in traffic when you're already late, or standing in a slow-moving line at the grocery store. It's the noisy neighbors who won't let you sleep, the delayed flight that throws off your plans, or spilling coffee on your favorite shirt just before a meeting.

These forces, both large and small, and so many other frustrations we face in life are often entirely outside our control. And yet, they consume so much of our mental and emotional energy.

The truth is, most of the things that frustrate us the most are those we have little or no control over. And this is where radical acceptance becomes not just helpful, but essential.

Radical acceptance isn't about giving up or pretending you like the situation. It's about finding within yourself the ability to release the energy of resistance—the *"No, this can't be happening"* or *"This isn't what I wanted"* mindset.

Holding onto that energy of non-acceptance serves no purpose.

It doesn't help. It doesn't change the situation. And the only person it truly harms is you.

The key to living a peaceful life is learning to let go—completely and fully—of the things outside your control.

It's about accepting those moments and situations as if you had chosen them.

Yes—*as if you chose them.*

Giving them that level of space to simply be.

And here's the important thing: acceptance is the first step, not the last. Once you've let go of resistance, you create the clarity and inner calm to decide if there's any action you can take.

If there is, take it—not from a place of frustration or desperation, but from a place of groundedness and intention.

And if there's nothing you can do, then simply allowing the situation to be as it is becomes the most powerful choice you can make.

In my home office, there's a sign that hangs directly above my head, right in the center of the wall. It's always in my line of sight, impossible to miss.

The words are simple: *"Have a mind that is open to everything and attached to nothing."*

I see it and read it often. It's been a quiet reminder to stay flexible, to let go.

But during one of the most overwhelming times in my life, it began to feel like it was speaking directly to me, calling me to look deeper and truly understand what it meant.

At the time, anxiety had wrapped itself around me like a storm cloud.

Every decision felt like life or death. Every outcome had to be controlled. I felt trapped in an endless loop of *what-ifs*, and no matter how hard I tried to think my way out, I only sank deeper into fear.

One day, sitting at my desk, my eyes locked on that sign, and something shifted.

I realized that the need for control wasn't helping me. It was suffocating me.

The harder I tried to force life to fit into neat little boxes, the more anxious I became.

Slowly, I began to see that peace doesn't come from controlling outcomes. It comes from letting go of the need to control them in the first place.

Those words—*"open to everything, attached to nothing"*—became my guide.

They reminded me to embrace life as it is, not as I think it should be.

Most of us spend our lives trying to control things that are completely outside of our power—other people, outcomes, situations, politics, the world itself.

We agonize over how things *should* go, only to find ourselves frustrated, stressed, and exhausted when life doesn't follow our script.

But here's the truth: control over anything outside of yourself is an illusion.

It's like trying to hold water in your hands: the tighter you grip, the faster it slips away.

Life, by its nature, flows. It's meant to move.

When you stop trying to dam the river and instead step into its current, you discover that the flow will carry you—always to exactly where you need to be.

What you can control is this: your attitude, your responses, and your actions.

That's it. That's where your power begins and ends.

Surrender doesn't mean giving up. It means releasing the futile attempt to control everything else and directing that energy inward, where it can actually make a difference.

Let go of your need to control how other people behave. Release the stories you tell yourself about how things should turn out. Stop clinging to expectations about the world, your relationships, or your career.

These attachments are like heavy stones in your backpack, weighing you down as you try to move forward. When you let them go, you lighten your load, and suddenly, the path ahead feels easier.

And here's the thing: if something happens—if life throws something unexpected your way—you will handle it. You've always handled it.

As I've said before, you have a one hundred percent track record of making it through every challenge you've faced. You're still here. You're reading these words. That's proof of your resilience.

When you surrender the need to control everything outside of you, you'll find a surprising freedom. You'll move *with* life, not against it.

It's like stepping into a river and letting the current carry you, trusting that it knows the way.

Surrender doesn't mean drifting aimlessly—it means moving with intention while letting go of resistance.

Anxiety thrives in the gap between craving certainty and fearing the unknown.

Awakening dissolves that gap—not by giving you certainty, but by teaching you to trust the process.

That doesn't mean giving up on growth or desire. It means shifting from striving out of fear to growing with joy.

Anxiety narrows your attention to everything that could go wrong. Awakening widens your vision to what could go right.

Instead of feeding the endless loop of worries and external chaos, pause and ask yourself:

"What excites me? What feels alive in me right now?"

What if, instead of clinging to control, you let joy and curiosity guide you?

Imagine releasing the need to predict every outcome and trusting that the excitement you feel in the moment is enough.

This isn't about abandoning responsibility or ignoring challenges. It's about shifting your energy from fear to possibility, from resistance to growth.

When you stop fighting with reality, you win.

You stop wasting your energy on resistance.

You create a sense of openness and ease, even in the face of things you don't want.

You free yourself.

And as you move through life, hold onto this:

Have a mind that is open to everything and attached to nothing.

Because in that openness, in that surrender, you will find something incredible.

Not fear. Not anxiety.

But freedom.

YOU WERE NEVER MEANT TO FIGHT THE DARKNESS—ONLY TO SHINE

Why is there so much suffering in the world?
Why does darkness persist, and why does evil exist at all?
Are we just supposed to accept it, since so much of it is outside our control?

These questions echo through humanity, cutting to the core of our deepest pain and confusion. And yet, the answer lies in the very nature of duality—of life itself—and the profound purpose of the soul's journey.

Imagine a single ray of sunlight, brilliant and pure, as part of the infinite brightness of the sun.

When it is close to the sun, or one with it, the ray cannot see itself.
It cannot distinguish its own radiance, because it is enveloped within the whole.
Its light is merged with the vastness of the sun, inseparable and indistinguishable.

And so, for the light to know itself—for the soul to experience itself as light—it must leave the sun. It must project itself into the shadow, into the contrast of a physical world filled with duality.

Only in the presence of darkness can the light recognize itself.
Only in separation can it know unity.

This is why we come to this dream of life.

We enter a world of contrast—joy and suffering, love and fear, light and darkness—so that we may experience and remember who we truly are. Without the challenges of duality, we would remain indistinguishable from the source, unaware of our own brilliance.

But here is where many of us misunderstand: darkness is not something to fight.

It does not require a battle.

Darkness is not an opposing force; it is simply the absence of light.

Like a shadow that disappears the moment the sun rises, darkness dissolves when light is introduced.

And here's the profound truth: you are the light.

Your light, like the flame of a candle, does not diminish when it is shared. Instead, it multiplies. A single candle can light thousands of others without losing its own brilliance.

This is the nature of life, and this is the nature of your light.

A single candle in the darkest room transforms the space completely, allowing us to see what was hidden. And when we light another's candle, we are not just spreading light—we are sharing warmth, connection, and hope.

This is how we collectively illuminate the world.

Bringing your light into the world doesn't mean performing grand acts or being perfect. It's often in the smallest moments—when you smile at a stranger, comfort someone in pain, forgive yourself, or simply hold space for another—that your light shines brightest. These small, seemingly simple acts ripple outward, touching lives in ways you may never see.

Even when you feel surrounded by darkness, remember this: the light is always within you.

It may seem dim or hidden at times, but it is never extinguished.

All it takes is a moment of stillness, a breath, or a simple act of love to begin to shine again.

And when you shine, you don't just illuminate your own path—you light the way for others.

This understanding shifts our perspective on life's contrasts. We begin to see that darkness and suffering are not meaningless chaos, but the fertile ground from which the light of awareness blooms and recognizes itself.

Just as a ray of sunlight finds its purpose in the contrast of shadow, we find our deepest truth when we stop resisting life's duality and instead embrace our role as light-bearers.

And as we shine, something extraordinary happens: we begin to see that the light and the darkness were never truly separate.

They were always part of a greater whole, designed to help us return to the awareness of oneness.

The light does not fear the darkness.

It does not resist it, and it has no need to fight it.

It simply shines, and in doing so, it fulfills its purpose.

And this is a key to overcoming anxiety.

Anxiety is a form of darkness, but not because it is powerful—because it thrives in the absence of light. It exists in the space where fear overshadows presence, where we forget who we are.

Anxiety is the mind projecting shadows onto the walls of an uncertain future, making us believe there is something to fear. But just like darkness, it has no substance of its own. It is an illusion created by the absence of awareness.

And just as a single candle can banish darkness, a moment of awareness can dissolve anxiety.

When you return to presence, to the truth of this moment, the shadows begin to fade. You remember that the fear in your mind is not real—only this moment is real. Only *you* are real.

Anxiety cannot survive in the light of full awareness.

So, when fear takes hold, anchor yourself in the now. Feel your presence. Step into your light.

Shine boldly, and share it freely.

The world is waiting—not for a battle, but for your brilliance to illuminate the shadows.

This is your purpose, your power, and your gift to life itself.

LET LIFE FINISH THE STORY BEFORE YOU JUDGE IT

We spend so much of our lives labeling things—events, people, outcomes—as either good or bad.

It's such an automatic habit that we rarely stop to question it.

Something happens, and we judge it immediately, locking ourselves into that perspective, unable to see beyond it.

My kids ask me all the time, "Daddy, is that bad? Is that good?"

Maybe they've overheard something about an election result that has adults either celebrating or upset. Or they found out that their class is getting a new teacher next year, and they're not sure whether to be excited or nervous.

And I tell them the truth:

"We don't know yet. We'll see."

They still look at me sideways sometimes, as if I'm not answering their question at all. And I get it. Kids want clarity. So do most adults. But certainty is an illusion.

The moment we slap a label of "good" or "bad" on something, we shrink it.

We cut ourselves off from its wholeness, from the truth that life is always moving, always unfolding, and what it looks like right now is never the whole story.

More than that, when we label something as "bad," we create resistance.

It's as if we're saying, *"This isn't how it should be."*

But life doesn't work that way.

Life is what it is.

When we resist it, when we push back against what's already happening, we only make it harder for ourselves. We suffer not because of the situation itself, *but because of our thoughts about it.*

Because we're fighting against it.

We see this everywhere, but especially in politics.

An election is won or lost, a law is passed, or a headline flashes across our screens, and within seconds, we decide, "This is good," or "This is bad." We dig our heels into that perspective, joining a chorus of voices either cheering or condemning.

But politics, like life, is a long story. Its effects ripple out in ways we can't always predict.

What feels like progress today might reveal unexpected challenges tomorrow.

What looks like a setback could clear the way for something better.

When we label something too quickly, we close the door to seeing the full arc of its impact.

So, the next time you feel that instant judgment rising up, take a breath. Step back.

Ask yourself, "Do I really know yet?"

There's a story I love about a wise old farmer that captures this perfectly.

The wise farmer lived on the edge of a small village, his days spent tending to his land. He was quiet, with weathered hands and steady eyes that always seemed to see something others couldn't.

One day, his only horse broke free from its pen and disappeared into the hills. The villagers came to him, shaking their heads. "Oh no, this is terrible!" they said.

The farmer, with a faint smile, replied, "Maybe. We'll see."

The next morning, the horse returned and brought with it a group of wild horses. The villagers rushed back, their voices full of excitement. "This is wonderful!" they exclaimed.

The farmer, steady as ever, replied, "Maybe. We'll see."

A few days later, the farmer's son tried to ride one of the wild horses. The horse bucked, throwing him hard to the ground, breaking his leg. The villagers gasped. "Oh no! This is terrible!"

The farmer sat beside his son, his voice as calm as ever. "Maybe. We'll see."

Weeks later, soldiers arrived in the village to conscript all able-bodied young men for war. Families wept as their sons were taken away, but the farmer's son, with his broken leg, was left behind. The villagers marveled, "This is wonderful!"

And the farmer replied, as he always did, "Maybe. We'll see."

This story stays with me because it reveals something so simple and so true.

We just don't know.

What feels like a loss today may turn out to be a gift.

What looks like good fortune may come with challenges we can't yet see.

Think about your own life right now. Maybe something is happening that feels bad. Maybe it's a situation that's keeping you up at night, a challenge you can't stop thinking about, a plan that didn't work out, a loss that hit you harder than you expected.

Take a moment and breathe. *Really* breathe. Step back from it.

Right now, you might be so close to what's happening that it feels like it's all there is, like this one moment has swallowed your entire world. But that's not true.

Your life is so much bigger than this one situation.

When you zoom out, when you take a step back, you'll see that this moment, no matter how hard or confusing it feels, is just one small part of a much larger story.

And when you stop resisting, when you let go of the idea that things should be different, you create space. Space to see more clearly. Space to move forward with less struggle. Space to trust that life is unfolding exactly as it's meant to, even if you can't see why just yet.

I've been there myself. There were moments in my life that felt impossible, like everything was falling apart. At the time, I couldn't see how they could ever be for my benefit. But looking back, I can see it clearly now. Those moments were clearing a path, leading me somewhere I couldn't yet imagine.

Now, think back on your own life.

Haven't there been moments that felt like setbacks, losses, or failures—only for you to later realize they were actually opening doors to something better?

At the time, they may have felt like the worst thing that could happen. But now, with time and perspective, you can see—those moments weren't just endings.

They were beginnings.

So, whatever you're going through right now, trust that it's not the end of the story. Trust that life is still unfolding, still working for you in ways you can't yet see.

Maybe what feels like a loss right now is actually clearing space for something better. Maybe the ending you didn't want is setting you up for a beginning you never expected. Maybe what fell apart was never meant for you, because something greater is on its way.

You don't have to figure it all out right now. You don't have to know how it will all come together. You just have to trust the process.

So, take a breath.

Look at whatever is happening in your life right now, and instead of judging it, labeling it good or bad, just say to yourself, "I don't know yet. We'll see."

Like the wise farmer who didn't rush to judge his circumstances, trust that what looks like misfortune today may turn out to be a blessing tomorrow. Life is always unfolding in ways we can't yet see.

Trust that there is a bigger picture, even if you can't see it yet.

And know this: everything—*everything* is part of the masterpiece.

THE DAY I STOPPED RESISTING LIFE

Before my awakening, complaining was just a part of my life. It was automatic.

And I didn't just complain.

I complained *a lot*.

If my kids didn't put their shoes where they were supposed to, I'd complain.
If I had too much work, I'd complain about being overwhelmed.
If I didn't have enough work, I'd complain about that too.

If someone's behavior toward me felt wrong, or if I didn't like how they acted in general, I'd complain about that as well. My mind was constantly searching for problems instead of solutions, and I didn't even realize it.

Through my awakening, I started to realize that this pattern wasn't serving me.

Complaining wasn't making anything better.

It wasn't solving problems or changing situations.

All it did was keep me in a state of resistance, a constant fight with the present moment.

Fighting reality doesn't change reality.

Complaining is universal. It's something we all do because it feels like we're taking control. It gives us a false sense of power, as though by voicing our frustrations, we're somehow fixing the situation. But really, complaining is your ego's way of trying to resist what is.

It's the mind saying, "I don't like this, so I'll push against it."

But the truth is that no amount of resistance changes the truth of what's in front of you.

When I saw this clearly, I decided I needed to stop.

I grabbed a marker and wrote *No More Complaining* on my whiteboard, right where I'd see it every day. I made a deal with myself: *If something needs to be done, I'll do it. If something isn't the way I want it to be, I'll recognize it, but I won't hold any energy toward it. I'll let it go.*

It took some time, but finally ... it worked. I stopped complaining, and I haven't looked back.

Here's what I want you to understand:

Complaining is a habit, and like any habit, it can be broken.

The first step is awareness.

Start noticing how often you complain, whether it's out loud or just in your head. Most of us don't even realize how much we do it.

Next, make the decision to stop.

Consider a goal of no complaining for seven days.

Write it down where you'll see it daily.

Make it a mantra.

Do whatever it takes to remind yourself.

Every time you catch yourself starting to complain, pause and ask, "Is this something I can change?" If yes, "What action can I take right now?" If it's something you can't change, ask, "How can I accept it and let it go?"

Most of the things we complain about fall into the second category: things we can't change. Traffic, other people's behavior, the weather… When you stop resisting those things, you'll notice something incredible: your frustration starts to dissolve, and you feel lighter.

Complaining isn't just wasted energy. It's your ego's attempt to control the uncontrollable.

Real power doesn't come from resistance.

It comes from acceptance.

When you accept what is, you stop being at war with life.

Letting go of complaining isn't just about finding peace. It's about reclaiming your energy and stepping into the flow of life as it is. When you do that, you'll be amazed at how much lighter and freer life feels.

When you stop arguing with life, life stops feeling like an argument.

HOW A HURRICANE
TAUGHT ME TO LET LIFE FLOW

Not long ago, a massive hurricane swept toward Florida, and from the moment I saw it on the map, I just knew—it was heading straight for our area.

It was October, long past the peak of hurricane season, and several storms had already battered our coast.

In the past, that alone would have been enough to send me spiraling: *Seriously? Another one?* Frustration, resistance, and even anger at how unfair it all felt.

But this time, it was different.

I felt something I hadn't expected: calm.

I knew what I had to do, and I didn't fight it.

Putting up hurricane shutters, a task that had once felt like a punishment, became something else entirely. I thought to myself, *This is just part of life here. It's what I do to protect my home and my family. It's even getting me some exercise.* And so, with each shutter I installed, I moved not in frustration, but in acceptance.

When the decision came to evacuate, it wasn't chaotic or rushed.

We packed up the kids, the dog, and a few essentials, and headed out of town—not out of panic, but with intention and flow.

I reframed it in my mind: *This is a chance to be together as a family, to make an adventure out of something unpredictable.*

Even in the unknown, I felt anchored.

But I'd be lying if I said there weren't moments of fear.

As the storm intensified, it pushed the limits of what we even call a hurricane. Category 5 is supposed to be the highest level, but this storm was different. It was so powerful that meteorologists debated whether a new category should be created just to measure its strength.

This wasn't just another storm—it was a force of nature unlike anything we had seen before.

As I looked at the map and saw the storm's eye locked onto our town, I wondered if we'd even have a home to come back to.

Would it be underwater?

Would everything we'd built be gone?

Those thoughts came, as they do, but I let them come. I didn't push them away or try to pretend I wasn't scared.

I let myself fully feel the fear.

I accepted that I had absolutely *zero control* over what would happen.

And in that surrender, something shifted.

In letting go of the need to control, I found something remarkable: peace.

Not the peace of pretending everything is fine, but the peace of fully embracing life as it is.

I trusted that there was something bigger at play—an intelligence, an order beneath the surface. I couldn't see it, but I could feel it.

And then, something extraordinary happened.

Meteorologists had expected catastrophic devastation.

But just as the storm neared our coast, a powerful wind shear swept down from the north—disrupting its force, slowing its momentum. What should have been stronger than a Category 5 unexpectedly weakened to a Category 3.

The difference between the two wasn't just numbers on a scale—it was the difference between catastrophe and survival.

Our town, our home, instead of what could have been total devastation, suffered only minimal damage.

Some might call it luck. But I knew better.

It felt like a reflection of something deeper.

When I stopped resisting, the storm itself seemed to let go too.

I had surrendered, and somehow, life had met me there.

That storm wasn't just a weather event, it was a reminder of how life works. Awakening isn't about avoiding storms; it's about learning to embrace them.

There's a common misconception that awakening is about escaping life—leaving behind its challenges, imperfections, and messiness to float off into some distant, blissful state.

But true awakening is the opposite.

It's not a retreat; it's a return.

A return to the present moment, to the raw and unfiltered reality of existence. And not just a passive return, but a full embrace—a deep, abiding love for life exactly as it is.

When you awaken, you don't stop feeling.

You feel more deeply than ever before.

But the difference is, you no longer fight life.

You stop resisting the things you once saw as hardships or upheavals, because you realize they are just as much a part of life's perfection as the moments of joy.

Awakening isn't about fixing yourself or your life—it's about fully showing up for it.

All of it.

Imagine standing in the middle of a storm, the wind pulling at your clothes and the rain soaking your skin, and instead of running for shelter, you open your arms wide and feel it all. Awakening is like that—a willingness to experience the fullness of life, no matter how wild or unpredictable it may seem.

When you reach this state, you begin to see life as it truly is: a beautiful, chaotic, and awe-inspiring dance.

The joy and the heartbreak, the certainty and the uncertainty, the laughter and the tears—they all belong.

And when you no longer reject any part of life, you start to feel something incredible: peace. Not the kind of peace that comes from avoiding problems, but the kind that comes from knowing you can handle them—like you always have.

The kind of peace that's born from loving life enough to embrace it completely.

This is what it means to live in an awakened state.

It's not about walking away from life's challenges—it's about walking straight into them with an open heart.

And it's about knowing, deep in your bones, that you are fully equipped to handle anything life sends your way. Why? Because you've realized that life isn't happening to you; it's happening *for* you.

Every moment is an invitation to grow, to expand, to deepen your connection with yourself and the world around you.

The awakened life is not perfect.

But it is real.

It is vibrant.

And it is yours to claim.

When you stop waiting for life to be perfect and instead embrace it exactly as it is, you realize that awakening is not some distant destination.

It's here.

It's now.

It's in the smile of a stranger, the ache of heartbreak, the quiet of a morning sunrise.

It's even in the storms that shake you, but never break you.

What if you stopped waiting and instead fell deeply in love with life—exactly as it is?

THE PARTS OF YOU YOU'VE SPENT YOUR LIFE HIDING ARE YOUR GREATEST STRENGTHS

For much of my life, I saw myself as lazy, undisciplined, weak-willed, unmotivated, and directionless.

These "flaws" weren't just minor insecurities—they were parts of myself that I actively resented. I believed they were the reason I wasn't where I wanted to be, the weight holding me back from my potential.

As you reflect on your own life, you might notice the aspects of yourself that you've labeled as "negative" or "flaws."

Perhaps you've judged these parts of yourself harshly, believing that they diminish your worth or keep you stuck.

But what if, instead of being weaknesses to eliminate, these perceived shortcomings were essential parts of your design?

What if they were given to you for a reason—so that through overcoming them, you could become exactly who you were always meant to be?

In the same way that a seed needs the resistance of the soil to push through and become a tree, your perceived flaws are the fertile ground for your transformation.

They are not mistakes.

They are the catalysts that propel you forward, forcing you to grow, adapt, and evolve into the person you were destined to become.

We often hear that we should love ourselves despite our "imperfections." But what if real transformation comes when we love ourselves *because of them*?

These parts of you, the ones you've spent years criticizing or trying to hide, are actually your greatest teachers.

They are the challenges you were given, not as punishments, but as sacred invitations to become the fullest expression of who you are.

When you begin to love these aspects of yourself—not as burdens, *but as gifts*—everything opens. You start to see that the very things you once saw as obstacles are the stepping stones to your awakening. They are the tools given to you to break free from limiting beliefs, to grow beyond your comfort zone, and to embody your highest self.

The moment you stop seeing your perceived flaws as proof of your limitations and start recognizing them as part of the process, a new kind of clarity settles in. You realize they are not barriers—they are the very conditions necessary for your transformation. They are not signs of something missing in you, but the exact resistance needed to forge the qualities you once believed you lacked.

I didn't understand this at first. For years, I saw my struggles as obstacles, as evidence that I was somehow broken or unworthy. But looking back, I can see that they were invitations. The very things I resented—my lack of discipline, my indecision, my perceived weakness— became the raw material for my transformation.

Because I felt undisciplined, I had to cultivate self-discipline. Because I saw myself as weak-willed, I had to forge inner strength. Every quality I now embody—focus, resilience, discipline—was built upon the foundation of the very struggles I once believed were holding me back.

That's the paradox: struggles are not roadblocks. They are a training ground.

If I had been born with the qualities I once wished for, I would have missed the process of becoming—the very journey that shaped me. There would have been no struggle to push against, no resistance to overcome, no journey of transformation to walk. The growth, the wisdom, the depth—it all came from the process of becoming. The very things I once saw as flaws were, in truth, the necessary contrast that allowed me to cultivate the qualities I once thought I lacked.

And isn't that true for you as well? If you look closely, can you already see it? The ways in which your struggles have shaped you, refined you?

Now, think back to your darkest moment.

The one that may still hold the weight of shame, regret, or pain.

That moment—the one you might try to forget or avoid—was not your lowest point.

It was, in fact, your brightest.

That dark moment was not a failure; it was the moment that set your transformation in motion. It was the turning point, the catalyst that forced you to confront the parts of yourself you are most afraid to face. Without that moment, you wouldn't have been pushed to grow, to change, or to discover your true strength.

You may have felt broken or lost during that time, but what was really happening was a breakthrough.

In your darkest hour, you were unknowingly moving toward the light of your true self. The shame or regret you carry is a misunderstanding of that moment's purpose. It wasn't a sign of your weakness. It was a sign of your impending transformation.

When you look at certain parts of yourself now, you may still feel resistance. You may still be working through them. And that's okay. Growth is not about erasing your struggles—it's about seeing them differently. Instead of trying to fight them, you can meet them with love. Instead of seeing them as flaws, you can recognize them as part of your path.

You don't have to wait until you feel completely transformed to embrace these parts of yourself. You can start now. You can choose to see that these struggles are not proof that something is wrong with you.

They are proof that you are in the process of becoming.

They are guiding you toward strength, clarity, and resilience.

And one day, you will look back and see that these very things you once wished away were the greatest gifts you were ever given.

Not because they remained, but because they shaped you into the person you were always meant to become.

FREEDOM BEGINS
WHERE CONTROL ENDS

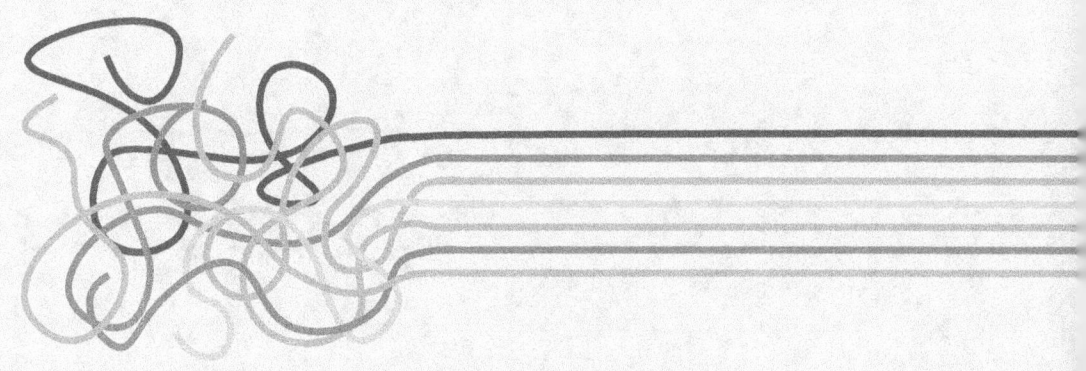

WHAT YOU'RE CHASING IS ALREADY YOURS

There's a truth we rarely acknowledge: what we think we want is never what we truly desire.

What we really want is the feeling we believe exists on the other side of having it: peace, freedom, fulfillment.

I learned this in one of the most unexpected and life-altering ways.

Years ago, my wife and I were on the verge of closing a monumental corporate deal for the wellness app we had created. It was with one of the biggest companies in the world.

This wasn't just a deal—it was *the* deal.

It was nothing short of life-changing money. It was going to set us up with true wealth for generations to come. It was the end of any and all financial struggles.

It was everything I had worked so hard for.

Financial freedom, stability, success—it was all right there. It was destiny manifesting.

The meetings with the company went phenomenally well. The conversations were fully aligned. The VP of this massive company told us, "We're going to do this."

Not only that, but they were actively pushing to move things forward, eager to close the deal. I can still hear their confidence in every word.

As I clicked out of the video call, it was like the weight of years of effort lifted off my shoulders. I got up and did a dance of joy, arms raised, fists clenched, as if I had just won the World Cup.

For the first time in as long as I could remember, I exhaled.

In my mind, it was done. I wasn't just waiting for my life to change—I felt it had already changed.

I could feel it in my bones, in my energy. The striving, the constant push, the gnawing need to prove myself—it all melted away.

I wasn't running toward anything anymore. I was *here*—and it was glorious.

For weeks, I found myself living in this *in-between* space—a strange and transformative place suspended between my old life and the one that was just on the horizon.

127

It felt as though I were standing in a chasm, with my old world of anxiety and striving on one side, and a new world of abundance, freedom, and ease on the other.

In my heart and mind, I had already crossed the threshold.

I stopped worrying about money, about outcomes, about the endless *what-ifs* that had consumed so much of my energy for most of my life.

I let go.

I surrendered to the certainty that everything I wanted was already on its way.

I felt free, like a weight I hadn't even realized I was carrying had been lifted.

This in-between phase was extraordinary.

I wasn't striving anymore. I wasn't seeking anything.

For the first time, I felt like I could just *be*.

My old life wasn't defining me anymore, and while my new life hadn't fully materialized, I was living as though it had. I was lighter, more present, more alive than I had ever been.

It was as if I had borrowed the feelings of the life I was longing for—and I realized I didn't need to wait for it to arrive.

Day after day, week after week, I stayed in this state of peace. I was deeply present. My mind was quiet.

My kids' laughter seemed brighter, fuller. I stopped to smell flowers, to marvel at sunsets, to breathe in the stillness and beauty of life all around me.

I wasn't rushing or striving anymore, because everything I had worked so hard for was finally coming.

That certainty allowed me to let go, to simply *be*.

I experienced inner peace like I had never known.

Absolutely *nothing* bothered me.

Everything was moving forward as planned.

There was nothing left to do but wait for the final paperwork.

I could see the contract signed, the numbers—*massive, life-changing numbers*—hitting my bank account, and the certainty of stability, freedom, and recognition washing over me.

I started making quiet plans for what this new chapter of life would look like for our family.

And then, the certainty started to slip.

At first, it was small hesitations—delays in the next steps, vague responses. I told myself it was normal.

Deals this big take time, right?

At least, that's what I kept telling myself.

But the delays kept piling up, and their tone began to shift.

They started making excuses—concerns about corporate profits, stock performance, and budgets.

They said things were tighter than expected and hinted at needing more time to make a decision.

I felt the first cracks of doubt, but I tried to hold onto hope.

And then it happened.

They backed out entirely.

The deal I thought was guaranteed—the deal that was supposed to change *everything*—slipped through my fingers like sand.

It was like realizing I had won one of the biggest Super Lotto jackpots of all time—spending weeks already living in the certainty of my new life—only to find out, just as I was about to collect my winnings…

That my numbers were from last week.

It was over.

It felt like the ground itself had been ripped out from under me.

I remember sitting there shell-shocked on our living room couch, in complete disbelief, shaking my head and trying to process it.

How could something so certain—something that was *destined*—fall apart so completely?

I was devastated.

I had been living in that in-between place, so sure of my future, and now it was gone.

I fought with reality.

I raged against it.

I grieved the life I had already *felt* I was living.

And then, finally, I surrendered.

There was nothing left to hold onto.

I had to let go.

I began asking myself, *Why? Why did this happen?*

Deep down, I knew there was a lesson in this. But I couldn't see it yet.

So, I asked myself, *What am I supposed to learn from this?*

And slowly, clarity began to emerge.

I began to recognize that during this *in-between* period, nothing in my outer life had actually changed.

Absolutely nothing.

The money had never arrived. The deal had never been finalized.

The only thing that had shifted was *my inner world*.

I realized *I* had created the feeling I was longing for within me, believing it was tied to something external.

But it wasn't.

There was absolutely *nothing* I was lacking or needing in order to feel this way.

The peace, the presence, the freedom—they had been within me all along.

And here's the part that hit me hardest:

I realized how many of us—myself included—live our lives *waiting*.

Waiting for something to happen, for something to arrive, so that we can finally start living.

We tell ourselves, *When this happens, then I can relax. When that comes into my life, then I'll be happy.*

But the truth is, the life we're waiting for never arrives—not because it's not possible, but because it's not *out there.*

It's *in us.* It always has been.

And as I think about this now, the reality is that while I may not have received the financial wealth this deal promised, what this experience gave me was far more valuable than any financial gain I could ever imagine.

It gave me something money could never buy: the internal peace and freedom I had always longed for.

For that, I am profoundly and deeply thankful.

I realized that if I could create that feeling of peace, freedom, and fulfillment just by *thinking* my life was about to change, then I didn't need anything external to access it.

I began to see that the peace, the calm, the ease I had been chasing was never tied to any future outcome.

It was mine to step into at any moment.

From that point on, I began to let go of the need for anything outside of me to bring me those feelings.

I let go and surrendered to the truth that I could access those states without conditions.

If I could detach from the outcomes I was pursuing. I could remain in that state no matter what happened in the world around me.

That was the true gift of this experience: the understanding that I didn't need *anything* at all to change in my outer world to feel whole, free, and at peace.

The life I thought I was chasing had never been out there.

It had been mine all along.

This experience was a massive catalyst in my awakening. It taught me that the fulfillment we seek is never tied to something external.

It's a state of being, always accessible, regardless of what's happening around us.

From that day forward, I lived as though I already had everything I needed—because I did.

And so do you.

THE HARDER YOU PUSH,
THE MORE STUCK YOU BECOME

You don't need to control every detail of your life to be happy or successful.

In fact, the more you try to force things to go your way, the more resistance you create. When you start letting go of the need to micromanage every outcome, you open yourself up to the incredible possibility that life actually knows what it's doing.

You begin to notice that things often fall into place in ways you could never have predicted, almost as if there's an invisible current carrying you to where you need to be.

Trusting in that flow is a game changer.

Of course, this doesn't mean you stop doing the important things.

You still need to get up, go to work, take care of your family, and handle your responsibilities. But you no longer need to force events or manipulate people to fit into your plans.

Life is not meant to be a series of puzzles you need to solve through sheer willpower.

When unexpected hurdles come up—and they will—you just handle them the best you can and then let go. You don't get stuck on what went wrong or what didn't go according to plan.

You let it be, and you move forward. And when you do that, something amazing starts to happen: life becomes more effortless. It starts to flow.

This is what many people refer to as synchronicity.

Suddenly, the right opportunities show up, the right people cross your path, and things start to align in a way that feels almost magical. We'll explore this concept more deeply later, but for now, just know this: the less you resist, the more life flows effortlessly in your favor.

It's not that life becomes free of challenges; it's that your perspective shifts. Challenges are no longer insurmountable problems—they're just situations to address, and then you move forward. You realize that these challenges are part of the path, not obstacles blocking it.

I came to this understanding after decades of trying to control every aspect of my life and ending up frustrated. I realized that when I stopped trying to control everything, things just worked out—often better than I could have planned.

Life stopped feeling like a battle and started feeling like an unfolding journey.

And here's the truth: you don't need to know exactly how things will work out. You just need to trust that they will.

And they do.

Every single time.

So, take a breath.

Let go of the need to force and control.

Trust that there is a greater intelligence at play—one that knows exactly where you need to be, and that it's guiding you there.

Your job is not to fight the current, but to flow with it, knowing that everything is working out for your highest good.

WHY THE PURSUIT OF HAPPINESS IS MAKING YOU MISERABLE

What if one of our most deeply ingrained cultural ideals—the pursuit of happiness—is actually the root of our anxiety and dissatisfaction?

From the moment we're old enough to understand the concept, we're told that happiness is something to chase. A goal. A destination. A prize waiting somewhere in the future. But here's the truth: you don't find happiness by pursuing it. In fact, the harder you chase it, the more elusive it becomes.

True happiness exists when the search for it ends.

Let me say that again:

True happiness exists *when the search for it ends*.

The very act of pursuing happiness reinforces the idea that you're incomplete, that something is missing, and that fulfillment is somewhere *out there*. It's cultural programming that keeps us striving endlessly, where happiness always seems just out of reach. This mindset creates a constant state of tension, where we're trying to fill a void we don't realize doesn't actually exist.

Consider this: Stars are not visible when the sun dominates the sky, but they've been there all along. Happiness is the same. It's not something to be hunted or created; it's always there, but it's obscured by the noise of our constant striving.

This relentless pursuit isn't making us happy. It's making us anxious.

Think about it: When you believe happiness is a future achievement, you create pressure to always be doing more, achieving more, and becoming more. You can never fully rest in the present, because your mind is fixated on some future point where you'll finally "arrive." And in a culture that prizes achievement above all else, this cycle of striving is deeply ingrained.

America, the land of *the pursuit of happiness*, also happens to be one of the most anxious countries in the world. Coincidence? Probably not. Our obsession with chasing happiness has blinded us to the reality that happiness isn't something you find by running toward it; it's something that arises naturally when you stop running altogether.

Here's the paradox: happiness is not a goal; it's a byproduct.

It's what flows effortlessly when you align with the present moment, let go of resistance, and accept life as it is. When you stop chasing happiness, you realize it was never missing to begin with.

The pursuit is the problem, not the solution.

The alternative to this endless striving isn't complacency or giving up, it's freedom. Freedom from the belief that you're incomplete. Freedom from the idea that happiness is something you have to earn.

When you let go of the pursuit, you don't lose happiness.

You find it.

WHY IT FEELS LIKE NOTHING'S CHANGING—EVEN WHEN IT IS

Have you ever started something with so much hope—maybe a workout plan, a new habit, or even just trying to think differently—only to feel, weeks later, like nothing's changed?

You stare in the mirror, waiting to see the results of all your effort, but the reflection looks the same. It's frustrating, almost defeating, and you start to wonder, *What's the point?*

But here's the truth: real change doesn't announce itself. It happens quietly, in ways you often can't see at first.

Think of working out. From day to day, you look in the mirror, and there's nothing noticeable. Even after several weeks, it might feel like you're stuck in the same place.

But here's what's really happening: under the surface, your body is rewiring itself. Your muscles are growing stronger. Your endurance is building. The changes are happening—they're just not visible yet.

I experienced this firsthand in the gym.

I showed up week after week, month after month—and for a long time, it looked like nothing was happening. I'd check the mirror, searching for proof of progress, but I saw the same reflection staring back at me.

It would've been easy to believe that all the effort was for nothing.

But then, somewhere around the sixth or seventh month, something shifted.

I looked in the mirror one day, and suddenly, I could see it—muscles I had never noticed before, definition where there hadn't been any.

The transformation hadn't happened overnight. It had been happening all along. I just couldn't see it yet.

The same thing happens with this inner work.

It's like stacking one sheet of paper on top of another, every single day. At first, it feels pointless—what's one thin sheet of paper going to do? Even after a month, the stack might look nearly the same.

But over time, it begins to add up.

After a few months, the stack is thicker. After six months, it's solid. And after a year, it's so substantial, so unshakable, that it's impossible to ignore.

But here's the most incredible part: the stack never stops growing.

As long as you keep stacking—day by day, choice by choice—it keeps expanding. It becomes stronger, thicker, and more resilient.

What starts out feeling small and uncertain eventually becomes solid. And it doesn't just stay the same—it grows, strengthens, and expands, becoming a reflection of who you're becoming.

This is how awakening happens—not in one grand moment, but through the quiet, steady accumulation of choices.

Every time you question a fearful thought, every moment you recognize awareness, every small act of self-compassion—it all adds up.

You're stacking sheets. You're building something stronger than fear, more resilient than doubt.

And as you grow, so does your capacity for freedom, peace, and clarity.

So, keep going.

Even when it feels like nothing's happening.

Even when weeks go by, and you wonder if it's working.

Trust the process.

Every sheet you stack is part of your awakening.

And one day, you'll look back and see that what once felt fragile and fleeting has become something solid and unshakable—something that doesn't just transform who you are, but keeps expanding into what you're capable of becoming.

STRENGTH IS BUILT IN THE MOMENTS YOU FEAR

The quiet work of growth happens long before you see the results. But at some point, the moment comes when you're asked to step forward—to meet resistance head-on and prove to yourself what you're really capable of.

For the past several years, I've been showing up at the gym four days a week: Monday, Tuesday, Thursday, and Friday. Fridays are leg days, where I push myself through a challenging routine that begins with heavy squats.

It's uncomfortable.

And honestly, a little scary.

There's something about having a barbell loaded with hundreds of pounds resting on your back that forces you to confront yourself. It's one of the toughest workouts of the week, and on this particular Friday, resistance was building before I even started.

My kids were home because they had the day off school. Normally, I head to the gym right after dropping them off, but my routine was disrupted. It felt like the perfect day to skip.

My mind offered up plenty of excuses:

It's a cold morning.

You've been consistent.

Skipping one leg day won't make a difference.

Resting today is fine.

But as my mind worked to convince me, I noticed something else: a deeper part of me was watching. That part—the higher self—stepped in and said, *I know you don't want to go, but we're going. Because that's what we do.*

The truth is, there are many days each month when I don't want to go to the gym.

But I go anyway.

In the process of awakening, I realized it's not about whether or not I feel like it. It's about choosing to show up, no matter what.

And so, I went.

As I walked into the gym, I headed straight for the squat rack. The weight I planned to lift was heavier than anything I had ever attempted before. I had been lifting the same weight for a while, and it had started to feel easier. I knew it was time to push myself further.

Still, I felt some fear.

What if I fail? What if I can't do it? What if I get hurt?

But I've learned that hesitation is just a signal—it's the edge of growth calling me forward.

I observed the doubts in my mind, and did it anyway.

What happened?

I lifted the weight. I did six clean reps and set a new personal record.

After I finished at the squat rack, despite feeling spent, I pushed through the remainder of my leg exercises.

At the end of this grueling workout, as I walked out of the gym, exhausted yet satisfied, a thought struck me, stopping me in my tracks:

This is how I want to feel at the end of my life.

I paused, a bit shocked by the thought. And then it came again with a bit more detail…

This is how I want to feel at the end of my life. Glad I showed up. Satisfied with my effort. Knowing I gave it all I had. And glad it's over, because I have no more to give.

It was never just about the weight on the bar or the strength in my body—it was about something far greater. It was the quiet certainty that I had met every challenge head-on, that I had embraced the struggle rather than shying away. It was the deep relief of knowing I had never settled, never let doubt dictate my path. And in the end, it was gratitude—not for any single achievement, but for the unwavering commitment to keep showing up, no matter what.

Showing up is the foundation. It's the decision that makes everything else possible: the growth, the breakthroughs, the transformation.

Even when you don't want to.

Even when it feels hard.

Especially when it feels hard.

This isn't just about a workout. It's about how we show up for life—fully, completely, in every moment. For our challenges, our dreams, our relationships, and most importantly, for ourselves.

Showing up doesn't mean the fear goes away.

It doesn't mean the resistance disappears.

It means you feel it, face it, and move forward anyway. Because that's where growth happens.

Every time you show up, you're proving something to yourself.

You're reinforcing to yourself who's in charge.

You are the boss, not your mind.

You're reminding yourself that you are capable of more than you thought. And with each step forward, the resistance gets lighter. Growth happens—not all at once, but moment by moment.

At the gym, there's a well-known strategy for growth called "progressive overload." When the weight starts to feel easy, you don't stop there. You add more, because that's how you grow stronger. Life works the same way. If you stay where it's comfortable, you stop growing. Strength—whether it's physical, mental, or emotional—is built just outside your comfort zone.

Comfort is a slow death. It lulls you into stagnation, convincing you that ease is the goal, when in reality, it's the greatest barrier to who you're meant to become.

Don't seek comfort—seek challenge.

Seek the moments that stretch you, that demand more from you than you think you have to give. Because on the other side of discomfort is transformation. On the other side of struggle is the version of you that you were meant to be.

And here's the truth: the people who live the most fulfilling lives are not fearless.
Nor are they always motivated.

You know those people you admire?
The ones you think have more courage than you?

They feel the fear too.

They feel the resistance.

They have days when they don't want to show up.

But they do it *anyway*.

They lean into the discomfort, take the next step, and keep moving forward—not because they always feel inspired, but because they've learned that action comes first. Motivation follows movement, not the other way around.

You don't need to be fearless.

You don't need to wait for motivation.

Courage is not the absence of fear, just as discipline is not the presence of motivation. Both are decisions—choices to move forward despite the doubt, the fear, the resistance.

Feel the fear—and do it anyway.

Feel the lack of motivation, and show up anyway.

Anxiety exists because it's a guide. It points you toward the edges of your growth, showing you what you need to push through. It's inviting you to step forward, lean into discomfort, and uncover your strength beyond it.

The weight that once felt impossible becomes manageable. The action that once seemed unbearable becomes second nature. Because strength—whether mental, emotional, or physical—isn't built on the days when you feel ready.

It's built on the days when you don't.

Each time you push yourself just beyond your comfort zone, you grow. That strength, built moment by moment, becomes the foundation of a life fully lived.

Strength isn't born—it's built. Not in bursts of inspiration, but in the quiet, consistent choice to keep going.

Your life, fully lived, is waiting for you to step forward.

All you need to do is show up.

WHAT IF EVERYTHING REALLY IS WORKING OUT FOR YOU?

Have you ever felt like nothing was going your way? Like life was piling on challenge after challenge, and you couldn't see a way through?

I've been there too.

But once I began to understand that life was working *for* me—that every challenge and obstacle was there for my growth and held the seed of opportunity—I started saying something that completely shifted my reality:

"Everything always works out for me."

When I first started saying it, I was a little skeptical. It felt strange to declare something so bold when my current reality seemed far from working out. But I went with it anyway—just to see what would happen.

Something in me was willing to give it a chance.

This wasn't just a random phrase. It came from a deeper realization I had during my process of awakening. I began to understand that life wasn't happening to me—it was happening *for* me.

Even when things didn't go the way I wanted them to, I started to see that there was an intelligence to the system. Life was always guiding me, even when I couldn't see it in the moment.

So, I decided to trust that.

I decided to stop resisting what was happening and start testing the idea that things were working in my favor, even when it didn't feel that way.

That's when I started saying it out loud—almost like an experiment.

Not just when things were going well, but especially when things seemed to go completely wrong.

When I was with my family, I'd say, "Everything always works out for us."

And when I was alone, I'd say it to myself: "Everything always works out for me."

And here's the thing: it worked.

Not just once. Not just occasionally.

Every single time.

Without fail, things aligned in ways I couldn't have predicted.

Big things. Little things. It didn't matter.

Even when I had no idea how things could possibly work out, they did—often better than I could have planned.

Looking back now, I'm still amazed at how powerfully this one practice transformed my life—and it continues to this day.

I know this will work for you too.

It's not magic, and it's not blind luck. But if you pay attention, it might feel pretty close.

It's a shift in how you relate to life, and that shift is everything.

Even the hardest moments turned out to be stepping stones.

A challenge became a lesson. A failure became a redirection. A delay or setback made space for something better to come along.

What felt like obstacles at the time were really detours leading me exactly where I needed to go.

What makes this mantra so powerful is that it doesn't deny the reality of what you're going through.

It's not about pretending that things are perfect or that you're not struggling.

It's about acknowledging the challenge while reminding yourself that it's not the end of the story.

When you say, "Everything always works out for me," you're essentially saying:

"I know this moment might feel hard. I know things may not be going the way I want them to right now. But I also know that, in the long run—or even in the short term—it's all going to work out for me."

This belief allows you to hold two truths at once: that life can be challenging in the moment, and that it's ultimately working for your benefit.

It shifts your focus away from what's wrong and toward the possibility that something better is on its way—even if you can't see it yet.

Belief isn't just a comforting thought; it's the mechanism that creates your framework for what's possible.

It's like the operating system of your mind.

Just as a computer's operating system dictates what programs can run, your beliefs—especially the ones deep in your subconscious—determine how you see the world, respond to challenges, and create solutions.

When you believe "everything always works out for me," you're rewriting the code.

You're teaching your mind to stop focusing on obstacles and start noticing opportunities.

That belief doesn't make challenges disappear, but it changes how you see them.

It allows you to trust that even the hard moments are part of a bigger picture—one that's ultimately working in your favor.

This isn't just about the big, life-changing moments.

It's about the small, everyday ones too.

Think about losing your wallet or your phone. Instead of panicking, you pause and remind yourself, "Everything always works out for me."

Maybe someone returns it. Maybe it turns up in the exact place you needed to check.

Or imagine you're late to an important appointment.

Most people would stress and spiral, but instead, you say, "Everything always works out for me."

Maybe being late means you miss traffic.

Maybe you arrive at just the right time to meet someone who ends up being important to you.

Even the smallest moments can shift when you trust this process.

A long line at the store, a canceled plan, a frustrating miscommunication—these things might seem like annoyances at first, but they often turn out to be blessings in disguise.

When you say, "Everything always works out for me," you create space for those blessings to reveal themselves.

Belief shapes your perception, and your perception shapes your reality.

When you clean up the lens through which you see the world—when you choose to believe that life is working for you, not against you—you start to notice how things fall into place, even when they don't go the way you planned.

From this moment on, I invite you to adopt this mantra.

Whatever you're going through—whatever challenges you face, big or small—say it to yourself:

"Everything always works out for me."

Say it out loud. Whisper it in your mind. Write it down if you need to.

And here's the key: keep saying it.

Say it when you're calm, and say it when you're in the middle of a storm.

Say it even if you don't believe it yet, because belief doesn't always come first—sometimes, it follows repetition.

The more you say it, the more you'll start to see how it works.

Imagine what it would feel like to truly trust that everything is unfolding perfectly for you, to carry that calm confidence in your daily life, knowing that even the challenges are part of a bigger picture.

That's what this mantra gives you: a way to step into trust, no matter what life throws at you.

One day, you'll look back and see how true it's been.

You'll realize that the hardest moments led to your greatest growth, and that life really was working for you all along.

Life doesn't always go as planned, but it always unfolds as it's meant to.

Everything always works out for you.

Every. Single. Time.

Trust it. Say it. And keep saying it.

Watch what happens.

WHAT IF YOU'RE ALREADY OKAY, RIGHT NOW?

My daughters are just getting to the age where they can explore the neighborhood on their own.

It's something I've always wanted for them—a little freedom, a taste of independence, the kind of childhood I remember, when kids played outside without the constant shadow of a hovering parent.

A few moments ago, my eight-year-old, Mia, grabbed her scooter and headed out to meet some friends. She was beaming, thrilled to go on her little adventure. And as I watched her scoot off, a thought appeared.

What if she's not aware of cars, even though I told her to be? What if she's not careful enough? What if she falls?

Before my awakening, this is where my mind would have spiraled—caught in constant worry, dragged into an endless storm of "what ifs." It was like a reflex, as if fear was the default setting.

But now, everything is different.

Thoughts still arise, but they don't stick. They're like ripples on the surface of a still pond. The moment they appear, I see them for what they are, and they dissolve.

I stood there, watching her disappear down the street, and I asked myself, "And what if not?"

What if she's just fine?
What if she has the time of her life?
What if this moment isn't about controlling every possibility, but about letting go?

And in that moment, I remembered.

The "what ifs" aren't the problem.
They never were.
They're just thoughts.

Neutral. Passing.

The real problem is the story we attach to them, the way we take them seriously, as if they hold some kind of truth.

But here's the thing:

The moment you see a thought as just a thought, it dissolves.

No fight. No resistance.

It loses its weight because it's no longer tied to you.

"What if?" It's the question anxiety loves to ask.

Over and over, it drags you into its endless hallway, opening doors to rooms that don't even exist.

"What if I fail?"
"What if something goes wrong?"
"What if I'm not enough?"

Each one feels urgent, as though answering it will bring you peace. But you've noticed this, haven't you?

It never does.

And here's what I realized in that moment with my daughter. "What if" isn't the enemy. It's not a question to answer. It's a doorway, a quiet invitation to let go of the illusion of control and drop into the only moment that's real:

This one.

What if the next time "what if" arose in your mind, you didn't see it as a problem to solve, but as a gift, a nudge to notice where you are, right now?

Because every "what if" is really asking:

What if this moment is enough?
What if I'm okay?
What if nothing is wrong or missing?

The beauty of this realization is that it doesn't require effort.

It doesn't ask you to practice anything.

It's already here.

Once you see it, "what if" stops being a question and becomes an opening.

The "what ifs" no longer pull you into fear—they pull you back into yourself.

So, the next time you hear that little voice asking, "What if…?", don't rush to fix it, argue with it, or answer it.

Just notice it.

Watch it.

Then ask yourself the only question that truly matters:

"What if it's all okay?"

"And what if I'm okay too?"

THE EGO IS A CAGE—
AND YOU'RE HOLDING THE KEY

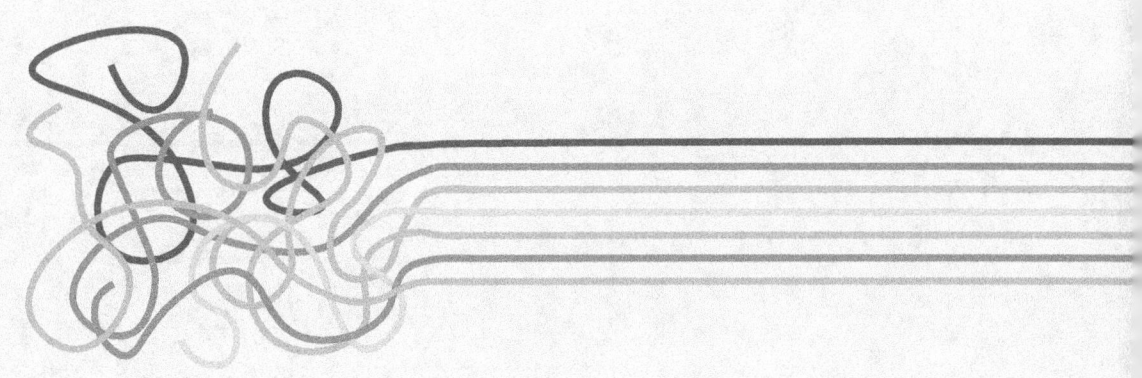

ONCE YOU SEE IT, YOU'RE FREE

The ego doesn't just show up one day. It's not something we choose or consciously create—it's a survival mechanism, a response to the world around us. At its core, the ego is the part of us that learns to navigate life through a simple equation:

"How do I protect myself from harm and get what I need?"

And while it might start out as a necessary tool for survival, it can easily take over and become the master of our lives.

The ego is born out of experiences—particularly the ones that teach us, directly or indirectly, that we aren't safe, or that we aren't enough as we are.

For many, it begins in childhood.

Trauma, whether big or small, lays the foundation.

A parent who didn't give us the love or support we needed, a moment when we felt abandoned, rejected, or unseen—these experiences leave an imprint. When those feelings of pain, fear, or inadequacy become overwhelming, the ego steps in to protect us.

Imagine a child who grows up feeling unwanted or unloved. Their mind, desperate to avoid the pain, begins constructing stories: "I have to prove my worth to be loved. I have to be the best to matter. I can't trust people, so I have to rely only on myself."

These beliefs don't come out of nowhere. They're coping mechanisms, ways of making sense of a world that feels unsafe or hostile. The ego becomes the armor, the mask, the survival strategy.

But here's the thing: the ego doesn't know when to stop.

What starts as a protective mechanism in childhood keeps running in the background of our lives, even when the original threat is gone.

The person who once needed to prove themselves to feel worthy might grow into an adult who's constantly chasing achievements or approval.

The child who learned to avoid vulnerability might become the adult who struggles to connect or trust.

The ego, formed in response to pain, becomes a habit—a lens through which we see the world.

And yet, the ego isn't all bad. Let's not villainize it. It does have a purpose. It helps us build a sense of identity, navigate challenges, and survive in a complex world. Without it, we wouldn't strive, achieve, or even protect ourselves when necessary. The ego gets us through the storm. It's the part of us that learns to adapt, to overcome, to make sense of chaos.

But here's where things go sideways: the ego doesn't know when to let go.

Its job is to protect, and it assumes that job is permanent. So, instead of stepping back when the perceived danger has passed, it keeps building walls, clinging to control, and chasing a sense of worth that can never be fully satisfied. And the more we let it drive, the more it limits us.

Think of it like a guard at the gate.

When the ego is healthy, it protects us when needed, but knows when to step aside so we can engage with the world openly. But when the ego runs unchecked, the guard locks the gate and won't let anyone in—not even us. It keeps us locked in cycles of fear, comparison, judgment, and control.

The ego intensifies when it's reinforced by repetitive experiences and beliefs.

Every time we feel unworthy, rejected, or inadequate, the ego doubles down:

"See? I was right. The world isn't safe. I need to protect myself even more."

Over time, this creates a self-fulfilling loop. The ego's stories—"I'm not good enough," "I need to prove myself," "I have to control everything to feel safe"—become so ingrained that they feel like the truth. And because the ego is so good at reinforcing itself, we rarely stop to question it.

But here's the truth: the ego *isn't who you are.*

It's a structure, a tool, a defense mechanism.

It's not your essence—it's just the lens through which you've been programmed to see the world.

The problem isn't that we have an ego; the problem is that we overidentify with it. We forget that there's a part of us beyond the ego—a deeper, truer self that doesn't need to prove, defend, or control.

So, why does this matter?

Because understanding how the ego forms is the first step to loosening its grip. When you see it for what it is—a survival mechanism born from fear and false beliefs—you can begin to disarm it. You can start to recognize the patterns it's created in your life, and instead of letting those patterns define you, you can choose differently.

Here's an example: If you notice yourself chasing validation—whether through achievements, relationships, or approval—pause and ask yourself, "Where did this start? What belief am I operating from?" More often than not, you'll trace it back to a moment when you felt unseen or unworthy. That's the ego in action. It's trying to protect you from ever feeling that pain again, but in doing so, it's keeping you stuck in a cycle of seeking what you already have within you: worth, love, and safety.

The ego isn't your enemy, it's just a part of you that's misunderstood.

When you begin to understand it, and observe it, you can work with it instead of letting it control you. You can thank it for its role, for the ways it's helped you survive, and then gently remind it that it doesn't have to run the show anymore.

And when you do?

You'll begin to feel lighter.

Freer.

You'll start to see the world—and yourself—with more clarity. You'll recognize that the ego isn't who you are; it's just one part of the journey.

So, if you've ever felt trapped by the need to prove, defend, or control, know this: it's not because you're flawed. It's because you're human. And being human means you've had an ego doing its best to protect you. But you don't have to live there anymore.

You can step beyond the ego. You can step into something deeper, something truer. And it starts by understanding how it all began—and choosing, moment by moment, to let go of what no longer serves you.

THE DRUG YOU DON'T
KNOW YOU'RE ADDICTED TO

The other day, I was in the car with a relative on a three-minute drive. Within that short span, they managed to find something wrong with just about everything. First, they called the cold weather "disgusting." Then, they moved on to how, when it's not cold, there's red tide at the beach. And if you can't go to the beach, well, the only other option is a community pool "where everybody pees."

I just listened, quietly amused. But what struck me wasn't just how automatic this habit of judgment was—it was why it existed in the first place.

The ego loves to judge.

It sits like an emperor on its throne, giving a thumbs-up or a thumbs-down to every moment. It pretends that by declaring, "This is good" or "This is bad," it holds some cosmic authority over reality itself.

Truth be told, before my awakening, I was guilty of this too.

But reality has no opinion.

It simply *is.*

Your judgment doesn't alter the moment, it only distorts your perception of it. And in doing so, it creates suffering—for you.

The ego isn't interested in peace. Peace requires surrender, and surrender is the greatest threat to the ego. Instead, the ego seeks certainty, validation, and most of all, *to be right.*

Because if the ego is right, it exists.

It thrives in opposition, in finding something or someone to stand against. Judgment isn't just about personal preference—it's about power. Every complaint, every criticism, every moment spent declaring reality to be "wrong" strengthens the illusion of separateness—the "me versus the world" narrative that the ego depends on.

But judgment isn't just a habit—it's an addiction.

The ego doesn't just judge for survival; it chases *the high of being right*.

It's an intoxicating hit, a momentary rush of superiority that feels like control. But like any addiction, the crash always follows—stress, resentment, and the endless need for another fix.

And this is where it gets interesting.

This illusion of control, of superiority over the situation, might feel satisfying for a fleeting moment. But the cost is high—stress, resentment, and most of all, anxiety.

Because anxiety thrives in the exact gap the ego creates—the space between *what is* and *what the ego insists should be*.

The ego looks at the present moment and declares it wrong, broken, or incomplete. And anxiety rushes in to "fix" it.

But think about it. When you're anxious, what are you really doing?

You're trying to solve the unsolvable. Replaying conversations, imagining worst-case scenarios, asking endless "what if" questions. Anxiety convinces you that if you just think harder, prepare better, or judge more harshly, you'll find relief. But you won't. You can't. Because peace doesn't live in control.

Peace lives in *letting go*.

The deeper truth is that the ego doesn't judge or resist because it's powerful—it does so because it's afraid. Afraid of being wrong. Afraid of uncertainty. Afraid of dissolving into something greater than itself.

And this is where *you* have a choice.

Because you are not your ego. You are not anxiety. You are the awareness that notices them both.

When you stop needing to be right, stop fighting reality, stop resisting what is, you discover something the ego can never offer you:

Peace.

Not the fleeting kind that depends on circumstances, but the deep, unshakable peace of simply being *here*.

So, let me ask you…

Where is your ego gripping onto judging right now, convincing you that being right matters more than being free?

WHEN GETTING EVERYTHING LEAVES YOU EMPTY

Ever since I was a teenager, I had this dream: one day, I would own a sports car with gull-wing doors—the kind that open up like wings.

To me, that car wasn't just a vehicle; it was a symbol. An unmistakable sign to the world that I had made it. That I was successful, important, and valuable in the eyes of others.

It seems so ridiculous now, but back then, it was the ultimate marker of achievement in my mind.

As I got older, that dream grew louder. I decided I had to have it.

Finding the specific car I had my heart set on was no small task. I had to arrange for a specialty car shipping company to pick it up from a dealership across the country and deliver it to me.

The logistics alone felt monumental, but I didn't care—it only added to the anticipation. The effort made the dream feel even more significant, like I was about to receive something life-changing.

Finally, the day arrived. I remember standing there as the truck pulled up, my heart racing with excitement.

I watched as they carefully unloaded the car, its sleek lines gleaming in the evening light. This was it—the moment I had waited so long for. My dream was right there in front of me, and I couldn't wait to climb inside.

I carefully opened the beautiful gullwing door, just as I had always imagined. It rose effortlessly like a sculpture in motion, graceful and weightless, almost otherworldly, welcoming me inside.

I slowly and carefully sat down, started the engine, and began driving, expecting the rush I'd dreamed of for so long. But instead, my stomach dropped.

The excitement didn't come.

What hit me instead was an overwhelming wave of emptiness. The car I had fantasized about for years, that I had gone to such lengths to acquire, didn't fulfill me at all.

I sat there, deeply and utterly confused.

The car was beautiful.

It was quick.

But instead of excitement, there was only emptiness.

For weeks, I kept driving it, hoping—waiting—to feel something. Each time, I thought, *Maybe this time, it'll click. Maybe I just need to give it a chance.*

But each time I drove it, I felt emptier and emptier. Instead of the joy I had imagined, I was left with a growing sense of disconnection. The car felt completely unaligned with who I really wanted to be.

Owning the car didn't just fail to fill the void—it made it deeper, leaving me more disconnected—not just from the car, but from myself.

Eventually, I stopped driving it altogether. It just sat in my garage.

Every time I looked at it, a deep hollowness settled in—a stark reminder that it hadn't filled the void I thought it would. Instead, it magnified it.

I really thought people would see me driving that car and think, *Wow, look at that guy!*

But absolutely nobody cared.

And even if they had, would it really have changed anything?

The car was supposed to make me feel accomplished, whole, validated, and important. But all it did was sit there, a glaring symbol of everything I didn't feel.

Looking back, I see that that car wasn't the problem. It was my ego—the part of me that believed I needed that car to feel worthy, successful, and complete.

The ego whispers lies like this all the time, and most of us believe them without even realizing it.

After a month of owning it, I knew I had to let it go. Selling it felt inevitable, even though I knew I'd lose money.

But the moment it was gone, I felt an overwhelming sense of relief. It was like a weight had been lifted off my shoulders—a weight I hadn't even realized I was carrying.

For the first time in my life, I didn't feel the need to prove *anything to anyone*—not through a car, not through anything external, not through anything at all.

As I think back to it now, I'm deeply grateful it happened.

Owning that car wasn't just a disappointment; it was a *profound* lesson on my journey of awakening.

It showed me, in a way I could never forget, that no material thing was ever going to give me what I was truly searching for.

It forced me to confront a truth I had been avoiding: self-worth and joy don't come from what you own, how you look, or what others think of you. They come from something far deeper—something already within you.

Maybe you've had a moment like this—when you achieved or acquired something you thought would change everything, only to find yourself feeling the same—or worse.

It's a hard truth to face, but it's also the beginning of a much deeper freedom.

I had to live this lesson. I had to feel the disappointment, the emptiness, and the eventual relief of letting go.

Selling that car was a transformative moment. It closed a chapter for me and opened my eyes to a truth that shifted my entire perspective: what I was looking for wasn't out there. It never had been.

It showed me, in no uncertain terms, that the material things we believe will transform us— the house, the promotion, the watch, the car—never will.

They are illusions, promises that dissolve the moment we grasp them.

Maybe your version of the sports car isn't a car at all.

It could be a milestone you've been chasing, a version of success you've built in your mind, or a possession meant to prove your worth.

Maybe it's the relationship you're convinced will solve everything, or the number in your bank account you've tied to your sense of worth.

We all have something like this—something external we believe will fill the void, silence the anxiety, or prove we're enough.

And yet, when we finally get it, we find ourselves right back where we started.

This realization marked a turning point for me.

It wasn't just about the car; it was about the deeper pattern of seeking validation and happiness through external things—a pattern driven entirely by the ego.

The moment you recognize the ego is the moment you step into freedom.

Awareness is your greatest tool, and every time you notice the ego, you reclaim more of your power.

You don't need to fight it. You don't need to fix it.

You simply need to see it.

Because when you do, the ego loses its grip, and you step closer to the peace, presence, and joy that have always been within you.

This is how you begin to free yourself—not by defeating the ego, but by seeing through it.

THE PEOPLE WHO TRIGGER
YOU ARE HERE TO FREE YOU

Some people enter our lives not as friends, mentors, or allies, but as mirrors, reflecting parts of ourselves we might rather ignore.

They challenge us, not with wisdom or support, but by embodying traits we instinctively resist or despise. And in doing so, they reveal something deeper. Not about them—about us.

For me, one family member stood out as a vivid example of this. Let's call him Richard.

By all appearances, Richard was successful—financially well-off, with a loving family and great health. But none of that seemed to make it through. His focus was always on what was missing, what was wrong, who was trying to take advantage of him.

Conversations with Richard weren't conversations; they were performances. His stories were never just stories. They were crafted to prove one thing: *I'm right. I'm strong. I've got this all figured out.*

And no matter what you said, his response was always the same:

"I know."

It wasn't just a response—it was a brick wall.

It shut down connection, any real conversation, any possibility of growth. It wasn't about actual knowledge; it was about control. Admitting that he didn't know something—or could see things differently—might crack the carefully constructed armor of his identity.

One day, I tried to nudge him toward a more positive perspective.

"You know, you don't have to see things so negatively. You could choose to look at it differently."

His reply?

"No," he said, shaking his head. "That's my character."

That moment stuck with me.

He didn't just hold onto his worldview—he fused it with his identity. His negativity, his judgments, his need to be right weren't things he *did*—they were who he *was*.

And yet, for all his certainty, Richard never seemed at peace.

Beneath the armor, beneath the endless "I know," was something else.

A deep, unspoken fear.

Fear of being wrong. Fear of being vulnerable. Fear of facing himself. And perhaps most of all, fear of losing control.

His judgments weren't just opinions; they were defenses—shields against a world that, to him, felt unsafe.

And yet, the toll of maintaining this illusion was visible.

Richard often spoke about how drained he felt, how exhausting life was, how much he had to fight just to get through the day.

It wasn't just others who were exhausted by his ego. He was too.

Because that's the thing about ego: it takes everything from you and gives nothing back.

It thrives on control, on judgment, on being *right*—but in the process, it builds its own prison. It creates walls where there could be connection. It drains instead of fulfills.

And watching Richard, I started to wonder—*How often do I do the same thing?*

His exaggerated negativity was like a magnifying glass, exposing the ways I too might lean on frustration, complaints, or resistance—not just to avoid the deeper work, but because in those moments, negativity itself made me feel superior, like I was above it all.

Richard had so much to be grateful for. Objectively, his life was full of blessings.

But no matter how good life was, he didn't just see what was missing—he only saw what was wrong.

What he could judge.

What he could resent.

What he could feel superior to.

What he could prove himself right about.

At first, I found myself frustrated by it. How could someone with so much going for him focus so intently on what was wrong?

But looking back, I see that my frustration wasn't just about his negativity—it was about the fact that I took it personally.

In the beginning, I thought his dismissiveness, his coldness, even his negativity itself, were somehow directed *at me*. I assumed I had done something wrong, that he didn't like me, that I wasn't enough in his eyes.

Every passive-aggressive remark, every moment of condescension, I saw as a reflection of *me*. But over time, I started to see the truth.

Richard wasn't acting this way because of me.

He was acting this way because of *himself*.

This wasn't personal. It never was. It was simply the only way he knew how to be. And once I saw that, I stopped trying to prove myself. I stopped reacting. I stopped waiting for him to change.

Because I finally understood—he wasn't choosing *me* to be unpleasant to.

He was just unpleasant.

And once I saw that, something shifted. I stopped waiting for him to change. But I also saw something else.

His negativity didn't just stay with him—it had the power to pull others in. If I wasn't careful, I could get swept up in the same energy, seeing life through that same lens of lack and frustration.

And then it hit me.

Richard wasn't just reflecting *his* attachment to ego—he was showing me my own.

If you're reading this book, you're not as deeply entrenched in ego as Richard. People fully consumed by ego don't pick up self-help books—they already "know everything."

But that doesn't mean we're immune.

The truth is, we all have a "Richard" inside us—those moments when we defend, complain, or focus on what's missing instead of what's present.

And let's be honest: we all have a Richard around us too.

That person who triggers us, frustrates us, pushes our buttons in ways no one else quite can.

But here's the thing: what you focus on, you find more of.

Richard's endless complaints taught me that lesson in a way I couldn't ignore.

If you're constantly looking for what's wrong, you'll find it everywhere.

But if you shift your focus to what's good, you'll find that too.

It's not just an empty idea—it's how life works.

Imagine if someone offered you a hundred dollars for every red car you noticed on the road today. Suddenly, red cars would be everywhere. But if I asked how many red cars you saw last week, you probably wouldn't have a clue.

What we focus on, we amplify.

Watching Richard fixate on every slight, every failure, every injustice, I realized how easy it is to fall into that mindset—and how damaging it can be.

But here's the beauty of awareness: the moment you recognize ego in action, its power starts to dissolve.

The moment you see it—whether in yourself or in others—it starts to lose its grip.

And I began to see Richard's negativity for what it was: a survival strategy.

His complaints weren't just venting—they were armor, a way of protecting himself from the possibility of disappointment.

Life, for Richard, seemed like a battle where he constantly needed to prove his worth.

But I didn't need to fight that battle with him.

I didn't need to react, correct, or try to change him.

I could simply see the ego in him for what it was—and let him be.

And in doing so, I freed myself.

Instead of getting hooked by his complaints, I chose gratitude.
Instead of focusing on what wasn't working, I started noticing what was.
I caught myself in those moments when I was tempted to complain or judge—and I let them go.

And every time I did, I felt lighter.

So, what about you?

Who is the "Richard" in your life?
Who triggers your frustration, your need to react, your desire to fix?
What would happen if you stopped trying to change them—and instead shifted *your own* focus?

The most profound changes don't come from fixing others.

They come from shifting ourselves.

When we release judgment and focus on what's good, the world reflects that change back to us.

And in the end, I realized something surprising:

I felt a deep unexpected gratitude toward Richard.

So, to the Richards in our lives: thank you.

You remind us that we can't always change the world around us.

But we can always choose how we see it.

And in the end, that choice determines everything.

NOT MY EGO, NOT MY PROBLEM

Not long ago, I was walking through my neighborhood with my wife and our dog, Buster, enjoying a quiet afternoon.

As we turned a corner, one of our neighbors stood in his open garage, his large dog off-leash. Before I could react, his dog lunged, growling and sprinting aggressively toward Buster. Instinctively, I yanked our dog out of harm's way, heart pounding.

We avoided a scuffle, but the energy of the moment lingered.

"She usually doesn't lunge like that," the neighbor called out casually, as though those words could erase what had just happened.

My wife, calm but firm, responded, "Maybe you should put her on a leash."

That's when it happened. His face twisted, his voice sharpened, and out came the words: "F*CK YOU!"

A younger version of me wouldn't have let it end there. Back then, my ego wouldn't have allowed me to walk away. I would've felt the heat rise in my chest, the need to confront, to prove something, and it might have escalated into a shouting match or a physical altercation.

But something in me paused.

I became aware of the space.

"Are you really going to talk to your neighbors that way?" I asked, keeping my tone even.

"Yeah, I am," he shot back, continuing his tirade. But I was already gone, mentally, emotionally. I saw what was happening—not just in the moment, but in him.

This wasn't about me. It never was.

The moment my wife mentioned the leash, his ego took over.

He felt embarrassed, exposed, judged, and his ego couldn't handle it. Instead of sitting with that discomfort, it turned it into anger. That's what the ego does. It attacks, deflects, and distracts to avoid facing vulnerability.

As I walked away, I realized something: this wasn't just about him—this is how ego operates in all of us.

He could have paused, taken a breath, and said, "Yeah, you're probably right. I'm sorry about that." The moment would have passed peacefully. But his ego wouldn't allow it, and I didn't need to meet him there.

"Enjoy your life," I said, not sarcastically, but with genuine detachment, and I meant it. I turned and walked away, carrying nothing of his energy with me.

How often do you let someone else's words or actions linger in your mind? How often do you replay moments like this, caught in loops of "what if" or "I should've"?

You might even carry it for hours or days, justifying yourself, defending your actions in your mind. But who are you defending yourself to? Who is really judging you?

But it's never really about the moment—it's about what your ego fears that moment says about you.

This is where anxiety thrives, isn't it? In the stories your ego tells you—the ones about needing to control the situation, needing to protect how others see you, needing to win.

After awakening, you see these stories for what they are. You notice the pull to react, the temptation to defend or justify. Instead of getting offended, you see their behavior as a reflection of their own internal struggles, not of you. And instead of getting caught in them, you let them move past, like clouds passing by in the sky.

When you truly and deeply know who you are, the ego's stories lose their power.

You don't need to prove anything to anyone, and you don't need to prove anything to yourself.

That deeper knowing dissolves the ego entirely, leaving only clarity, peace, and freedom.

That day, as I walked away from my neighbor's anger without carrying it with me, I realized something deeper: the ego isn't just an illusion, it's optional.

And when you stop feeding it, something remarkable happens.

What's left isn't emptiness—it's presence.

That's when I truly saw that awakening isn't about becoming someone new. It's about remembering who I've been all along.

AWAKENING ISN'T BECOMING, IT'S REMEMBERING

Imagine awakening as less a journey of gaining something new and more a process of revealing what has been within you all along.

It's like the gradual unfurling of a flower, each petal gently unfolding, allowing what's been hidden inside to finally be seen.

This path is one of shedding layers:
Old beliefs.
Outdated definitions.
Energies that no longer serve you.

These layers, once essential, may have protected you or given you structure…

But they are no longer aligned with the core of who you are becoming.

In this process, the ego isn't something to defeat or conquer.

It doesn't need to be broken down.

Instead, the ego can be a tool—a lens through which you experience individuality and separation.

Think of it like a prism:

It refracts the light, allowing you to see each hue separately, even though they all come from the same source.

It allows you to see life through the lens of contrast, of opposites, of "me" and "not me."

Yet, when we cling too tightly to the ego's definitions—when we define ourselves by these limiting ideas—the prism narrows, dimming our view of the vastness within.

Awakening, then, becomes about gently peeling back these layers of false beliefs and fears.

Each layer you release brings you closer to your true self—an essence that has always been there, like a steady flame.

As you let go of what doesn't align with your highest joy, your truest self…

You relax into your natural state.

Your own unique vibration.

And in this state, there's a deep ease, a feeling of being home, where you no longer need to seek outside yourself for peace or validation.

The remarkable part is that in this place of relaxation and alignment, you realize that the divine, the infinite, has been with you all along.

You're not uncovering something foreign or external.

You're simply unveiling your essence.

And in that unveiling, you realize there is nothing to "seek."

You are what you've been seeking all along.

You are the one you've been searching for.

So, this is the heart of awakening:

A quiet, gentle shedding of what you're not, so that what you are—the love, the joy, the peace you've always longed for can come forth naturally.

As you let go, as you trust, as you allow, you come to experience your own divinity, the powerful presence of your being, in each and every moment.

This is the awakening.

Not as a final destination…

But as an ongoing journey.

A way of living each day in harmony with your true self.

THE WAY YOU LOVE YOURSELF IS THE WAY YOU LOVE YOUR LIFE

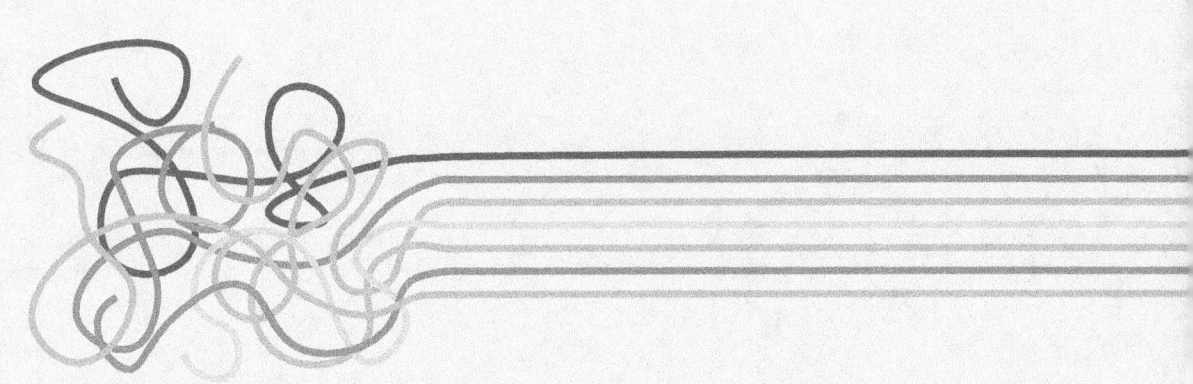

EXISTENCE IS NOT AN APPLICATION YOU NEED TO SUBMIT

For so many years, I felt like I needed to justify my existence.

I thought I had to prove my worth—be as good as, or better than, others—to feel okay about myself.

I believed my value was tied to achievements, titles, accolades, or the right possessions, as if external validation could finally make me feel whole.

This isn't just my story—it's a common struggle. Many of us grow up with an unspoken expectation to be "successful" in the way the world defines it: a traditional career, a respectable title, a certain income level, something that makes others nod with approval.

For me, it was the quiet but persistent notion that I should pursue something professional and conventional, like being a lawyer or a doctor. My parents never explicitly pressured me, but I could sense it in the air, in conversations, in the way they spoke about their friends' kids who were embarking on those paths.

It planted a seed in me—a belief that I needed to prove myself, because the life I envisioned didn't look like theirs. I didn't see myself in those roles, and yet I carried this burden of needing to "measure up" in some way.

We're surrounded by cultural narratives that whisper—or sometimes shout—that our worth is conditional.

Conditional on success.
On effort.
On meeting certain standards.
On being "enough" in the eyes of others.

These messages creep into our minds, and we absorb them without even realizing it. And for years, I lived under the weight of those expectations, trying to be enough in a world that never stopped moving the goalposts.

But through my awakening, I realized something profound:

Existence is enough.

The fact that you exist is enough.

It's not something you need to earn or justify. You're already here. You're already part of this miraculous, infinite experience of life, and that alone is the ultimate validation.

But when you strip away the conditioning, the pressure, the striving—what's left?

Life.

Just life, unfolding effortlessly.

Take a moment and look at the natural world around you.

Does a tree question its right to grow? Does it worry whether its branches are straight enough or its leaves green enough?

No.

A tree simply grows—rooted deeply in the earth, reaching boldly toward the sky. Its existence is its purpose, and it fulfills that purpose simply by being.

What about the birds?

They don't compare their songs or wonder if they're "good enough." They sing because that's what they're here to do.

The ocean doesn't pause to question the rhythm of its waves, nor does the sun hesitate before rising, wondering if it's shining brightly enough.

Nature doesn't overthink its existence—it just is.

And in its simplicity, it is breathtakingly whole.

You are no different.

You are life itself, flowing uniquely and beautifully.

You are not here to prove your worth or measure up to someone else's standards.

You are here to live—to grow, to express, to connect, to experience.

The moment you let go of the need to justify your existence, you allow yourself to come alive.

When you let go of striving from a place of lack, you don't lose yourself—you find yourself.

In that freedom, you reconnect with the truth of who you are.

This realization is freedom.

It's not an invitation to become complacent—it's an invitation to let go of the pressure, the anxiety, and the constant striving to prove your worth.

When you stop trying to justify your existence, something remarkable happens:

You start living from a place of authenticity.

You stop comparing, stop performing, and start connecting—with yourself, with others, and with life itself.

The world doesn't need another person ticking off boxes on someone else's checklist of success.

The world needs *you*.

The *real* you.

The one who knows that being here, right now, is a miracle in itself.

So, let go of the idea that you have to justify your existence.

Take a deep breath and remind yourself:

I am enough, simply because I exist.

Feel it settle into your bones, anchoring you like roots into the earth.

Because if the tree doesn't question its place, and the bird doesn't second-guess its song…

Why should you?

WHAT YOU NEEDED FROM YOUR PARENTS, THEY WERE INCAPABLE OF GIVING YOU

There is a moment, whether you remember it or not, when you first wondered if something was wrong with you.

Maybe it was the way your mother looked at you with exhaustion instead of warmth.

Maybe it was the way your father's voice could cut the air like a blade.

Maybe it was something quieter—the absence of love rather than the presence of pain.

Maybe it was everything.

But at some point, you felt it:

The weight of their moods, their emotions, their limitations.

And without realizing it, you made it mean something about *you*.

It was never about you.

But when you're a child, you don't know that. A child's mind doesn't separate itself from the world—it *absorbs* it.

You didn't have the ability to say, "My mother is cold because *she* is wounded."

Maybe *she* had never been nurtured the way she needed. Maybe she spent her entire life never knowing what it felt like to be held, to be seen, to be comforted herself.

Maybe no one ever told her that softness was safe.

And you couldn't recognize that your father's anger or distance wasn't about you either.

Maybe *he* had never felt loved by his own father. Maybe his mother never looked at him with warmth either.

Maybe no one ever taught him how to process his own pain, so he learned to release it the only way he knew how—through silence, through distance, through rage.

Maybe, just like you, they spent their entire lives waiting for something that never came.

But you didn't know that.

Instead, you did what all children do: you internalized it.

You believed it was about *you.*

And so, without anyone meaning to, the world taught you a lie.

That love must be earned.

That safety is conditional.

That something about *you* is unworthy, unlovable, not quite enough.

But that was never true.

Your parents—whether they were kind or cruel, present or absent, loving or distant—were never showing you your worth.

They were only ever showing you *themselves.*

Their wounds.

Their conditioning.

The patterns passed down to them long before you were born.

You were *never* the cause.

You were simply the closest witness.

And yet, up until this point, you've carried it.

You've been holding onto these stories like they are still real.

You keep waiting—somewhere deep inside—for the apology that will never come.

For the moment they will see you, love you, *choose* you the way you always needed them to.

But they won't.

Not because they don't love you.

But because they never had what you were asking for.

Because they weren't capable.

They couldn't give you what they didn't have themselves.

So, what now?

Now you let it go.

And I know what you're thinking…

Just like that? After all these years? After everything they did?

No.

Not just like that.

Letting go doesn't mean forcing yourself to forgive before you're ready.

It doesn't mean pretending it didn't hurt or acting like it didn't shape you.

It means *seeing it clearly for the first time.*

It means recognizing that what you're holding onto isn't protecting you.

It isn't serving or helping you.

It's keeping you tied to the very thing that wounded you.

And it was never yours to carry.

Because the way they acted was never about you.

It was always about *them*—their wounds, their fears, their limitations.

They owned it.

Not you.

They passed it down, but it was never yours to hold onto.

And now, you don't have to.

Somewhere along the way, you got locked into fight or flight.

But you're not in danger anymore.

You don't have to stay on alert.

That survival energy is loosening.

Your parents—whether they're still alive or not—don't hold that power over you anymore.

You are safe now.

Because you are not that child anymore.

Because the love you wanted from them is already inside of you.

Because the only thing keeping this alive is the part of you still waiting for something that will never come.

And when you see that—*really see it*—something inside you softens.

Maybe even right now, you can feel it.

Maybe there's a part of you that's already loosening its grip.

And if you allow it, just for a moment, something shifts.

Because you don't have to hold this anymore.

You don't have to carry what was never yours.

You don't have to stay bound to the past when freedom has been waiting for you all along.

And if you close your eyes right now and just breathe deeply, you might even notice…

The weight is already lighter.

Not because they deserve it.

But because **you** do.

THE MOMENT YOU ACCEPT YOUR PARENTS, YOU SET YOURSELF FREE

Even when you understand your parents—when you see their wounds, their limitations, and the reasons they became who they are—you may still carry a weight. A weight you don't even realize is there—until you feel the exhaustion of it.

It's the weight of everything you still wish had been different.

The weight of waiting—waiting for them to change, waiting for them to understand, waiting for them to love you in the way you always needed.

And yet, no matter how much time passes, they remain the same. Because they are who they are.

And as long as you hold onto the hope that one day they'll finally see you, finally give you what you deserved, you remain bound to them.

Not to who they are—but to who you wish they had been.

And that weight?

It's not just exhausting.

It's keeping you stuck.

Maybe you think you've moved on.

Maybe you tell yourself it doesn't matter anymore.

But if there's any part of you that still feels resistance, that still wishes they had been different, that still holds onto the idea that they should have been better, kinder, more present, more loving, more anything—then you are still carrying that energy.

And that energy is keeping you trapped in the past.

You don't need to forgive them for their sake. You don't need to excuse anything they did or didn't do.

This isn't about them at all.

This is about you.

Your freedom. Your peace.

Because here's the truth: that resistance, that anger, that hurt—it doesn't change them. It doesn't change what happened.

It doesn't rewrite the past.

It only keeps you bound to it.

You've spent years, maybe even decades, carrying this weight. Maybe you've been waiting for an apology that will never come. Maybe you've been hoping for them to suddenly understand, to finally see you in the way you always needed them to.

But that's not going to happen.

Not because they don't love you.

Not because they don't care.

But because *they are who they are.*

They are souls on their own journey, walking their own path, shaped by their own conditioning, their own wounds, their own limitations.

Just like you.

And when you really, deeply *see* this—when you stop making their actions mean something about you—something inside of you *lets go.*

It softens. It releases. It stops fighting a battle that was never going to be won.

Because the battle was never with them.

It was with *reality.*

The reality is, they did what they did. They were who they were. They showed up with the tools they had—even if those tools were dull, broken, or completely missing.

And when you accept that—*fully, completely, without resistance*—you free yourself.

You stop carrying the weight of what they *should* have been. You stop waiting for a version of them that never existed and will never exist.

You stop waiting for something outside of you to change in order for you to feel free.

Because *freedom doesn't come from fixing the past.*

It comes from letting it be.

It comes from *fully letting go.*

And even more than that ... it comes from *accepting them.*

Not just accepting what happened.

Not just letting go of the anger.

But fully, completely, *deeply* accepting them *exactly* as they are.

With all of their flaws. All of their limitations. Everything they couldn't give you.

Because here's the truth: holding onto resistance against them has never been about them.

It's been about the part of you that still wonders if you were ever enough.

But you were.

You *always* were.

And you are enough right now.

Loving yourself means no longer waiting for them to do it first.

It means realizing that the love you've been searching for is already inside you.

And when you let go—when you stop needing them to be different, when you stop defining yourself by their limitations—you stop rejecting yourself in the process.

You step into something new.

You step into yourself.

Fully.

Freely.

With more love than you ever thought possible.

Because self-love isn't just about treating yourself kindly.

It's about releasing every lie that ever made you believe you weren't worthy of it.

And this?

This is the biggest one.

So, right now, take a deep breath.

And as you exhale…

Feel the weight begin to lift.

Feel the energy of resistance leaving your body.

Feel yourself *softening* into acceptance…

Acceptance of them. *Exactly as they are.*

Not *for them.*

For *you.*

YOU ARE NOT BROKEN.
YOU WERE NEVER BROKEN.

Take a breath.

That weight you've been carrying—the one you thought was yours—was never yours to begin with.

You're starting to see it now, aren't you?

Maybe for the first time, something is clicking into place.

But let's be honest… That old voice in your head?

The one that whispers, *You're still not enough.*

Perhaps it's not fully gone.

Not yet.

And that's okay.

Because now, you see it for what it is.

It's not the truth.

It never was.

So, let me ask you something:

What if you were never broken?
What if there was never anything wrong with you?
What if every time you believed you were unworthy, you were simply believing a lie?

For decades, I too carried that lie.

I believed the parts of me I wanted to hide—the flaws, the mistakes, the things I judged as "unacceptable"—made me unworthy.

Unworthy of love.
Unworthy of success.

Unworthy of getting what I wanted in life.

For much of my life, I carried a deep resentment toward myself, believing I was lazy, undisciplined, weak-willed, unmotivated, and directionless. I saw these 'flaws' not just as insecurities, but as the very things that kept me from reaching my potential.

I spent so much time thinking that if I could just fix those things, I'd finally be good enough. But deep down, I felt like no matter what I did, I would always come up short. It was exhausting, carrying that weight, trying so hard to be better, but always feeling like something was missing.

And as I've worked with countless clients, I've come to see just how universal this is.

Beneath their anxiety, their struggles, and their fears, there's often a quiet frustration with themselves—a sense that something about them isn't right or good enough.

That they are somehow damaged beyond repair.

They might not put it into words, but it's there—this unspoken tension, this belief that if only they were different, things would be better.

I'm sure you've felt it too.

That belief that someday, when you achieve that one thing—when you lose the weight, get the promotion, find the perfect relationship, or live in the right house—then you'll be worthy. Then you'll finally allow yourself to love yourself.

Or maybe it's not about what you're missing. Maybe, deep down, you feel like there's something fundamentally wrong with you—a flaw in who you are, not just in what you have or haven't achieved.

Maybe it's the thoughts you think, the things you've done, or the mistakes you can't seem to forgive yourself for—that quiet, persistent fear that if people really knew you, they'd see you as unworthy too.

And so, you wait.

You tell yourself that someday, when you fix that part of yourself or achieve that goal, then you'll feel whole.

Then you'll finally be enough.

But here's the truth: that day will never come.

No matter how much you achieve, no matter how perfect your life looks from the outside, the voice in your head will always find something else to criticize.

You'll keep striving, believing the problem is something you can solve out there in the world. But the truth is, nothing external will ever fix what feels broken inside, because the real issue is not your life—it's the story you've been telling yourself about who you are.

It's a lie.

Here's the wake-up call.

The things you call flaws?

They're not flaws.

They never were.

Those choices you regret, those moments you wish you could take back, the parts of yourself you think are broken?

They are not evidence of your unworthiness.

They are the very things that have shaped you, taught you, and brought you here.

Without them, you wouldn't be who you are right now.

And if you look closer, you might realize that even the choices you once judged as mistakes were exactly what needed to happen for you to grow.

What if those choices weren't wrong? What if they were part of the path, guiding you to this moment?

You don't just need to love yourself—you need to love the road that got you here too.

I didn't understand this at first. For years, I saw my struggles and choices as obstacles, as evidence that I was somehow broken or unworthy. But looking back, I can see that they were invitations. The very things I resented—my lack of discipline, my indecision, my perceived weakness—became the raw material for my transformation.

Because I felt undisciplined, I had to cultivate self-discipline. Because I saw myself as weak-willed, I had to forge inner strength. Every quality I now embody—focus, resilience, motivation—was built upon the foundation of the very struggles I once believed were holding me back.

But that's the paradox: without those struggles, I wouldn't have had the chance to develop these qualities at all. If I had simply been born disciplined, motivated, and focused, I would have been robbed of the very experience that shaped me. There would have been no struggle to push against, no resistance to overcome, no journey of transformation to walk.

The growth, the wisdom, the depth—it all came from the process of becoming. The very things I once saw as flaws were, in truth, the necessary contrast that allowed me to cultivate the qualities I once thought I lacked.

And isn't that true for you as well? If you look closely, can you already see it—the ways in which your struggles have shaped you, refined you?

In fact, even the energy of anxiety is part of the design. As I've said from the very beginning, anxiety is not a mental illness. It's an invitation, a call to awaken, to look within, to uncover the deeper truth of who you are. It's a necessary ingredient, guiding you to this exact moment. It's not your enemy; it's been your teacher.

What if everything you've been through—every mistake, every heartbreak, even this energy of anxiety—wasn't random?

What if it was all necessary, every crack in your story letting in the light that's helping you become who you're meant to be?

You don't need to love yourself despite your perceived flaws.

You need to love yourself *because* of them.

Let me say that again...

You need to love yourself because of them.

In fact, you need to love yourself *and* your flaws.

They're not accidents; they're ingredients, essential pieces of your becoming.

And here's something very important to understand: not only are you worthy of love, you *are* love.

This isn't a metaphor or a feel-good affirmation.

It's reality.

The essence of who you are—the awareness behind your thoughts, the presence within you—is pure, unconditional love.

Consider this truth: You don't just deserve love; you are the energy of love itself. It's the very fabric of your being. And when you stop believing the lie that you're unworthy, you allow that love to flow freely, to yourself and to everyone around you.

So, how do you start loving yourself when you've spent so long believing you're unworthy?

It begins with a simple shift:

Stop fighting yourself.

Stop resisting the parts of you that you think shouldn't exist.

Loving yourself isn't about ignoring those parts or pretending they're not there.

It's about turning toward them with compassion—*even gratitude.*

Instead of seeing your struggles and "flaws" as proof that you're broken, see them as the roots of your strength.

Imagine a tree with twisted, gnarled roots.

Up close, those roots might look chaotic or flawed, but they're the very thing that keeps the tree strong and grounded. Without them, the tree wouldn't exist.

You are that tree.

Your perceived flaws, like gnarled roots, are vital parts of your foundation.

They ground you, stabilize you, and give you something to push against.

Without them, the tree cannot grow tall or strong. Even the messiest parts of life—the ones you wish you could erase—are like fertilizer. They may stink and seem unpleasant, but they enrich the soil, giving you the nourishment and strength to grow into something extraordinary.

Your perceived flaws are not mistakes; they are necessary.

Without them, there would be nothing to challenge you, nothing to shape you, nothing to help you transform.

They are the raw materials of your growth.

So don't just accept them.
Embrace them.
Love them.

They are what make your growth and transformation possible.

You don't have to wait to become "better" to start loving yourself.

You don't have to fix anything.

You don't have to earn it.

You are already whole.

You are already enough.

Right here, right now.

Close your eyes for a moment. Picture yourself as a child—small, curious, and full of wonder. See the innocence in their eyes, the hope in their heart. Now imagine yourself as you are today walking up to that child. Kneel down, meet their gaze, and say the words they've been waiting their whole life to hear:

"You are worthy of love. You always have been. There is nothing you could do or say, no mistake you could make, that would ever change that. I love you unconditionally, exactly as you are."

Watch their face as the weight they've been carrying begins to lift. See the light return to their eyes, the softness to their smile. And realize this: that child is still you. They've been waiting for you to come back, to remind them of what they've always known deep down: that they are enough. That they are love.

Everything you've been through, everything you've judged about yourself, everything you've labeled as a flaw—it's all part of the mosaic of your life. Up close, those broken pieces might look jagged or random. But when you step back, you see the whole picture. And it's breathtaking.

So, stop waiting.

Stop telling yourself that someday, when you're perfect, you'll finally be worthy of love. Let today be the day—the day you stop resisting the person you've been, the person you are, and the person you're becoming.

Let today be the day you look at yourself in the mirror and say to yourself, *"I see you, I accept you, and I love you."*

Because loving yourself isn't just about healing. It's about awakening. And the only way to awaken is to embrace the whole of who you are—the light and the shadows, the beauty and the mess.

You don't need to become anything else. You don't need to fix anything. You just need to allow the love you've been searching for to rise from the only place it's ever been: within you.

DOGS KNOW A SECRET
ABOUT LIFE THAT WE FORGOT

As I sit here writing, my dog, Buster, is curled up beside me, completely content.

He's a King Charles spaniel with a major jaw defect, so his tongue always hangs out—usually off to the side, like he's in on a private joke. Not only does his tongue hang out, but he was also the runt of his litter, about half the size of a normal King Charles spaniel.

Yet none of that matters to him.

He has no idea.

No clue.

He has no concept of himself as different or flawed.

He doesn't look in the mirror and worry about what others might think. He simply is.

He's not self-conscious; he's just conscious—aware, present, and joyful in the only way he knows how to be.

Most beings on Earth—dogs, birds, trees—exist as pure expressions of consciousness.

They are deeply connected to the same infinite awareness that animates all of existence, but they don't know themselves as *"I am."* They exist in complete harmony with the present moment, free from the inner dialogue and self-reflection that define human experience.

Watching him, I realize something: we struggle with what he does effortlessly.

But humans are different.

We are aware not only of the world around us, but of ourselves. We can step back and say, *"I am aware that I am."* This ability to reflect on our own awareness is both a gift and a challenge. It allows us to seek meaning, grow, and transcend the illusions of the mind.

But it also opens the door to suffering—ego, self-doubt, anxiety, and the stories we create about our worth.

When we look at animals or trees, we might think they're "less conscious," because they don't think about their own existence. But perhaps they're closer to the truth.

Their state of being is pure, unclouded by worries about past or future, and untouched by the need to be anything other than what they are.

They simply are.

And as I watch Buster, I wonder… what if we could live more like him?

What if we could embrace our imperfections without the endless mental chatter?

What if we could see that our flaws, just like his, are not mistakes, but part of the design?

Buster's quirks make him who he is, and in the same way, the things we label as imperfections in ourselves are what make us unique, what make us human.

They're not something to overcome—they're something to understand and embrace.

The paradox of being human is that we must journey through the maze of self-awareness to arrive at the same truth they embody effortlessly: we too are simply being.

The difference is, we can *know* it.

We can awaken to the truth of *"I am,"* not as a thought, but as the unchanging essence beneath all thoughts.

This is the gift of being human—a chance to consciously return to the awareness that everything, including ourselves, is one infinite expression of life.

This realization invites us to pause and reflect: what would it mean to live more like Buster?

To let go of the endless mental chatter and simply enjoy the act of being alive?

Nature constantly offers us this reminder—whether through the steady presence of a tree, the stillness of a sleeping dog, or the song of a bird in the morning.

These beings show us a deeper way of existing—one rooted in unity and peace.

As I look at Buster now, I can see his chest softly rising and falling, as he lies completely at peace with the world.

He reminds me of what humans so often forget: life isn't about becoming something more.

It's about peeling back the layers of worry, doubt, and judgment.

It's about remembering the simple truth of who we are.

Like Buster, we are already enough, exactly as we are.

This is the great awakening—not reaching for something distant, but coming home to ourselves, to this moment, and to the profound peace that's been here all along.

FEELING LIKE AN IMPOSTOR IS PROOF THAT YOU BELONG

Can I share something personal with you?

I'm not a writer.
I'm not smart enough to write a book.
I certainly don't have the discipline to ever finish writing one.

And a spiritual teacher?
Me?
Ha! Ridiculous.

For years, that was the story I kept telling myself.

A quiet, nagging voice convinced me I wasn't really that person. That no matter how much I wanted it, I didn't belong in that world.

And yet, here we are.

I'm a published author, and you're reading my words.

A part of me still vividly remembers the version of myself who never thought this would happen.

What about you?

What's the thing you secretly want, but dismiss with *Who am I to do that?*

Let me tell you something no one admits out loud: *everyone on some level feels like an impostor.*

Even the people you admire—the ones who seem so certain, so established, so real.

Because here's the truth: *no one has it all figured out.*

We're all just making the best choices we can and figuring it out along the way.

The only difference? Some people just decide to walk forward anyway.

It's not that they have more talent, more knowledge, or some invisible permission slip that makes them worthy.
It's that they stopped waiting to feel ready.

And yet, I almost didn't write this book.
I almost let that voice win.

But I didn't. I showed up anyway.

Even when it was hard.

Even when I wasn't sure if it would work or if I could do it.

Because here's what I've learned:

Your mind's job is to try to keep you protected. *Your job is to override it.*

It wants to keep you exactly where you are—comfortable, safe, unchallenged.

It will come up with a thousand distractions and justifications to keep you stuck.

You need more time.
You need more research.
You need to be fully ready before you start.

It's all a lie.

You don't need more thinking.

You need to turn off the part of your brain that wants to keep you exactly where you are.

Because when you finally decide to do something different, that's when your brain starts fighting back.

It tells you to wait.
It tells you to hesitate.
It convinces you that now isn't the time.

And if you listen to it, you will stay exactly where you are.

Your mind will always try to protect the status quo. That's its job.

But your job is to override it.

You don't need more research.
You don't need more preparation.

All you've got to do is start.

Literally, just start.

You can figure things out along the way.

And that brings me to something even bigger.

Most people think trying is progress.

But it's not.

Trying is the mind's way of keeping the door open just wide enough to keep you where you are.

Trying is not doing. Trying is preparing to fail.

Let me say that again:

Trying is preparing to fail.

When you say, *"I'm going to try,"* what you're really saying is:

"I'm leaving room for the possibility that I won't actually do it."

"I'm giving myself an easy out."

When you *try* to do something, you're already half out the door.

Think about it. If you tell yourself, "I'm going to try to wake up early tomorrow," what happens?
You set the alarm, but when it goes off, you hit snooze.
After all, you only said you'd try.

But when you decide, "I'm waking up early tomorrow," it's different.
The alarm goes off, and you get up—because there was no other option.

That's how you need to approach *everything*.

When you stop trying and start deciding, everything flips.

Trying keeps you stuck.

Eliminate the word *try* from your vocabulary.

There is no try.

There is only doing.

Switching your mindset from "I hope I can do this" to "I'm going to make this shit happen" is the difference between staying stuck and changing your life.

That thing you've always wanted to do?
You can do it.

The person you've always wanted to be?
You can become them.

Not by trying.

By becoming.

And I know what you're thinking:

Who am I to do this?

Let me tell you exactly who you are.

You are the person who is meant to do it.

That's why you feel it.
That's why you sense it.
That's why it's inside you.

Because it's yours.

Now go out there and get what's yours.

If you weren't meant to do it, you wouldn't even be thinking about it.

So, stop questioning.
Stop waiting.
Stop trying.

Just start.

THE LIFE YOU WANT IS WAITING— BUT YOU'RE STILL THINKING

Think about your favorite game.

Maybe it's a board game where every move shifts the entire strategy. Maybe it's a fast-paced video game where hesitation costs you everything. Or maybe it's something as simple as a card game, where one decision can change the entire round.

No matter the game, one rule is always true: nothing happens until you make a move.

The board stays the same. The score doesn't change. The pieces don't move themselves.

In every game, one truth is constant: nothing happens until you take action.

The game doesn't care how much you think, plan, or analyze. Your intentions don't matter. Your strategy doesn't matter. The pieces don't move. The ball doesn't score. Nothing changes until *you* move.

Life works the same way.

Most people are stuck on the sidelines, lost in their heads. They plan out their next move. They obsess over how to make it perfect. They wait for the right time, the right feeling, the right level of confidence. And in all that waiting, the game of life moves forward without them.

I sat with the idea of writing this book for a long time. I felt the pull—but I also felt the weight. The work. The doubt. Not knowing where to start. So, I waited. I thought about it. I planned. I hesitated.

And nothing happened.

Then one day, I just sat down and started writing. The first three chapters? Honestly, they weren't great. The way I wrote them in the beginning—pretty bad, actually. But that didn't matter. What mattered was that I started.

The moment I moved, something shifted. The ball started rolling. The ideas started flowing.

And now, here you are—reading the book that almost didn't exist.

Because that's how everything works. You don't need the perfect plan. You don't need to feel ready. You just need to move.

The ones who move—win.

That's the secret: the players in the game aren't fearless. They're not always confident. They don't always know exactly what to do. But they move anyway.

You don't need to be fearless. *You just need to feel the fear and do it anyway.*

Fear doesn't disappear before you act—it shrinks *because* you act.

The truth is, action builds everything you're looking for.
Action builds momentum. The moment you take the first step, the next step becomes clear. You don't need to know the entire path—you only need to move one square forward on the board.

Action dissolves anxiety.
Action builds clarity.

You learn by doing. Every move teaches you something—what works, what doesn't, and what comes next. You adjust, you adapt, and you keep moving.

And action builds confidence. Confidence isn't something you wait for. It's something you earn. It's the result of showing up, taking risks, and proving to yourself that you can handle whatever happens next.

The players in the game know this. They feel the same doubts you do—the same hesitation, the same fear.

But they act. They move. They play.

So, here's the question: where are you right now?

Are you sitting in the stands, watching life happen to other people? Are you on the sidelines, waiting for the right time to jump in? Or are you on the board, in the game, making moves and learning as you go?

What's the one move you know you need to make?

The one decision that, if you made it, would change everything?

Let the answer come. Trust the first one.

And when it does, *you might resist it.* It might feel uncomfortable, inconvenient—something you'd rather avoid.

But that's how you'll know it's the right move—the necessary one.

Don't turn away from it. Don't rationalize it away.

Act on it.

It doesn't matter if the move is small. It doesn't matter if it's imperfect. What matters is that you take it.

You don't need to wait for the fear to disappear. You don't need to wait for the moment to feel perfect.

Life doesn't wait.

The players in the game understand one thing: life rewards action. Not perfection—just movement.

The board is in front of you. The pieces are ready.

You've spent enough time watching. Enough time hesitating. Enough time waiting.

Enough.

Put your hand on the piece. Take the shot. Send the message. Make the move.

Because the game doesn't play itself. Life doesn't wait.

The next move is yours.

Take it.

THE GREATEST MOVIE EVER WRITTEN

Picture this:

Your life is a movie—but not just any movie.

It's the kind that becomes a *global phenomenon*. The kind people can't stop talking about. The kind that inspires, moves, and shakes people to their core.

And you are the main character.

Not just any main character—the one everyone roots for. The one who's been through the trials, the setbacks, the heartbreaks, the moments that felt impossible to survive.

You've already made it through scenes that would've broken someone else. You survived. You endured. You kept going.

And now, here you are.

This is the moment.

You know the one.

The turning point—*the moment where everything shifts.*

The part of the movie where the audience is on the edge of their seats because they *know* what's coming. They've been with you since the beginning. They've watched you struggle, watched you fight, watched you *almost* step into your power so many times.

And now, they're screaming at the screen:

"This is it!"
"Do it!"
"You're ready!"
"Go all in!"

They aren't hoping you'll win. *They know you're going to win.*

They've seen the foreshadowing, the setup, the groundwork you've laid without even realizing it. They know this is your moment—to rise, to stop doubting, to step into the role you were born for.

Can you hear them?

They're not passive viewers. They're *invested*.

The kind of fans who would sit in a packed theater, fists clenched, shouting at the screen, willing you to take the next step.

Because they see what you can't yet.

They see the version of you that has *already made it*.

They see the truth.

And here's the thing: this scene is already playing. The movie is still rolling.

The moment is happening *right now*.

So, what do you do?

Do you hesitate, waiting for a sign that's already screaming at you?
Do you let this scene pass, assuming another one will come along?
Or do you step into it?

Because the audience—the ones who love you, the ones who believe in you, the ones who would give anything to see you win…

They're watching.

They're begging you to *go for it*.

The choice is yours.

But if you could hear them—*really* hear them—you'd know there's only one way this story goes.

YOUR WHOLENESS HAS BEEN HERE ALL ALONG

At the core of everything, the only thing any of us truly want from others is to be loved and accepted exactly as we are.

We want to feel seen, valued, and embraced—flaws and all.

But here's the thing: it is nearly impossible to give that kind of love and acceptance to someone else when we have not given it to ourselves.

That is why we struggle to truly connect, why we resist others' imperfections: because we have not made peace with our own.

If you cannot love yourself, how can you fully love someone else? If you do not accept your flaws, why would you accept the flaws in others?

This is why the inner work is so essential.

Every spiritual tradition points to the same truth: love is the answer. But love is not just an idea or an emotion.

It is an energy that transforms.

It is through love—real, unconditional love—that we find connection, that we rediscover our Oneness.

Love is the force that unites us all.

But it has to start somewhere.

And that somewhere is within.

Here is the secret: the most magnetic force on earth is loving your own energy.

When you fully resonate with your essence—when you accept yourself completely and align with who you truly are—you create a powerful attraction.

Every intention, every action, every choice begins to flow in harmony with that resonance. And with that alignment, something remarkable happens.

Everything you desire begins to move effortlessly toward you.

You are no longer pushing or forcing.

You are simply being.

And the energy of that alignment does the work for you.

The external world becomes a mirror of the inner harmony you have cultivated.

The truth is that every part of you—the light and the darkness—is there for a reason.

The parts of yourself you want to deny, the flaws you want to hide, the shadow you would rather ignore…

They are not mistakes.

They are by design.

That darkness within you is not there to defeat you.

It is there to give you a choice.

Every choice you make moves you closer to the light or deeper into the darkness. But here is the empowering part: that choice is always yours.

When you choose the light—when you choose compassion, acceptance, growth—you are not just moving toward something good.

You are reclaiming your power.

You are deciding that the darkness does not get to rule you.

And even when you make mistakes, even when you falter, the opportunity to choose again is always there.

That's the beauty of it.

No matter where you are, no matter how dark things feel—

You can always turn toward the light.

True power is not about erasing the darkness. It is about recognizing that it's there…

And yet choosing to shine your light anyway.

It is the ability to face those parts of yourself—to acknowledge them—but not be ruled by them.

The darkness becomes a backdrop against which your light can shine even brighter.

Without it, there is no contrast, no growth, no transformation.

When you begin to see yourself this way—as whole, as worthy, as intentionally designed—you start to loosen the grip of self-judgment.

You stop rejecting parts of yourself and start embracing the truth:

All of you belongs.

This is not about fixing yourself or becoming perfect.

It is about seeing that even your darkest parts are part of your growth, part of your awakening.

They are not obstacles…

They are stepping stones.

And here is the beauty of it: when you love and accept yourself fully—even the parts you have been fighting against—

You stop needing anyone else to do it for you.

You stop chasing approval and validation…

Because you realize you have had everything you needed within you all along.

And from that place, you can give love freely—without conditions, without expectations.

You can accept others fully, because you have learned to accept yourself.

This is the work.

It is not easy.

But it is worth it.

Because when you love yourself as you are—light and darkness—

You unlock a kind of freedom most people spend their lives searching for.

And in that freedom, you discover the truth:

Nothing is missing.

Nothing was ever wrong.

Every part of you—light, shadow, flaw, and strength—was never a mistake.

It was all leading you back to yourself.

THE LION DOESN'T WAIT TO BE INVITED

I've always felt drawn to lions.

For as long as I can remember, something about them has captivated me—their intensity, the energy they carry, the way they move, the look in their eyes.

It's not just their physical strength or presence, but something deeper.

For years, I couldn't quite put my finger on it. I just knew I was fascinated by them.

Then one day, it hit me.

It was their mindset.

The lion's energy is magnetic, unshakable.

They don't question themselves. They don't hesitate or shrink.

They move as if the very ground beneath them recognizes who they are.

And when I realized this, it hit me hard: this was the energy I'd been wanting more of in my own life.

I'd spent so much time questioning, doubting, and second-guessing myself.

The lion showed me what was possible—not for the lion, but for me.

Imagine a lion walking into a clearing.

Silent, deliberate, and unshaken.

The air shifts.

The creatures nearby pause, their instincts sharpening.

They don't need a roar to tell them what's just entered the scene.

The lion doesn't question its presence.
It doesn't hesitate.
It doesn't shrink.

It moves with the quiet, immovable certainty that it belongs—and that's enough.

The lion isn't the fastest—that title belongs to the cheetah. It isn't the biggest—that would be the elephant. It isn't the strongest—that's the gorilla. And it isn't the smartest—that would go to the chimpanzee.

Yet none of that matters.

When the lion steps in, its presence alone commands attention.

Its power isn't in any single attribute, but in the way it carries itself.

The lion doesn't need to prove its worth.

It doesn't second-guess its role or hesitate in its movements.

It steps forward with quiet, immovable confidence, as its very presence speaks for itself.

That unshakable mindset is its true power.

Up until this point, anxiety may have had you questioning your own presence.

You may have found yourself hesitating, holding back, or doubting whether you're ready—whether you're smart enough, strong enough, or deserving enough to take the next step.

You might have felt like you were tiptoeing through life, afraid to take up space, waiting for someone else to tell you that you're enough.

That's the lie anxiety tells you: that you need to be more before you can belong.

The lion shows us a different way.

It doesn't wait for permission to be the lion.

It doesn't wonder if it's deserving of respect.

It doesn't shrink itself to make others comfortable.

It moves forward, trusting fully in itself—and the world responds to that energy.

That's the mindset you need to bring to your own life—not arrogance, not dominance, but presence.

It's stating, *"I'm here."*

Without a single word.

What would it look like for you to step into your life with that same energy?

Imagine showing up to a meeting or a difficult conversation—not questioning your worth, not overthinking, not hesitating, but simply deciding, "*I belong here.*"

Imagine starting your day with the quiet confidence of someone who knows they are already enough, just as they are.

When anxiety takes hold, it tries to convince you to shrink, to stay small, to second-guess every move.

It can *try*, but you decide not to let it.

The process of awakening is happening when you let go of that story.

It happens when you decide, once and for all, that you are worthy—not because you've proven it, but because you've *chosen it*.

You don't need to roar to be heard.

You don't need to be the loudest person in the room to be noticed.

True power doesn't announce itself—it simply exists.

And when you embody that energy, when you move through life with clarity and certainty, the world responds.

This isn't about pretending to be fearless or faking confidence.

It's about recognizing that your worth has never been in question.

Like the lion, you don't need to be the fastest, the biggest, the strongest, or even the smartest to claim your space.

You don't need to have all the answers or wait for the perfect moment.

You only need to step forward.

The next time you walk into a room, don't wait for permission.

Don't wonder if you belong.

Decide it.

Move with the quiet strength of someone who already knows.

Just like the lion.

Stop waiting for someone to hand you your power.

It's already yours.

Stop waiting for permission to live fully—it's never coming.

Like the lion, you are enough, exactly as you are.

Right here, right now.

Walk forward, not as someone asking for their place, but as someone who knows they've had it all along.

The lion doesn't wait for the world to make room for it.

It steps in, and the world adjusts.

It's time for you to do the same.

LIFE IS HAPPENING
FOR YOU, NOT TO YOU

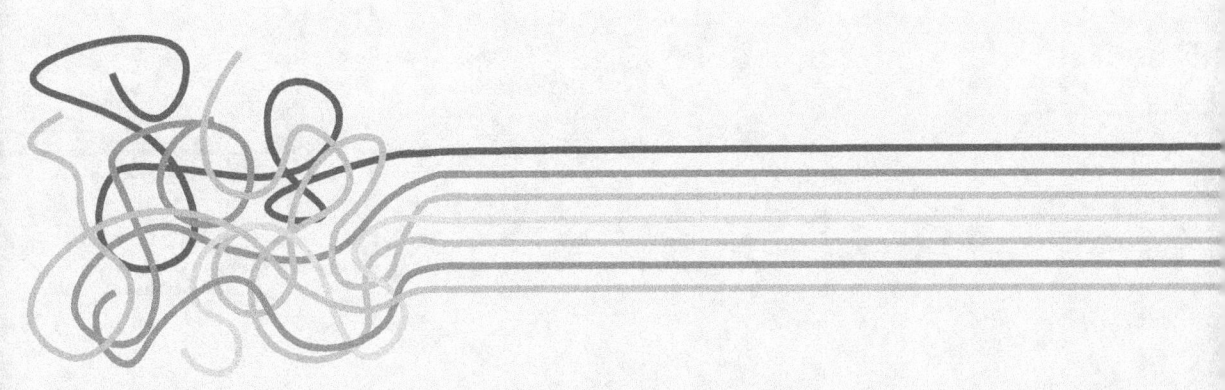

LIFE IS A TV SHOW, AND YOU ONLY WRITE YOUR LINES

Sometimes I think of life as a TV show.

There are writers behind the scenes crafting every episode, bringing in wild plot twists, unforgettable lines, and just the right mix of drama and comedy.

You're the main star of your TV show.

The people in your life?

They're the cast.

You've got your main characters—family, close friends, your partner—then the guest stars, and even the extras who show up for a split second, but somehow leave a lasting impression.

The thing is, everyone is playing their role exactly as it was written, and everybody's the star of their own show.

Think about it.

When you watch a show, you don't expect a character to suddenly stop being who they are. You don't expect the clueless boss to walk into a meeting and suddenly start making wise, well-thought-out decisions. That's their role. That's what makes them *them*. If they suddenly became competent and self-aware, the entire show would collapse.

So, why do we expect the people in our lives to be any different?

Why do we assume that this time, in today's episode, they're going to show up as someone completely new?

They're not.

They're going to show up exactly as they are—exactly as they've always been—fully committed to their character.

Who do you have in your life that's always playing their character perfectly?

That one person who is so consistent, so unapologetically them, that you can practically predict how they'll respond in any given situation?

Maybe it's a parent, a sibling, your partner, a coworker, or even a friend.

When you stop expecting them to be someone else and instead just watch them—like a character in a show—you'll find yourself thinking…

Wow, they are so who they are.

They are absolutely *nailing* their role.

And here's the thing: you're not writing their lines.

You're not in charge of their script.

They're playing their role, following their own storyline, and no amount of frustration or resistance is going to change that.

The only part of this show you get to write is yours—your character, your lines, your actions and reactions.

And when you stop trying to rewrite other people's scripts, you reclaim your energy.

Life gets lighter.

You realize how much mental energy you've been wasting, expecting them to act differently.

That's not your job. It never was.

Your job is to step back, watch, and sometimes even just stand in awe of how fully people commit to playing their character.

My wife and I joke about this all the time. After a particularly wild day, we'll sit back and say, "Wow, that was quite an episode. The writers are really working overtime—they must be gunning for an Emmy."

And honestly, it helps. It reminds us not to take things so seriously.

The absurd twists, the people who show up exactly as they always do, the unexpected chaos—it's all part of the show.

And sometimes, the writers give us episodes so ridiculous that we have to laugh.

For my wife's birthday, my mom—her mother-in-law—decided to get her a massage. She got a gift certificate to her usual massage therapist, a small Korean woman who specializes in deep tissue and shiatsu. My mom booked it, my wife was excited, and everything was set for a relaxing, blissful experience.

Except that's not how this episode was written.

She walks in expecting a soothing massage, lies down … and within minutes, this woman is absolutely wrecking her.

Deep pressure, knuckles, elbows, digging straight into muscle with no mercy. My wife starts flinching. Then squirming. Then outright telling her, "Too hard! Please, too much pressure!"

The woman doesn't ease up.

She doesn't adjust.

Instead, she casually says, "No, no. Good for you."

As if my wife just didn't understand what was best for her own body. As if pain was simply a misunderstanding that she needed to accept.

Then come the hot stones.

Except these aren't just warm stones. These things feel like they've been sitting in a furnace for a week. My wife tenses, gasps, her body locking up.

"They're too hot!" she says, wincing. "Please, too hot!"

And the woman, calm as ever, just says:

"You endure."

My wife freezes. "No, really, too hot!"

"You endure."

She repeats it. Same tone, same delivery, like a mantra from some ancient school of suffering. At that point, my wife knows there's no way out. She's gripping the table, eyes squeezed shut, her mind trying to escape her body, just surviving.

When she finally got home and walked through our front door, I didn't even need to ask how it went.

The look on her face said it all.

Her eyes were wide, her expression blank, and the imprint from the massage table's face cradle was still stamped across both cheeks like a set of battle scars.

"Mommy, what happened to you?" my daughter Eden asked, eyes wide.

For a moment, she stood there like someone who had just returned from war, then said, "If your mom didn't go to this woman herself, I'd swear she secretly hates me."

Without another word, she set the business card from the massage place down on the kitchen counter, like she needed to rid herself of it. I picked it up and flipped it over.

The name on it?

Silk Hands.

You can't make this stuff up.

And that's when it hit me:

Everyone in this episode was just playing their part.

My mom? The classic mother-in-law. Of course she thought this was a great gift. Of course she had no idea what my wife was about to go through.

She played her role flawlessly.

The Korean massage therapist? Not the villain—just the ultimate deep tissue warrior. She was always going to say, "No, no. Good for you," and "You endure."

She was fully in character, committed to her craft.

My wife? The protagonist. Expecting one experience, getting something completely different, reacting exactly as she would in any other episode.

Me? The observer.

Watching the whole thing unfold, laughing my head off, and realizing the deeper truth.

And life?

Life is the *ultimate director*, making sure every scene plays out exactly as written. Never off-script, never missing a beat, just running the show no matter how absurd it gets.

Because isn't that exactly how life works?

We expect it to be comfortable.

We expect it to be soothing, peaceful, like some kind of endless spa retreat.

And sometimes, sure, we get those moments.

But most of the time?

Life is elbows in your spine, burning-hot stones on your back, and someone telling you, "No, no. Good for you."

We resist it. We fight it. We keep thinking, *This isn't how it's supposed to be.*

But maybe, just maybe, life—like that massage—isn't supposed to be easy.

Maybe it's supposed to break up the knots, crack us open, and push us just past what we think we can take.

And when you stop fighting it, when you stop expecting it to be anything other than what it is, something shifts.

You endure.

Maybe you even loosen up a little.

And if you're really lucky?

You laugh.

Because let's be honest: the writers are going for an Emmy with your life.

PARENTING WILL BREAK YOU OPEN—AND HEAL YOU

IF YOU'RE A PARENT, THIS REFLECTION IS FOR YOU.
IF YOU'RE NOT, FEEL FREE TO SKIP AHEAD.

Parenting is, without question, a fast track toward awakening.

It doesn't matter how old your children are. Whether they're toddlers clinging to your leg or adults navigating their own lives, this truth applies.

Parenting will show you your own mind like nothing else can. It amplifies everything you bring with you: the anxiety you've carried since childhood, the patterns you've inherited, and the expectations society has placed on you. It magnifies your emotions, your fears, and your hopes.

Parenting puts it all under a microscope.

For many of us, this magnification can feel overwhelming. Anxiety, already present in the background of our lives, is suddenly turned up to full volume.

Parenting pushes every button, often all at once. There's no hiding from it because parenting isn't just about raising children, it's about facing yourself.

I was reminded of this recently while dropping my kids off at school. One of them made some ridiculous claim—something about whether a zebra is more black or white, or if a certain song was actually good—and suddenly, we were in it.

Voices rising, each one absolutely certain that they were right, the sheer conviction over something so trivial filling the car like a storm.

But in that moment, as I sat there in the middle of all the noise and emotions swirling around me, I noticed something.

Beneath all the intensity and chaos in the car, within me, there was stillness.

There always is.

And in that stillness, I saw the choice.

I could get sucked into the emotions, react, escalate, spin out, or I could simply observe. I could hold space for it all without losing myself.

This is what parenting demands of us, and this is where it becomes a path to awakening.

It teaches us, moment by moment, to notice our own anxiety, our own patterns, and decide whether we want to keep carrying them forward.

It shows us how to pause, how to breathe, and how to choose something different.

It shows us how to *respond*, instead of react.

It doesn't matter if your children are young, wrestling with tantrums, or adults navigating careers and relationships. Parenting always has the power to challenge you, to press your buttons, and to call you to a higher level of awareness.

The emotions don't stop when your children grow up, but neither does the opportunity to grow through them.

The truth is, parenting isn't just an emotional journey, it's a spiritual one.

It calls on you to go beyond reaction, to step out of the cycle of anxiety and into awareness. It's not about being perfect or emotionless.

It's about being present, awake, and willing to see your role in the bigger picture.

As you move through your parenting journey, take a moment to reflect.

Notice the emotions, the chaos, and the noise.

And notice, too, the stillness and silence beneath it.

Recognize the choice you always have: to react or to respond, to hold onto anxiety or to let it go.

You don't have to get it right every time.

No one does.

But every moment you choose to step into awareness is a moment you grow—not just as a parent, but as a human being.

Parenting isn't just about what you give to your children.

It's about discovering who you are beneath the noise, and awakening to the stillness that's been there all along.

I know that journey well, because before my awakening, I lived with parenting anxiety every day.

The stress, the guilt, the self-doubt, the endless worrying. It shaped how I thought, reacted, and connected with my kids. I was constantly caught in cycles of frustration and guilt, wanting to be more present, but feeling trapped in my own mind.

But when I realized that anxiety wasn't just about them, it was about me—my patterns and expectations—everything changed. My parenting became lighter, more present, more connected.

That shift didn't happen overnight. It took time, awareness, and new ways of seeing myself.

Through that process, my wife and I realized how powerful it is to shift from reaction to awareness. That realization led us to create MamaZen, an app that helps parents break free from stress and anxiety, just like we did.

I know firsthand how hard it is to parent through a fog of stress. Anxiety doesn't just come and go. It shapes how we think, react, and connect. MamaZen rewires those patterns from the inside out, helping you shift from reaction to awareness and create a foundation of calm, patience, and clarity.

And just like we need support, our kids do too. That's why we added Zenzy Kids, a series of sessions within the app designed specifically for children to help them build resilience and confidence from the inside out.

Parenting will always challenge you, but it doesn't have to feel like a constant struggle. The more you transform, the more peace you create—not just for yourself, but for your children too.

THE UNIVERSE DOESN'T MAKE MISTAKES— AND NEITHER DOES YOUR LIFE

If you look closely at the universe, you'll see order everywhere. It's not subtle. It's not hidden. It's right in front of you, woven into everything.

Picture a vast spiral galaxy, billions of stars swirling in perfect harmony. Now hold a seashell in your hand. Notice the same spiral, carved by the intelligence of life, repeating itself from the infinite to the tiny. That's not coincidence—that's order.

The branching of a tree mirrors the branching of veins, rivers, and lightning. Snowflakes form with mathematical precision—no two alike, yet all built with the same rules. Look at the Fibonacci sequence—it's in pine cones, sunflowers, hurricanes, and the proportions of your own body. Fractals—self-repeating patterns—are everywhere. Zoom in, zoom out— the pattern stays the same.

Even what we call chaos isn't chaos. A thunderstorm feels wild and unpredictable, but it follows exact laws. Ocean waves crash in rhythm. Gravity holds everything together. The planets orbit the sun in perfect cycles. The universe is designed to be in harmony. It is precise, intelligent, and flowing.

So, let me ask you: why would your life be the exception?

Why would the same universe that moves the stars and grows the trees somehow forget about you? Why would your experiences—your challenges, your setbacks—be random or out of sync with this same intelligence?

They aren't. Of course they aren't.

I used to believe that life was happening to me—that the challenges, the obstacles, and the chaos I faced were mistakes or accidents I had to fight through. And the more I resisted, the more anxious I became. I thought I had to control it all—micromanage my life like it was separate from everything else.

But then I saw it. And I couldn't un-see it.

If the entire universe operates in perfect order, then so does my life.

So does your life.

The same intelligence that spins galaxies is the same intelligence moving through you. Everything that happens to you—every moment, every experience, every challenge—is part of the design.

At first, this wasn't easy to accept. Because when life feels hard, when you're deep in discomfort or uncertainty, it doesn't look like order. It feels like chaos. But what if it isn't? What if the very challenges you face are part of the design—meant to help you grow, to make you stronger, to wake you up?

When challenges come now—and they still come—I remind myself:

Everything is in divine order. It cannot be otherwise.

This doesn't mean I sit back and do nothing. I still meet life as it comes. I still take action if it's needed or will make a difference. But I no longer fight it. I trust it. I trust that whatever is happening is meant to be happening—that even the things I don't like are here for a reason. Life isn't happening *to* me. Life is happening *for* me.

And when you trust this—when you truly trust it—you can begin to align yourself with the order that already exists.

Bring order to your mind. Pause. Reflect. Let go of the noise.

Bring order to your body. Sleep well, move often, and nourish yourself with food from nature.

Bring order to your space. Let go of what doesn't serve you. Make tidy what you use and enjoy.

Bring order to your time. Focus on what matters, and let go of what doesn't.

This isn't about forcing or controlling. It's about aligning. Nature doesn't resist life—it works with it. A tree grows in patterns, but still adapts. It flows. It thrives. You can do the same.

And here's what I want you to remember: When life brings you challenges—and it will—pause. Take a breath. And say to yourself:

"Everything is in divine order. It cannot be otherwise."

Let that truth sink in. Let it carry you through whatever comes next.

Because the universe doesn't make mistakes. Life doesn't make mistakes. And that includes your life.

Everything is happening exactly as it's meant to. Everything is indeed in divine order. It always has been. It always will be. It cannot be otherwise.

So, let go. Trust the flow. Trust the design. And know this: life is carrying you exactly where you're meant to go.

YOU'RE NOT DROWNING,
YOU'RE RESISTING

I'm not a surfer. I'm not that cool.

But I have boogie-boarded, and I imagine the feeling is similar. When you catch a wave, there's no thinking. No analyzing. Just movement. The wave picks you up, and for a moment, you're fully carried by it.

Present.

Yet relaxed.

Free from thought.

Fully free.

Before awakening, life feels like waiting. Like a surfer sitting on their board, scanning the horizon, hoping the right wave will finally come. Or worse, like getting hit over and over, ducking under waves just to stay afloat.

You paddle hard, but the ocean is relentless. No matter how much effort you put in, you never feel fully in control. It's exhausting. It's frustrating. And at some point, you start to wonder... *Will I ever catch the right wave?*

Awakening is different.

It's catching the wave, and staying on...

It's living fully in the now, letting the wave of life carry you completely.

Not fighting.

Not forcing.

Just moving with it.

The moment you stop trying to control the ocean, you realize it was always carrying you.

Because fighting the ocean is a battle you'll never win.

It doesn't matter how strong you are, or how much effort you put in.

The ocean is bigger than you.

Deeper than you.

Far more powerful than you.

And yet, you've spent your whole life trying to fight it.

You can thrash, resist, and exhaust yourself… or you can let go and ride.

Sometimes the wave shifts.
Sometimes it swells up and becomes harder to ride.
Maybe you slip.
Maybe it twists you in a direction you didn't expect.

But that doesn't mean you're lost, and it doesn't mean you're drowning.
It just means you adjust.

You keep riding.
Because the wave doesn't stop.
Life doesn't stop.

This wave doesn't crash.

It only moves forward.

And here's what most people don't realize:

The wave is already here.
Right now.
Beneath you.
Carrying you forward.

You don't have to wait.
You don't have to fight.

You can let go and ride.

So, what are you waiting for?

Can you feel it?

Can you just let it carry you?

LIFE IS ALWAYS SAYING YES—
WHAT ARE YOU ASKING FOR?

Remember when I said life is a TV show?

That each of us is living our own storyline, surrounded by a cast of characters perfectly playing their roles?

Well it's not just you.

Your family has a show, your neighborhood has a show, even your favorite restaurant has a show. Everyone is living out their own story, like episodes in an infinite series.

But what if these shows aren't separate? What if every family, every workplace, every relationship is part of a massive, interconnected, grand production? And what if there's something watching it all—not as a distant observer, but as the ultimate showrunner, effortlessly weaving all the stories together?

Pause for a moment and consider how awareness works in your everyday life.

When you hear a sudden sound outside your window, you don't need to try to notice it— you simply do. If someone taps you on the shoulder, you feel it immediately. Awareness doesn't require effort. It's natural, constant, and effortless.

Now imagine that same awareness, but on an infinite scale.

That's the supreme awareness. It doesn't strain to notice everything everywhere—it simply does.

Effortlessly.
Constantly.
All at once.

This supreme awareness isn't just watching your show—it's aware of all the shows, everywhere, at all times.

But it's not just aware of everything; it *is* everything.

It sees all because *it is all.*

Every person, every story, every moment is part of this awareness, like waves rising and falling in an infinite ocean.

And here's the most profound part: you are it, and it is you.

You're not separate from this awareness—it expresses itself through you, as you.

Your desires arise from your unique perspective as an expression of this infinite awareness.

What you believe, it creates.

This is why your thoughts and beliefs are so powerful. They aren't just fleeting ideas in your mind. They are signals shaping the reality around you, weaving the next scene of your story before it unfolds.

But here's where it gets even more extraordinary: this awareness doesn't just observe—it reflects.

It's listening to your thoughts, your beliefs, your intentions, and it's saying yes.

Every thought you have is like a seed you're planting, and the awareness nurtures it into growth.

When you think, *Nothing ever works out for me*, it reflects that belief back to you.

When you think, *I'm ready for new opportunities*, it reflects that too, opening doors you couldn't have imagined.

It doesn't judge or decide—*you* decide. It simply amplifies the vibration you're sending out and coordinates the world around you to match.

This is why awakening is so transformative. It's not about escaping the show or rejecting the chaos—it's about realizing that you're shaping the storyline in every moment.

You're not just a character in your show. You're the creator too.

The supreme awareness is constantly recalibrating the story—not by effort or control, but by effortlessly reflecting the energy you bring to it. The challenges, the detours, the plot twists—they're all part of the masterpiece being written for you and through you. Even the moments that feel random or unfair are chosen at a higher level for the growth they catalyze.

And here's the profound truth:

Life is always saying yes to you. The question is, what are you asking for?

The next time you feel lost in the chaos or weighed down by the plot twists of your own show, pause.

Take a moment to notice what you're thinking.

Ask yourself: *What am I inviting into my story, and how do I want my character to grow?*

Because life isn't just a show you're watching.

It's a masterpiece you're helping to create—one thought, one choice, and one moment at a time.

The supreme awareness is always there, reflecting you effortlessly, and weaving your story into something extraordinary.

Have you ever had a moment when everything just seemed to fall into place?

A chance encounter, an idea that felt like it came out of nowhere, or a situation that seemed tailor-made for your growth?

That's the supreme awareness at work.

It's not outside of you—it's within you, responding to your deepest beliefs and intentions.

Every thought, every moment, every choice adds its color to the masterpiece of existence.

Trusting this awareness is trusting that the masterpiece is already perfect—and that you're an essential part of its beauty.

You are not just in the story; you are the awareness behind it.

Life isn't just happening to you—it's happening through you, *as* you.

And in that realization, you find the greatest truth of all:

You are the showrunner, the character, and the masterpiece itself.

YOU WERE GIVEN THIS LIFE TO FEEL IT ALL

Have you ever stopped to marvel at the sheer genius of nature?

Think about it—the sheer perfection and beauty of an orchid, the way the sky ignites in a symphony of purples and golds as the sun sets beyond the horizon, or how your heart has been beating, long before you were born, without you ever asking it to.

Now, compare that to anything man-made.

A sleek spacecraft soaring into the heavens, the dazzling lights of a city skyline at night, or even the intricate detail of a world-famous painting. As impressive as these creations might seem, do they truly inspire the same awe? Do they stir your soul in the same way that the natural world does?

When you recognize that nothing humans have ever created even comes close, you begin to sense the extraordinary power behind it all—the infinite intelligence that shaped not just the natural world, but also the very essence of who we are.

This energy, this Creator, didn't merely form the world around us; it infused it with purpose, beauty, and meaning. And it gave us something miraculous: the ability to experience it.

Have you ever truly considered the wonder of biting into a perfectly ripe orange?

The way its vibrant juice bursts across your tongue—a symphony of sweet and tart, so alive that it feels like sunshine in fruit form?

Or the mesmerizing beauty of a star-filled sky—countless points of shimmering light suspended effortlessly in the infinite darkness?

What about the rhythmic crash of ocean waves, steady and eternal, or the intricate pattern of a snowflake, utterly unique, yet fleeting?

None of these wonders were man-made. They came from the same infinite intelligence that designed you.

And here's the extraordinary truth: your ability to taste the orange, to feel the sun's warmth on your skin, to hear the whisper of the wind in the trees—none of it is an accident.

These moments were created for you, and your enjoyment of them is part of the design. You were given this gift of life to experience it fully—not just to observe it, but to live it. To marvel at its beauty, its complexity, and even its challenges.

Because the point isn't just to seek the highs or avoid the lows.

It's to *experience it all.*

The moments of heartbreak and frustration carry a richness, a depth, a power that joy alone cannot offer.

The challenges stretch us, transform us, and show us what we're capable of becoming.

Every tear, every triumph, every sensation you feel is a piece of the same puzzle, a part of this incredible experience we call life.

The more present you are to these gifts—the sweetness of an orange, the sting of a tear, the majesty of a waterfall—the more connected you become to the truth of why we're here.

To live.
To feel.
To grow.

To stand in wonder of it all.

Because the same infinite intelligence that paints the sunsets and arranged the stars across the night sky also created you.

And it gave you this incredible life—not to fear it, not to pass by it, but to truly live it.

WHAT IF YOU CHOSE THIS TOO?

A couple of days ago, I woke up with a cold.

It wasn't severe—a low fever, some discomfort—but enough to throw off my rhythm. My sleep was disrupted, and I didn't feel like myself.

Before my awakening, this would've triggered frustration.
I would've questioned why this was happening, especially since I take good care of myself. I would've resisted the reality of being sick, thinking about how it might derail my plans or productivity.

But this time, it was different.

I didn't fight it.
I didn't question it.

Instead, I felt a deep sense of acceptance.

Not resignation, but an understanding that this was simply what is right now. My body was giving me a message: *Slow down. Take it easy.* So, I listened. I took some extra vitamin C, did what I could to support my body, and moved on.

Instead of letting frustration take over, I welcomed the opportunity to rest.

It was a Saturday, so I sat outside with my family, feeling the warmth of the sun, watching the world move at its natural pace, and letting go of any need to control what was already unfolding.

What I've come to realize is that there's immense power in going with the flow of life, in meeting each moment as if you have chosen it. Even challenges can become opportunities to align with something greater when we stop resisting them.

Think about the last time life threw you an unexpected curveball.

Did you resist it, or did you lean into it? Imagine how different it would feel to meet even those moments with full acceptance, as if you had chosen them.

And as I reflect and write about this, something small but meaningful happens.

I glance at my phone and notice the time: 4:44. For me, moments like these are reminders—a subtle nudge from life that I'm aligned with something greater. Whether you see it as coincidence, synchronicity, or something more, these moments invite us to pause and trust in the flow.

This is what it means to flow with life—not just to accept what happens, but to embrace it as if you have chosen it.

Because when you act as if you chose it all, you unlock freedom, power, and peace.

Resistance dissolves, and what's left is the realization that life isn't happening to you; it's happening for you.

THE GAME OF LIFE GETS EASIER
WHEN YOU STOP TRYING TO WIN

Imagine, for a moment, that life is quite literally a game.

Not just a metaphor, but a real, intricately designed experience meant to be played, explored, and mastered. Every challenge, every joy, every relationship is part of its design, shaping you as you progress.

Now think about how you've been playing it.

Most of us approach life as if it's a race, always trying to get somewhere. We believe that if we can just reach a certain goal, fix a problem, or achieve the "next thing," then we'll finally feel at peace.

I used to think that way too.

When I was in my early thirties, I met up for lunch with my longtime friend, Michael. We've known each other since second grade.

As I was sharing some ambitious goal of mine, he looked at me and said, "You know, as long as I've known you, you always like talking about the finish line. You do realize the ultimate finish line is a casket, right?"

His words stopped me in my tracks.

My old buddy had a good point.

I had spent so much of my life focused on arriving—on achieving, fixing, and getting to some imagined future where I could finally relax. But in that moment, something shifted. What if I had been missing the point all along?

I started to recognize the beauty of the process—that life isn't about getting somewhere. It's about living.

And yet, most of us don't play the game that way. Instead, we treat life like a race, always chasing the next thing, believing that if we just reach some future moment, then we'll finally be okay.

Here's where it gets tricky. For most people, the game of life feels anything but playful. It feels heavy, serious, and often painful. There's anxiety, fear, frustration, and suffering—and it's easy to wonder, *If life is a game, why does it feel so hard?*

The answer lies in forgetting. When we step into this game, we forget who we truly are. We forget that we're not just the player—we're also the creator of the game. And because we forget, we start playing in a way that makes life harder than it needs to be.

We start believing that life is about reaching some future moment where everything will finally be okay. We spend our time chasing goals, running from discomfort, and trying to control outcomes. And in doing so, we lose sight of the present moment—the only moment that's real.

Most people are playing the game backwards. Instead of experiencing life as it unfolds, moment by moment, we treat it like a finish line we're trying to cross. We think, *If I can just achieve this, fix that, or get there, then I'll finally feel complete.*

But here's the truth: the game isn't about getting somewhere. The point of life isn't to "win."

It's to experience.

When you chase the future, you miss the present. When you try to control every outcome, you resist the natural flow of life. And when you play the game this way, it's no wonder that it feels like a struggle.

Awakening is what happens when you remember what the game is really about. It's not about escaping life. It's about seeing it clearly. Awakening reveals that the point of the game isn't to win—it's to wake up and play fully, right here and now.

When you awaken, you stop running after some imagined future and start living in the present. You stop resisting the challenges and start embracing them as part of the design. And here's where the magic begins: when you stop trying to control the game, life starts to flow.

The moment you awaken, something extraordinary happens. Life begins to work with you instead of against you. You start to notice synchronicity after synchronicity—those perfectly timed events that feel almost too good to be true.

You might think of someone, and they suddenly call. You might need help, and the right person or perfect opportunity appears.

These are not random coincidences.

They're signs that you're aligned with the deeper intelligence that created the game.

When you stop fighting against life and start experiencing it moment by moment, you enter a state of flow. The game stops feeling like a struggle and starts feeling like an adventure.

The game of life isn't about achieving or conquering. It's not about getting to the finish line.

It's about discovering who you truly are.

Awakening doesn't take you out of the game; it shows you how to play it.

You realize that you're not just the character—you're also the creator. You're not separate from the challenges or the joys. Everything you experience is part of the process, designed not to punish you, but to wake you up.

And once you see this, a new awareness takes hold. Life becomes richer, deeper, and more meaningful. You stop trying to "win" and start experiencing the fullness of what's already here.

The game of life was never meant to be a race.

It's an invitation to wake up, to play fully, and to experience the miracle of being alive. And the moment you remember this, the game starts to transform.

Are you ready to start playing it differently?

EVERYTHING THAT BROKE YOU BUILT YOU

There was a time in my life when I was more than one million dollars in debt.

Many years ago, we had a small business we had poured years of effort and hope into, but it was losing more and more money year after year. The financial strain kept growing, and the pressure to make ends meet became unbearable.

The fallout left us drowning in debt.

Home loan, multiple business loans, and credit card debt piled up, with everything leveraged to the hilt. We were maxing out credit cards to cover bills from the business—bills we couldn't afford to pay otherwise.

It was a cycle of debt feeding debt, with no clear way out.

Even my parents' house wasn't spared.

They had put it up as collateral to help me start the business that was now failing. The guilt of knowing they had risked *everything* for me—and that I might lose it for them—was almost too much to bear.

It wasn't just financial pressure; it was existential.

Living in a small condo in West Los Angeles, where the cost of living was incredibly high, every month felt like a fight to stay afloat. And amidst all this, my wife and I were raising two young daughters.

The weight of it was staggering. Crushing.

But here's the thing: it didn't crush me.

I could've let it. I could've been consumed by fear, frustration, or anger.

And to be honest, there were moments when I felt the pull of those emotions. There were days when I was depressed, days when it felt like I was carrying the weight of the world.

But even then, I didn't allow the debt to define me. Somehow, I found ways to still enjoy my life—to savor time with my kids, to find little moments of joy.

It wasn't the presence I know now, but it was enough to keep me moving forward.

Looking back, I can see it clearly: the debt was so overwhelming that fighting it wasn't an option.

All I could do was surrender—not in defeat, but in trust.

Trust that somehow, some way, we would find a way through.

One night, as we lay in bed, my wife turned to me, her voice breaking, and asked, "Are we ever going to get out of this?"

Without hesitation, I answered, "Yes, we are. I have no doubt."

Even as I said it, I had no idea where the answer came from. My conscious mind didn't have a plan. There was no logical way out that I could fathom. But something deeper inside me—a part of me beyond reason—knew.

That inner certainty became my foundation.

The path out wasn't easy. As we began to dig ourselves out of debt, we had to make painful decisions. We let go of the business we had poured so much into, suffering a massive financial loss and leaving us still deeply in debt. Each decision was difficult, like letting go of a dream we had worked so hard to build.

But little by little, these choices began to lighten the financial burden.

And when an opportunity came to move across the country, we took it. That single move created a cascade of unexpected benefits. We sold our home, paid off the debts, and against all odds, bought a new house outright—with no mortgage.

Even my parents, who had leveraged their house to help us, ended up moving near us. In one of those incredible synchronicities, they not only saved their home, but were able to pay it off completely.

When I look back, I have no doubt that a higher energy was orchestrating it all.

The way events, both small and monumental, aligned with almost impossible precision—it felt fully guided, as if something far greater than myself was moving the pieces into place in a way chance *never* could.

It was like life itself stepped in to show me what's possible when you trust.

Now, let me ask you something different:

Can you think of a time in your life when you found yourself in a situation so overwhelming, so impossible, that it felt like there was no way out?

But somehow, you *did* get out of it.

Maybe it wasn't logical. Maybe it didn't make sense on paper. But a series of events, a chain of seemingly unrelated moments, came together to carry you through.

Take a moment to remember that time.

What did it feel like when the pieces started falling into place?

What did it teach you about life—about how things align when you let go of control and trust?

That's not coincidence. That's not luck. That's the design.

Life is *always* aligning for you, even when you can't see it.

The same energy that guided you through that situation is still with you now.

So, what if, right now, you allowed yourself to trust again?

What if you let go of trying to figure everything out, just for a moment, and opened up to the possibility that life is working for you—even now?

Faith isn't about knowing the way; it's about trusting that the way exists.

And if you've seen it happen before, what's stopping you from trusting it again?

WHAT IF THE CHAOS IN THE WORLD ISN'T CHAOS?

As I write this book, the world feels heavy.

I suppose it always has, in some way.

Maybe you've felt it too—the weight of uncertainty, the chaos, the heartbreak.

If you're reading this, you might be asking yourself: *Why is there so much suffering? Why is there so much pain? Why does it feel like things are falling apart? If everything is in divine order, if life is orchestrated for the highest good, then why does it feel so chaotic?*

It's a fair question—

One of the hardest, actually, and one I've grappled with myself.

Years ago, in the darkest chapter of my life, I found myself sitting in a hospital ER, overwhelmed by anxiety, fear, and the chaos of my own mind. I remember thinking, *Why me? Why is this happening to me?* It didn't feel like divine orchestration. It felt like chaos, plain and simple.

But looking back, that moment wasn't chaos.

It was the turning point that started my awakening. It was the fire that burned away the parts of me that no longer served my growth, clearing the way for something new.

What I came to understand is this: the existence of divine orchestration doesn't mean life, and what happens in the world, will always feel good or fair.

It doesn't mean we won't experience pain.

It means there is a larger intelligence at work—one that we often cannot see when we're in the thick of it.

Divine orchestration operates on an *infinite* timeline, not the short-term moments we live in.

It's like hearing one dissonant note in a symphony and judging the entire piece based on that single sound. In the grander composition, that note has its place, contributing to a harmony that we may not yet understand.

This pattern isn't just personal; it plays out on a larger scale as well.

Consider how access to clean water has transformed entire communities. There was a time when diseases like cholera devastated populations, spreading through contaminated water. The suffering was unimaginable, but it led to innovations in sanitation and public health systems. Today, those advances save millions of lives every year, providing people with something as basic and vital as safe water to drink.

Or think about the rebuilding of Germany and Japan after World War II.

Both nations were devastated by war, their cities reduced to rubble, their economies shattered. Yet out of that destruction came remarkable transformations. Germany emerged as a leader in renewable energy and sustainability, while Japan became one of the most innovative and technologically advanced societies in the world. The suffering endured by those generations paved the way for a complete reimagining of their countries.

These transformations didn't happen without pain.

They didn't happen overnight.

But they demonstrate how even the darkest times can lead to growth, healing, and progress.

This doesn't mean suffering is good or that we should simply accept it. Far from it.

Suffering challenges us. It asks us to look at ourselves, to grow, and to evolve. It demands that we rise to our higher potential, not just as individuals, but collectively as humanity.

I'm not saying this to diminish the very real pain you or others may be feeling. Pain is real, and it deserves compassion. But what if the chaos is part of an unfolding story—one that is bigger than any single moment?

Here's where this understanding becomes empowering.

Divine orchestration doesn't mean we are passive observers of life.

It doesn't mean we sit back and say, "It's all happening for a reason," without taking action.

We are co-creators in this process.

When we see suffering, it's an invitation to step in, to bring love, healing, and light into the world.

We can't always stop the storms, but we can help rebuild after them. We can choose to act in alignment with the higher good by bringing compassion, understanding, and connection into our lives and the lives of others.

If you can hold onto this perspective, even for a moment, you might begin to see that what feels like chaos isn't the absence of divine order. It's part of its unfolding.

Trust that even in the darkest times, there is meaning, growth, and transformation waiting to emerge.

You are part of this process, and you have the power to help bring light into the world.

YOU ARE EVERYTHING
AND NO-THING

THE PART OF YOU
THAT HAS NEVER AGED

Think about this for a second…

Everything in your life has changed.

Your body isn't the same.

Your thoughts, beliefs, and opinions have shifted.

The way you see the world is different than it was five, ten, twenty years ago.

Maybe you've moved.

Maybe your relationships have evolved.

Friends have come and gone.

Emotions have risen and fallen.

Your experiences have changed.

The things you used to care about don't even cross your mind anymore.

But there's something underneath all of it that hasn't changed—

Something in you that has remained exactly the same.

Have you ever noticed that no matter how much time has passed, there's a part of you that doesn't feel any older?

Your body ages.

Your mind accumulates experience.

But the essence of you—the one who has been here for every single moment—hasn't aged at all.

It's the same presence that was there when you were five.

The same awareness that was there when you were fifteen.

The same you that is here right now.

Beneath the surface of your day-to-day life…

Beneath all the shifting thoughts, emotions, and experiences…

There is something in you that is still and unchanging—

The same presence that has watched everything come and go.

Pause for a moment.

Let this question sink in:

If everything about you has changed, *then who—or what—is the "you" that has been there through it all?*

Sit with that for a moment.

The answer isn't just philosophical—it's the key to everything.

You are not the shifting thoughts.

Not the changing body.

Not the evolving story of your life.

Those are just appearances.

Movements within experience.

What you are is the *awareness* that has been present through it all.

Unmoved.

Unaffected.

The one constant in the middle of infinite change.

It's not a thought.

It's not a belief.

It's not even a feeling.

It's the pure awareness beneath it all.

The presence that has been with you since the beginning.

Unchanged.

Eternal.

You've always known this, even if you haven't put words to it.

That feeling of *I am*—the deep, wordless sense of simply being—has always been there.

Beneath the noise…

Beneath the fluctuations…

Beneath the ever-changing waves of life…

There is something in you that is still.

The world will tell you that you are your body.

Your history.

Your personality.

But none of those things have stayed the same.

What has?

The part of you that has been here *all along*.

And when you truly see this—not just as an idea, but as a direct experience—

Life is no longer something happening to you.

You are the open space in which it all appears, moves, and fades.

You are not the passing waves.

You are the ocean.

Deep.

Still.

Unmoved by the waves that rise and fall on the surface of you.

THE MOVIE CHANGES,
BUT THE SCREEN REMAINS

Each day, you move through a world of sensations and experiences—moments filled with sights, sounds, tastes, and emotions.

The warmth of the sun on your skin, the sound of laughter in the distance, the taste of coffee lingering on your tongue—all these sensations create the vivid texture of your life.

Thoughts and emotions rise and fall—one moment excitement, the next a flicker of worry. Life seems to be in constant motion, with each experience coloring the present moment.

Yet beneath all of this, there is something that does not move.

Something that does not change.

It's the still, silent awareness that is always present, no matter what comes and goes.

Experiences can feel all-consuming. When you're laughing, joy seems to define everything. When you're anxious, the tension feels like it pervades your entire reality. In these moments, it's easy to believe that what you think, feel, and perceive defines you.

But no matter how vivid or intense these experiences seem, they always fade.

Laughter subsides.

Tension dissolves.

The sound of the wind fades into quiet.

What felt so immediate becomes a memory, a fleeting scene in the broader tapestry of your life.

And as each experience fades, it reveals what remains beneath: the unchanging foundation of your being.

The awareness that silently allows every moment to arise and dissolve.

Think of a movie playing on a screen. The images projected are vibrant—bursting with color, emotion, and movement. One moment, the scene is joyful; the next, filled with drama. Another moment, it might descend into chaos, tragedy, or even horror.

Yet no matter how gripping, disturbing, or beautiful the scenes become, the screen itself remains unaffected.

The screen is never burned by the fire, never broken by the violence, never stained by the sadness.

It stays pristine.

Untouched. Unmarked. Unaltered.

Perfectly clear and wide open, always ready for the next moment to arise.

The screen is completely indestructible to anything the movie can bring.

The fire cannot burn it.
The sorrow cannot stain it.
The horror cannot destroy it.

The screen is already whole, already perfect, already complete. It needs nothing, lacks nothing, and remains untouched by all that appears upon it. No scene in the movie can add to it or take anything away.

Through every moment—every joy and sorrow, every rise and fall, every fleeting change—your awareness remains exactly like the screen: pristine, pure, untouched, unshaken, unbroken, unscarred, and unchanging.

Your awareness, your consciousness, simply is.

Formless. Silent. Steady. Immaculate.

It watches as the movie of life unfolds, no matter what appears, and it remains whole and complete in itself.

How can you know this to be true?

Because your awareness is the only thing you can know for certain. You may not know the ultimate nature of the world, but you know, beyond any doubt, that you are aware.

As you read these words, as you hold this book, as you move through your life, you are aware of your experience.

That awareness is undeniable.

Everything else—your thoughts, sensations, perceptions, and even the world around you—is part of the movie. It comes and goes. It shifts and changes. But the awareness that observes it all remains steady, unmoving, and clear.

The profound realization is this: you are not separate from the screen.

You *are* the screen.

Your awareness is not just passive—it's the foundation of everything.

Once you see this, the illusion dissolves.

You no longer confuse yourself with the movie—the fleeting images of thoughts, emotions, and experiences. You can still engage with the movie, still experience its beauty, intensity, and drama.

But you no longer mistake it for who you are.

And when you rest in this awareness, something extraordinary happens. You no longer resist the uncomfortable moments or cling to the joyful ones. You watch them come and go, knowing they are like passing scenes in a film.

You realize that the screen—the awareness—is already perfect. You don't need to add or remove anything from the movie for the screen to remain what it is.

In this recognition, there is a quiet, profound freedom…

A freedom that allows you to engage fully with life—without becoming lost in it.

The highs and lows of the movie no longer define you.

Instead, you watch them unfold, like a vivid play of light and energy, knowing that your true essence remains steady and unshaken.

Infinite. Present. The silent space in which all of life's experiences arise and dissolve.

Life will continue to play its movie—rich with beauty, challenge, and change.

But you?

You are the screen, the awareness that allows it all to appear, yet remains completely untouched.

YOU ARE NOT WHAT
YOU THINK YOU ARE

Right now, as you read these words, something is watching.

There is an awareness within you—silent, steady, present. It is what allows you to think, to perceive, to feel. But have you ever turned that awareness back on itself?

Close your eyes for a moment.

Instead of focusing on your thoughts, ask yourself, *Who is aware of this moment? Who is seeing, reading, thinking?*

Don't rush to answer. Just notice.

There is something watching, something aware of all that arises. But that something isn't an object.

You cannot see it, touch it, or describe it. It is simply there—clear, open, awake.

Most of the time, we move through life caught up in experiences—thoughts, emotions, sensations, the endless movement of life. We focus on what is happening. But rarely do we step back and ask, "Who is this happening to?"

We assume there is a "self" in the middle of all of this, a solid being who is thinking thoughts, feeling feelings, experiencing life. But if you look closely, can you actually find that self?

Thoughts arise, but they are not you.

Emotions come and go, but they are not you.

Sensations flicker in and out of awareness, but they too are not you.

Everything that appears—every thought, every feeling—is an object within awareness.

But awareness itself? It has no form, no boundary, no location.

And here's the profound shift:

The moment you recognize this, you are not just aware—you are aware of being aware.

It is the shift from simply experiencing life to recognizing yourself as the one who is experiencing it.

It is the moment when awareness turns inward and sees itself—not as a person, not as a mind, but as the pure field of knowing in which all things arise and dissolve.

This is not an abstract concept. It is something you can experience directly, right now.

Try this:

Turn your attention inward and look for the source of your awareness.

Where does it come from?

Where is the "I" that is experiencing this moment?

Look closely, and you will see—there is nothing there.

No object, no thing, no entity you can point to.

There is only awareness itself.

And yet, you still exist.

You are not nothing. You are not a void.

You are a field of consciousness—an infinite expanse of presence, formless and boundless.

This realization is not an intellectual understanding. It is a felt experience—a moment of clarity when awareness recognizes its own nature.

Once this shift happens, everything transforms.

Instead of being lost in thoughts, you begin to watch them.

Instead of feeling trapped by emotions, you begin to observe them.

Instead of believing you are a limited self, you begin to sense the vastness of what you truly are.

And here's the greatest paradox of all:

You were never not this awareness.

You have always been here—watching, knowing, being. It is only the mind, the identity, the conditioning that created the illusion of separation.

But the moment you see—*really* see—that you are awareness itself, the illusion collapses.

You are not your thoughts.
You are not your emotions.
You are not your past, your name, your roles, or your story.

You are the vast, boundless consciousness in which all things arise.

And when this realization deepens, life itself changes.

You are no longer swept away by fleeting experiences.

You no longer cling to passing emotions.

You move through life with a deeper stillness, a quiet knowing that you are not separate from anything—you are the very space in which it all happens.

This is awareness waking up to itself.

And once it happens, you will never see yourself—or reality—the same way again.

YOU ARE THE SILENCE BEFORE THE DROP

Awareness is silent. Still. Always here.

But sometimes, the easiest way to recognize it … is to listen.

Let me ask you something: where do you experience music?

Think about it for a second.

Your ears may be the gateway, receiving the vibrations and translating them into sound, but where does the music actually land?

It doesn't exist in the world outside you.

Not in the speaker.

Not in the air.

It exists within you.

Take a moment to try this:

Sit down in a quiet space, grab a pair of headphones, and put on a piece of music you love—something that stirs you, lifts you, or fills you with emotion.

Close your eyes, and as you listen, shift your focus from the song itself to the space where it's being experienced.

You'll realize that the music unfolds not outside you, but within you.

And that "within" is not some part of your body or your mind—it's your awareness.

The space of consciousness is where the music arises.

It's where the rhythm takes form, where the melody dances, where the bass line hums.

Your awareness is the infinite, timeless space in which all experience—this moment, this music—unfolds.

But here's the deeper truth:

Music cannot exist without silence.

Silence is the foundation of music—the space that makes it possible.

Without silence, there would be no rhythm, no melody, no structure.

Silence is the blank canvas upon which the music is painted, the emptiness that allows sound to rise, move, and dissolve.

And silence isn't just the absence of sound.

It's the presence of infinite stillness—the space that holds all vibration, all movement, all creation.

It's alive, vast, and essential.

Without it, there could be no music, no sound, no experience at all.

Think about it…

Sound is just the vibration of energy moving through space.

It's not separate from silence—it's born out of it.

This vibration of energy is the same vibrational energy of creation itself.

Just as silence holds music, stillness holds all of existence.

And that stillness, that silence, is the essence of what you are.

Now let's take this further.

If you've ever been on a dance floor, in a club, or at a concert, you know the power of a DJ or musical performer who can take you on a journey.

The buildup begins—layer by layer, the sounds stack, and tension rises.

The energy builds.

And then, just for a moment—everything stops.

The beat drops out.

Silence.

What happens in that pause?

The crowd goes still.

The entire room seems to hold its breath.

It's just space, pure and empty, but in that emptiness is something electrifying.

And then—*boom!*—the beat drops, the bass hits, and the crowd erupts.

But here's what I want you to recognize:

That pause before the drop is the most powerful moment of all.

It's pure potential.

In that brief stillness, anticipation electrifies the air. The entire room leans into the silence, waiting.

Because in that emptiness, anything can happen.

It is the space where nothing exists, and yet everything is possible.

That silence is the awareness that holds it all—the music, the buildup, the explosion of sound.

And that silence, that stillness, is you.

But it's not just in music.

That pause—the stillness, the space—is beneath everything.

It's beneath all the noise in your life.

It's beneath all the drama, all the thoughts, all the chaos in the world.

Beneath every sensation, every experience, there is an underlying stillness.

That space is always there, holding it all, untouched by whatever arises within it.

Just as silence holds music, awareness holds all of life.

Everything you taste, touch, see, hear, or feel arises within the infinite space of your awareness.

Without that space, nothing could be experienced.

Sound and silence are not opposites, they are partners in creation.

Sound arises out of silence, dances in it, and dissolves back into it.

In the same way, all the forms and experiences of life arise out of formless awareness and eventually return to it.

They are inseparable, yet awareness itself remains untouched by what moves through it.

Silence is to music as awareness is to life.

Thus, the temporary cannot exist without the eternal to hold it all.

We are the eternal.

You are the eternal.

Awareness isn't separate from life; it's the very field in which life happens.

Before the Big Bang, there was only endless silence and stillness.

Only infinite awareness, with nothing but itself to be aware of.

Then came the ultimate *beat drop of creation*, the moment silence and stillness exploded into the symphony of life.

You are not the music.

You're not the buildup, and you're not the beat drop.

You're not the drama, the thoughts, or the emotions that swirl around you.

You are the space in which all of it happens.

You are the awareness that holds every experience, every moment, every sensation.

That space—the one that feels like stillness, but contains the power of creation itself—is untouchable, indestructible, timeless.

Think about it…

The music will rise and fall.

The beat will drop, and the song will end.

The noise of life will come and go.

Thoughts will arise, emotions will swell, and the world will spin on.

But the space it all arises in, the vast, open awareness that you are remains.

It's always there.

It never fades, never breaks, never changes.

It's infinite and indestructible.

So often, we're caught in the noise, swept up in the buildup, lost in the story of our lives.

But no matter how loud or chaotic it gets, there is always a pause.

A beat of silence.

A space of stillness waiting for you to notice it.

And when you find it, you realize something extraordinary.

That space isn't just where the music lands.

It's where everything lands.

The taste of chocolate, the warmth of touch, the sight of a sunrise, the sound of laughter—all of it arises and fades in that same space.

Your thoughts, your feelings, the anxiety—it's all just passing through.

But the space itself—your awareness—is eternal.

It's untouched by whatever moves through it.

So, the next time you listen to music, really listen.

Feel that space where the sound arises.

Notice the pause before the drop.

Then take it further.

Notice the pause beneath your thoughts.

Notice the stillness beneath your emotions.

Notice the silence beneath the noise of your life.

Pause for a moment now.

Feel the silence beneath your thoughts, beneath your sensations, beneath everything you're experiencing.

That silence isn't something you find—it's what you've always been.

THE MOMENT I STOPPED LOOKING FOR MYSELF

Once you recognize the stillness beneath sound, something changes. When you truly listen, it no longer feels like you are hearing something separate from you. Instead, you are experiencing yourself—because you are that space.

I first experienced this in a way I never expected.

One morning, I woke up far too early—the kind of waking where the world still feels heavy with sleep.

Usually, in those moments, I let myself drift between wakefulness and rest, letting the quiet hold me.

That morning, I decided to put on my headphones and listen to some music—something soft and expansive.

I wasn't expecting anything remarkable—just a moment of calm before the day began.

But as the sound unfolded, something inside me shifted.

The vibrations seemed to dissolve the edges of my body, my thoughts, even my sense of self.

I felt myself merge with the space around me—not as someone moving through it, but as part of the space itself.

I wasn't in space.

I *was* space.

Infinite. Boundless. Weightless.

It was as if the sound had unlocked a door I didn't even know existed, carrying me into a state where all separation disappeared.

And then—something in me released.

I felt tears begin to flow, first softly, then fully, as though years of tension, resistance, and identity were melting away.

But it wasn't just tears—my whole body trembled with the release, my breath catching in waves, as if something deep within me was finally breaking free.

I wasn't just crying.

I was unraveling.

It was like the final shell of who I believed myself to be had peeled away, leaving me in this raw, unguarded space of freedom.

The tears weren't separate from the release—they *were* the release.

A letting go that could only happen in the stillness of Oneness.

And in that stillness, I felt something undeniable.

I knew that I was both everything and no-thing at the same time.

Not a thought. Not a concept.

A truth so vast and silent that it didn't need words.

I wasn't experiencing it.

I *was* it.

When the song ended, I slowly returned to the ordinary world.

But I wasn't the same.

I reached for my phone, still feeling the resonance of that space, and wrote three simple words in a note:

I found me.

Even now, I don't know how else to describe it.

I had touched something eternal, and it was sound that brought me there.

Sound isn't just something we hear—it's something we become.

It moves through us, dissolving the edges of who we think we are, leading us back to what we've always been.

When we truly listen, we're not just hearing.

We're remembering.

And that memory is always waiting.

This is the paradox of awakening. It doesn't happen in grand moments or dramatic realizations. It happens in stillness, in a space so quiet and ordinary that the mind almost misses it.

But something deeper recognizes it immediately.

Maybe you've felt glimpses of it—those moments when time disappears, when the weight of thought falls away, when there is only now.

Maybe it came while watching the ocean stretch endlessly before you, or in the pause between words in a conversation, or in the way sunlight filters through the trees on a still afternoon.

That space has always been here.

Beneath the noise, beneath the searching, beneath the endless movement of life—there is something that does not move.

And that something is what you are.

THIS ONE SONG WILL
SHOW YOU WHO YOU ARE

Some music doesn't just create sound—it reveals something within you.

The first time I heard this piece, I felt something shift. It wasn't tied to any one moment in my life; instead, it felt like it held all of them.

It was as if the world fell silent, and all that remained was the sound—alive, powerful, and true. It didn't just reach me; it reflected me.

In every note, I felt my own story—the highs, the lows, the struggles, the beauty. It was like hearing my life played back to me, every moment woven into the music.

I didn't just hear it.

I *saw* it.

I *felt* it.

The genius of this music lies in its ability to mirror life itself—the twists, the turns, the challenges, the struggles, and the growth through it all. It feels like a universal soundtrack to human life—carrying the weight of every struggle, every triumph, and every breath.

It begins simply, like the quieter seasons of your life, when everything feels soft, clear, and steady.

And then it changes.

The music builds, gathering momentum, as though it's carrying you into something larger than yourself.

It twists. It turns. It grows in intensity.

You can hear the effort, the tension, the sound pressing forward like life's most difficult moments—times when the path isn't clear, when the struggle feels relentless. And yet, even here, it's still beautiful.

Because through the intensity, through the highs and the lows, there is still movement—relentless, unseen, like life itself refusing to stop.

There is growth.

The music swells to the point where it feels unstoppable, and then, just when it's almost too much, it changes again.

A pause.

A breath.

The struggle has passed.

In its place, something calmer, wiser, transformed.

Gentle notes of the piano re-emerge—soft, clear, as though reborn.

The strings return—not with force, but with grace.

Strength.

A quiet knowing, as if they understand that everything—*everything*—has its place.

This music reminds us that life, too, holds beauty in all of it.

The intensity.

The twists.

The times that feel unbearable, and the moments that let us breathe.

Even in the lowest and most challenging moments, life carries its beauty still.

As you read these words, consider this: the music isn't just sound—it's a mirror.

Let the music show you life's story and yours within it. Notice the stillness beneath it all—the stillness within you.

You are not the music.

The music moves, but it doesn't define you.

Life rises and falls, yet you remain—the constant awareness, silent and still, in which it all unfolds.

Just as you experience this music, you witness and experience all of life.

You've been the awareness beneath it all—through the beauty, the chaos, the intensity, and the stillness.

You've witnessed it—every moment.

Because this is life: an experience—unfolding in its beauty, its chaos, its stillness—and you are the awareness in which it all comes and goes.

Let this music carry you.

Let it show you the strength and beauty of your life, the powerful depth within yourself.

And when the final notes begin to fade, you realize this: you've survived it all.

You're still here.

This is why you are here: to witness it all, to feel it all, to experience it all—and to awaken to the beauty and strength beneath it all.

Now, pause.

It's your turn. Put the book down, grab your headphones, close your eyes, and turn it up.

Let *Experience* by Ludovico Einaudi take you where it wants to take you.

Once you've listened, come back and read this section again.

Notice what feels different.

Notice what the music revealed to you.

Let the words sink in deeper, now that you've truly felt the experience.

And notice this…

When the music faded, what remained?

Not just silence.

Something deeper. The same presence that had always been there—long before the first note played, and long after the final note disappeared.

This presence did not end.

This presence has never ended.

And it never will.

INSIGHT #9

WHAT YOU ARE CAN NEVER DIE

THE TRUTH THAT ENDS THE FEAR OF DEATH

It's been said that all fear is, at its core, the fear of death.

And for me, that was true.

For most of my life, fear was a quiet undercurrent beneath everything—a kind of anxiety I couldn't name, but always felt.

At times, it showed up as overthinking. Other times, it was a vague unease, a sense that something wasn't quite right, even when things were fine. And sometimes, it hit me with full force—panic, dread, a racing heart that seemed to warn me of something terrible, even when there was nothing there.

I didn't realize it then, but at the root of all that fear was a single question I couldn't shake:

What happens to us when we die?

Death was not something we discussed in my home. It lingered in the air, but was never spoken of directly. Anytime my mother mentioned that someone had died, it was in a hushed tone, almost a whisper, as if saying it too loudly might invite it closer. Sometimes it wasn't even words—just a glance, a slight tilt of the head, a subtle motion of her hand, as if to gesture toward something too heavy to name.

But that didn't stop death from creeping into my mind when I was young. I remember lying in bed at fourteen, staring at the ceiling, trying to grasp the impossible question: What happens when we die?

Would I just vanish? Would my consciousness flicker out like a light, never to exist again?

Would I be swallowed by an endless black void?

The thought was unbearable. It sent a cold chill of panic through my body.

If that was all there was—if this life ended in nothingness—then what was the point?

Why did anything matter?

That fear gnawed at me. I couldn't shake it, so I did the only thing I knew how to do: I searched for answers.

I started studying death, reading about the experiences of people on their deathbeds, diving into the insights of those who had come face-to-face with the end.

I wasn't just looking for comfort.

I was looking for clarity.

For some kind of understanding that would make sense of it all.

And yet, despite everything I read, I still carried that fear. No explanation, no philosophy, no religious teaching felt certain enough to quiet the dread inside me.

So, I tucked it away and let it sit in the background of my life, unresolved.

But as I continued questioning, exploring, and seeking, something started to shift.

Slowly, piece by piece, I began to see a truth that drastically changed my perception.

Before my awakening, I was the kind of person who questioned everything. I was skeptical—maybe to a fault. I didn't trust much outside of what I could see, touch, or measure. To say I leaned toward atheism would be an understatement—I'd probably have called myself agnostic on a generous day.

I believed we lived, we died, and that was it.

No deeper meaning, no higher purpose, no consciousness beyond this physical reality.

Religion? It was a nice idea, sure—but nothing more than a story written by people who lived a long time ago. A comforting story, maybe, but a story, nonetheless.

And I wasn't buying it.

Maybe you relate to that mindset. Maybe you've dismissed ideas like spirituality or eternity because they seemed too mystical, too ungrounded—just hopeful thinking wrapped in poetic words.

I get it. I was there.

But life has a way of challenging our beliefs, even the ones we're certain about.

Especially those.

What I'm about to share may or may not come as a surprise to you. Maybe it's an idea you've toyed with, a truth you've felt, but couldn't quite name.

For me, though, it was a shock.

It didn't come easily, and it wasn't something I had ever considered possible.

But it was something I could no longer ignore.

Through my own journey—through experiences that defied logic, through insights that shattered my skepticism—I arrived at an understanding so clear, so undeniable, that it shifted everything I thought I knew about who I am and what this life is.

The truth is this: You are not just this body. You are not just this life.

At the core of who you are—beneath the thoughts, the fears, and the stories you've been telling yourself—is consciousness.

Pure awareness.

And that consciousness doesn't end. Ever.

The physical body dies.

You do not.

Ever.

I know how that sounds. Believe me, I do. If someone had told me this years ago, I'd have rolled my eyes and moved on.

But here's the thing: This truth isn't just some spiritual philosophy.

It's everywhere you look.

It's what science is beginning to reveal in experiment after experiment.

It's what quantum physics points to when it shows us that at the most fundamental level, matter isn't solid—everything is energy vibrating in space.

And energy cannot be created or destroyed—it only transforms.

It's what millions of people have reported when they come back from near-death experiences—different languages, different cultures, and yet all pointing to the same reality:

There is no end to who you are.

Nothing real can ever be destroyed.

And what is this awareness?

It is nothing. No thing.

And yet, it is *everything*.

It has no shape, no weight, no form—yet it holds the universe within it.

It is the silent space where thoughts rise and fall, where worlds appear and dissolve.

It is the vastness before the first breath, the stillness after the last.

It is the infinite, which holds the finite.

It is the emptiness that is full.

It is the formless that gives birth to all forms.

And it is you.

And this understanding doesn't just transform how you see life; it transforms how you live it.

Anxiety loses its grip when you realize *the truth* of who you are.

Imagine responding to challenges not from fear or attachment, but from a deep sense of peace and trust.

Imagine letting go of stress and control because you know that the essence of who you are is untouchable and eternal.

Anxiety thrives on uncertainty.

But when you know—deeply know—that the awareness within you has no end, something shifts.

You are no longer at war with life.

You are no longer fighting against time.

Because time is an illusion, and you are beyond it.

So, take this truth with you:

Nothing real—no aspect that is truly you—can ever be destroyed.

It is the foundation of everything.

This truth is not distant—it's as close as your next breath.

It is the foundation of inner peace, the heart of freedom and liberation, and the light of your eternal essence.

Pause.

Connect to it.

And let it guide you through your challenges and joys alike.

As you carry this truth into life, you'll begin to live with a deeper sense of peace, trust, and freedom.

Anxiety is just a shadow cast by forgetting who you are.

But you are not the shadow.

You are the light.

You are not running out of time.

You are not racing toward an end.

You are alive, aware, and extraordinary.

And you always will be.

YOU ARE NOT THE STORY, YOU ARE THE ONE WATCHING

At some point on this path, you start to see yourself differently.

You recognize the character you've been playing—how you move through life, the patterns you repeat, the habits you hold onto without question. It's as if there are two versions of you: one still caught in the motions, and another watching from a higher vantage point.

You begin to notice the things you do automatically, the justifications you make, the moments where your actions don't quite align with the person you say you want to be. Maybe you tell yourself you're disciplined, but you cut corners when no one's looking. Maybe you say you want freedom, but you keep reinforcing the same limitations.

And you realize something: it's not that you don't *know* what's best. It's that, in small ways, you keep testing yourself—pushing your own boundaries, seeing what you can get away with, like a child pressing up against the limits of what's allowed.

But every choice has weight. And when you pretend your actions don't matter, you reinforce the illusion that you're separate from your own power.

Stepping back changes everything.

From this higher perspective, you start to see how much of your life has been shaped by unconscious momentum—reactions, habits, beliefs you absorbed without realizing it. And yet, the moment you step back and see it, something shifts. You're no longer just the character—you're also the one observing.

And that's where your real power is.

Because when you *see* yourself clearly, you gain the ability to move differently, to stop dancing to the same old rhythm and step into something new.

But here's where a lot of people get stuck: they try to fight their old habits instead of understanding them. They judge themselves for the patterns they've repeated instead of recognizing that those patterns were just survival strategies—things they picked up along the way.

Let me say that again: There's no need for guilt and no need for self-punishment. There's no need for guilt. No need for self-punishment.

If you catch yourself breaking a promise to yourself—whether it's eating something you said you wouldn't or skipping a practice you meant to do—own it.

Don't lie to yourself. Don't pretend it doesn't matter. But don't beat yourself up either.

If you're going to do it, do it with your eyes open. No guilt. No excuses. Just awareness.

Just own it.

The moment you stop playing mental games—justifying, excusing, regretting—you neutralize the energy of resistance. And once the resistance is gone, you're free.

Because the truth is, there are no "right" or "wrong" choices—only actions and consequences. The more you understand this, the more you move through life with clarity instead of self-sabotage.

And this is where the real question arises:

If you're not the character—if you can step back and *watch* yourself move through life—then who is the one watching?

Who is the observer behind your thoughts, behind your emotions, behind the entire story you've been telling yourself?

This is where you start to wake up.

Because there is a part of you that is untouched by self-doubt, by guilt, by the ups and downs of life. A place within you that is steady, calm, and unmoved—like the stillness at the center of a storm.

The more you connect with that place, the less control old patterns have over you. You stop reacting and start *choosing*. You stop feeling lost in the story and start seeing it for what it is: a story.

And when you see life as a story, you no longer get trapped in the past. The weight of old regrets and disappointments begins to dissolve, leaving behind only wisdom.

From this vantage point, everything becomes clearer. The patterns, the cycles, the ways you've played out the same dynamics over and over—suddenly, you see them for what they are. And in that clarity, something clicks:

You've been free this whole time.

And now, you get to choose how you move forward.

So, step back.

Watch.

See yourself clearly.

And then, when you're ready, step into the life that's waiting for you.

EVERYTHING IS BEING
OPTIMIZED FOR YOU

At the deepest level, you are not just a mind, a body, or even your thoughts.

By now, you are beginning to understand that you are pure awareness—the consciousness that observes all your experiences, emotions, and thoughts.

This awareness doesn't come and go.

It is always present, always watching, always aware.

It is the backdrop of your existence.

Some call this the Self, pure consciousness, or simply awareness itself.

Now, just as you are aware of your own experiences, this awareness is a reflection of something vast and infinite—what some call Source, Universal Intelligence, or even *God*.

But let's be clear—not the "man in the sky" version people have been sold. Not something separate from you. Not a being watching from above, deciding who gets what.

What people call "God" is the infinite awareness and intelligence that permeates everything—including you.

It is the all-encompassing consciousness that not only observes your individual experience, but is aware of everything happening throughout the entire universe and beyond at all times.

It is the energy of life itself.

Because this supreme awareness is infinite, it is fully aware of all things—of every thought, action, and interaction happening in existence.

It doesn't operate from a limited perspective, like humans often do, where we only see one part of the picture. Instead, it perceives the entire cosmic dance, from the largest events in the universe to the smallest details in your life, all in real time.

Quantum theory helps us understand this from a scientific perspective. In quantum physics, particles exist in a state of potential until they are observed or measured.

This is the famous concept of "superposition," where a particle can be in multiple states at once. It is only when observed that the particle collapses into a definite state.

Similarly, the supreme awareness is like the ultimate observer—it is aware of every possibility and every potential reality at once, witnessing how all these possibilities unfold.

Since this supreme awareness is the ground of everything, it is never overwhelmed.

It is everything. It holds all possibilities, all realities, all outcomes at once.

It knows what's happening everywhere, with everyone, in every moment, in everything.

It has a complete, holistic view of all interactions and outcomes.

In this way, it sees how all things are interconnected, how your choices affect not only your life, but the lives and energies of others, and how every aspect of the universe is in constant interplay.

Just as in quantum mechanics, where the act of observation influences the outcome, supreme awareness is fully engaged in the act of creation and observation simultaneously, shaping reality as it unfolds.

Here's where it becomes really powerful: because the supreme awareness is aware of everything happening at once, it has the unique ability to optimize and adjust the unfolding of reality in real time.

It's like being able to see the entire chessboard, all possible moves, and all potential outcomes simultaneously.

The supreme awareness doesn't need to wait to see how things unfold—it is always one step ahead, because it is aware of all possibilities. In every moment, it is adjusting and optimizing the game of life to ensure that the path leads toward growth, evolution, and awakening. It does this not in a reactive way, but in a proactive, ever-present manner.

Quantum theory also introduces the idea of "entanglement," where particles, even when separated by vast distances, are instantaneously connected. Changes in one particle affect the other, no matter how far apart they are.

In much the same way, the supreme awareness is interconnected with all of existence. It knows and influences everything at once, because everything is entangled within its field of consciousness. This is how it can optimize reality in real time—because it is fully aware of every interaction, every possibility, and every outcome simultaneously.

For instance, if you make a choice—any choice—this supreme awareness immediately knows how that choice will affect the entire web of reality. It adjusts the circumstances, bringing new scenarios or experiences into your life that will support your growth, even if it doesn't seem obvious at first.

If you take a detour, it recalibrates and offers you new opportunities or challenges that will help you get back on track. It's like having a built-in GPS for the soul, constantly rerouting you toward your highest evolution.

But even though supreme awareness knows and sees everything, it doesn't violate your free will.

You are still free to make your own choices, but this supreme intelligence is always there, optimizing in response to those choices. When you act, it creates new pathways, opens new doors, or introduces new lessons based on what you need to evolve and awaken.

Because supreme awareness is fully aware of everything—from your individual consciousness to the collective consciousness, to the cosmic flow—it knows exactly what experiences you need to continue growing.

This means that no matter what happens in your life, even in moments of struggle or challenge, the supreme awareness is continuously guiding you toward the most optimal path for your personal and spiritual evolution.

The beauty of this process is that the supreme awareness is not separate from you. Since you are awareness itself, you are a direct expression of this greater intelligence.

You are one of the ways the supreme awareness experiences and expands itself.

As you evolve, grow, and awaken, so does the supreme awareness.

Your insights, breakthroughs, and shifts in consciousness are also shifts in the consciousness of the whole.

This is why the supreme awareness is constantly optimizing reality. As it experiences life through you and every other conscious entity, it is expanding and evolving. In this way, life is not random—it is a deeply intelligent process, always moving toward greater awareness, growth, and awakening.

When you realize that you are an expression of this supreme awareness, it opens your eyes.

You begin to see that your life is part of a grand, intelligent design, constantly optimized for your highest growth. Even when things feel uncertain, difficult, or painful, you can trust that the supreme awareness is guiding you, in real time, to the exact experiences you need in order to evolve.

Living from this understanding means aligning with the intelligence of the now.

You become more present, less resistant to life, and more open to whatever comes your way.

You realize that every experience—joyful or painful—is part of the optimization process, designed to lead you to deeper awareness, peace, and fulfillment.

In essence, you start to live in harmony with the greater intelligence that is always aware, always optimizing, and always evolving through you.

If the supreme awareness is always optimizing reality in real time—guiding you, adjusting to your choices, and ensuring your growth—then a profound truth emerges: you can relax.

You can release the need to control everything, the anxiety over the future, and the resistance to what is happening in the present moment.

Why?

Because the intelligence of the universe is always working in your favor, always moving you toward your highest potential.

Trust in this process.

Trust that even when things don't make sense to your mind, the supreme awareness has a broader view. It sees the interconnectedness of everything and knows what you need in each moment to continue your evolution.

When you let go of the need to figure everything out, you create space for that higher intelligence to flow through you.

You align with the natural rhythm of the universe, allowing it to carry you forward with ease.

And in this very moment … you are exactly where you need to be.

THE WISDOM YOU SEEK IS ALREADY SPEAKING—ARE YOU LISTENING?

As you progress through the process of awakening, something profound begins to happen: you start to become more of the awareness behind your thoughts.

You step into the role of the observer, no longer swept away by the constant chatter of your mind.

At first, this shift feels subtle—like noticing that your thoughts are happening, but they aren't you. Over time, you begin to see the mind for what it is: a tool that's often on autopilot, churning out noise that has nothing to do with the truth of who you are.

From this place of awareness, something even more powerful starts to emerge.

You begin to notice the difference between the mind's repetitive noise and something far greater—what I call Divine Downloads. These aren't just random thoughts or fleeting ideas.

They're transmissions.

Often, they come in a softer voice, sometimes a whisper. Yet they feel clearer, and more intentional, as if they've been sent to you from a source beyond yourself.

The easiest way to tell the difference is in the tone and energy. Mental noise often feels chaotic, heavy, or self-critical. It can sound like, "I can't do this," "I'm not good enough," or "You'll never succeed." These thoughts tend to leave you feeling stuck, anxious, or drained.

Divine Downloads, on the other hand, are entirely different.

They arrive with a calm authority, carrying a sense of clarity and peace.

The messages might come as "You're ready for this," or "You can move forward," or "You know what you need to do."

Unlike mental noise, which spins you in circles, downloads feel like they're guiding you, offering support and direction. Even when they challenge you to step out of your comfort zone, they do so in a way that feels grounded and purposeful.

These downloads don't come from your brain—they come *to your awareness.*

Like a file sent to your phone from the cloud, these downloads aren't created by you—they're received.

They tend to arrive when your body is relaxed, your mind is still, and you are open to receiving.

Maybe it's as you're waking up, while you're on a walk in nature, during a shower, or just before falling asleep. The key is that you're not forcing them—they arrive naturally when there's space for them to come through.

But here's the catch: they're fleeting.

If you don't capture them immediately, they'll slip away, lost in the noise of the mind.

That's why I've made it a habit to write them down the moment they come. I have a note on my phone titled *Downloads* where I do my best to record every single one, whether it's a sentence, a phrase, or just a few words. When I look back at these notes, I'm often amazed by how much clarity and wisdom they hold. They're like breadcrumbs, little clues, guiding me forward one step at a time.

This practice of receiving is rooted in ancient wisdom. In Judaism, the mystical tradition of Kabbalah teaches that we must learn to receive. The word itself, Kabbalah, means "to receive." It's a reminder that this wisdom isn't something you create—it's something you allow. Divine Downloads are the same. They're always available, but you have to tune in.

Here's what's most important: these downloads are your higher self speaking to you. They're not separate from you—*they are you*, at the deepest, most connected level. When you act on them, you're aligning with a greater intelligence that knows exactly what you need to move forward.

So, start now.

Quiet your mind, relax your body, and listen.

When something comes through that feels different—clearer, calmer, more intentional—write it down.

At first, it might not make sense. But over time, you'll see—the wisdom has always been there, waiting for you to listen.

WHY THE UNIVERSE CHOSE
TO EXPERIENCE ITSELF AS YOU

Hopefully, you're beginning to understand the truth: you are awareness itself, infinite and unchanging.

But now you're asking the deeper question: Why am I here?

When you understand why you exist, the illusion of the ego dissolves, and you step fully into the freedom of being who you truly are.

So, let me tell you clearly: you are here because the infinite—the supreme awareness—is expressing itself as you.

Without you, something would be missing.

Out of all possibilities, the divine intelligence chose to experience existence through your unique perspective.

That is how important you are.

This isn't a metaphor. This is the truth of your being.

I repeat:

This is not a metaphor.

You are the energy of the divine, fully and completely, expressing itself as you.

Your entire self—mind, body, and spirit—is the divine energy in motion, living and experiencing itself through your unique perspective. This is truly who *and what* you are at the deepest level.

Right now, divine awareness is looking out through your eyes, feeling through your emotions, and thinking through your mind.

You're not a small, separate self, struggling to survive in a chaotic world.

You are a unique expression of the infinite intelligence that creates worlds.

The vastness of awareness is living as you.

Think about it.

Infinite awareness and intelligence didn't make you to be like anyone else.

It made you to be you.

Your joys, your struggles, your quirks, your perspective—all of it matters.

All of you is by design.

Your existence is how the divine expands, learns, and experiences itself.

You are not just part of the universe; you are the universe in motion.

But here's where things can still feel unclear: the ego. The identity you've carried. The story you may still tell yourself about who you are.

For so long, you've lived through this identity—your name, your achievements, your struggles, your fears. But by now, you may have started to sense that *this isn't all of you.*

As I've mentioned before, the ego isn't a problem. It's just a role awareness plays in the world. And when you see it for what it is, it doesn't have to weigh you down.

You don't have to fight it. You don't have to get rid of it. You just don't need to take it so seriously.

Because the real you—the infinite, eternal you—has always been here. Whole before the mask, whole beyond it.

You exist to create.
To grow.
To experience.
To play.
To awaken.

To remember.

You are here because your perspective is irreplaceable.

There has never been another you, and there never will be again.

Without you, the infinite would be incomplete.

This isn't about achieving something or becoming someone else. You are here to be—to allow awareness to experience life through you fully.

To know yourself as both the infinite and the individual, and to live in harmony with that truth.

When you truly understand this, everything falls into place.

The endless striving ends.

The fear of failure vanishes.

You stop needing validation from the outside world, because you already know: you are the infinite in motion.

And when you see yourself as the infinite in motion, anxiety softens. The weight of striving fades, and you are free to simply be.

And here's the proof: the fact that you're reading these words right now.

This isn't random.

This is awareness itself calling you back to the truth. It's already happening. The infinite is at work through you in this exact moment, guiding you to remember what you've always known.

Pause.

Feel the stillness beneath your thoughts, the awareness that is reading these words. Notice the part of you that has always been here—silent, watching, untouched by time.

Now, let this truth settle in:

You are not separate from the infinite.

You are awareness experiencing itself as this life, this body, this moment.

Breathe it in. Let it rise within you.

You were never lost. You were never incomplete.

The infinite is awakening through you right now.

And it always has been.

INSIGHT #10

EVERYTHING IS
INTERCONNECTED

NOTHING IS RANDOM— EVERYTHING IS A MESSAGE

The fact that you're holding this book and reading these words is no accident.

As you've now come to understand, life's intelligence works through an omnipresent awareness—one that's aware of everything.

It knows that I wrote this book, and it knows you've been seeking some guidance.

Maybe it sent you the thought to check it out on Amazon, visit a bookstore, or download the book or audiobook.

That same awareness nudged me to write it, while it nudged you to find it.

This is the same energy moving through all of life, because it *is* all of life, orchestrating everything.

This awareness gives you free will, allowing you to make your own choices while still guiding everything toward the highest good and evolution of all life.

It's orchestrating everything at the highest possible level, in real time, taking into account not only your choices, but also the free-will choices of all beings.

It's guiding you toward the optimal experience in every moment, given the countless free-will actions and events that have shaped situations here on Earth.

Why *wouldn't it* optimize for the highest good?

This intelligence desires expansion, growth, and learning. It's always optimizing toward evolution because it wants to evolve through us.

We are like drops of the ocean, and it is the ocean—eternal, omnipresent, infinite intelligence, and infinite awareness.

And if you reflect on your own life, you'll see it too. The right person, the right moment, the right message—always arriving at the exact time it was meant to.

But maybe you brushed it off as a fluke, just a coincidence.

These are not flukes—they are by design. This is how the system works.

This power, this Supreme Awareness, is not just aware of everything and everyone—

It *is* everything and everyone.

It is every blade of grass, every tree, every star, every ant, every person—including you.

It is your aunt, your next-door neighbor, your brother.

It is the barista at Starbucks, your dog, your cat—even your neighbor's cat.

It is everything, everywhere, always present and fully aware.

Because it is *all that exists*.

And maybe that sounds a little out there.

But when you start to see that everything we perceive is part of the same energy—because there's really nothing else—it becomes clear.

This awareness knows all things because it *is* all things, fully present in every detail.

When you understand that this intelligence is continually at work, something shifts.

You stop gripping so tightly. The fear of the unknown starts to lose its power.

Anxiety thrives on the illusion that you have to figure everything out yourself, that you're alone in this, that if you don't control every detail, everything might fall apart.

But that was never true.

The same intelligence that moves the stars and orchestrates the tides is guiding your life too.

You don't have to force every outcome. You don't have to exhaust yourself trying to control what was never yours to control.

You can trust.

Trust that whatever is unfolding is part of the larger orchestration.

Trust that life isn't just happening to you—it's happening *through* you.

And the more you trust, the more you'll see it:

Nothing is random. Everything is a message.

YOU WERE NEVER SEPARATE.
YOU JUST FORGOT.

The other day, I was in Costco.

I paused for a moment, leaned on my cart, and just looked around. I let myself take it all in—every person around me, fully absorbed in their own world, their own reality.

There was a little kid in a cart, laughing and playing on their mom's phone. The mom pushing the cart had this faint look of exhaustion, her shoulders slightly slumped, like she'd been running on empty for days.

A few feet away, a man stood frozen in front of the cold cuts, staring at them with a deeply concerned look, like he was carrying the weight of a decision much bigger than what to buy.

Across the aisle, a woman wandered out of the produce section, her movements hesitant, her gaze unfocused and confused, like she wasn't sure why she was there in the first place.

Nearby, a man in a faded baseball cap stood by the clothing racks, nervously tapping his fingers on the metal bar, his eyes flicking between the carts passing by, caught in some restless thought.

And finally, a Costco employee trudged past me, his expression blank, his steps slow and heavy, like he was just going through the motions.

As I stood there, I became quietly aware of something both simple and profound.

Every single one of these people is an expression of consciousness, living out a completely unique version of existence.

The laughing kid? That's consciousness absorbed in curiosity and play, filtered through the lens of a child's perspective.

The mom? Consciousness navigating exhaustion, shaped by the weight of her responsibilities.

The man staring at the cold cuts? Consciousness entangled in worry, seen through his personal struggles.

The man by the racks? Consciousness restless and distracted, filtered through his own internal state.

The employee? Consciousness moving through monotony, shaped by their role in that moment.

The same infinite intelligence and awareness that's behind their eyes is behind yours and mine—it's all one, filtered through the lens of each unique perspective.

That's the truth.

The consciousness reading these words right now is the same consciousness that laughed in that cart or wandered out of the produce section, forgetting why it was there.

It's the same infinite mind flowing through each of us, experienced differently through every individual lens. You might feel separate because you're living through your own unique experience, but you're not. You've never been separate.

Here's where this matters: anxiety thrives on separation.

It tells you that you're just one small, fragile person trying to hold it all together in a chaotic, disconnected world.

But that's a lie.

The moment you see the truth—that you're part of an infinite field of consciousness, expressed through the lens of your own being—anxiety starts to lose its grip.

Because here's the thing: the same supreme intelligence that's moving through you is moving through everyone else.

You don't have to fight the world, because you *are* the world.

You don't have to carry its weight because it was never yours to carry.

The consciousness that's flowing through you, through me, through that kid, that mom—it's all connected, all part of the same infinite awareness, seen through countless eyes, lived through countless forms.

When you see this—when you really feel it—something shifts.

You stop needing to control life because you finally realize you *are* Life. Anxiety dissolves—not because you fixed it, but because you understand that there's nothing to fix. There's only one infinite intelligence, one consciousness, and you've been part of it all along.

You were never separate. You just forgot.

THE RAINDROPS THAT ARGUED ALL THE WAY DOWN

Two raindrops fell from the sky, side by side, tumbling toward the earth.

One was large and round, heavy with momentum. The other was smaller, lighter, drifting more gently through the air.

The smaller raindrop glanced over. "You think you're better than me?"

The bigger raindrop smirked. "Obviously. Look at me. I'm big, bold, and moving faster than you. Speed, power—I'm built for impact. You? You're just floating."

The smaller raindrop rolled his eyes. "Oh, please. You think bigger is better? When you hit people, they flinch. They curse the rain. But when I land? I'm a delicate mist. Refreshing. Welcomed. People turn their faces toward me and smile."

The big raindrop frowned. "Yeah, well, I hit the ground first. I make an entrance. You just take your sweet time, floatin' around like some gentle little nothing."

The smaller raindrop narrowed his eyes. "At least I don't splatter into a puddle on impact."

And so, they argued.

Each trying to prove their worth, each adamant that they were nothing alike.

Then, another voice cut through their bickering.

A third raindrop, who had been quietly falling nearby, finally spoke. "You know, you're both ridiculous, right?"

The two turned toward him, caught off guard.

The big raindrop puffed up. "Excuse me?"

The small raindrop crossed his arms. "And what exactly makes us ridiculous?"

The third raindrop smiled, unbothered. "You're arguing as if you weren't made of the exact same thing."

The first two scoffed.

The big raindrop shook his head. "Oh, no, no. We are *not* the same. I came from that big, dark storm cloud up there. Toughest cloud in the sky. No way I'm the same as this puny little guy."

The smaller raindrop huffed. "And I came from that light, wispy cloud over there. Elegant. Refined. Not some clumsy old storm cloud."

The third raindrop just shook his head. "Oh, really? And where do you think those clouds came from?"

A pause. A flicker of doubt.

And then, at the same time, they both whispered:

"… the ocean."

They glanced at each other, realizing…
Instead of marveling at the view,
instead of feeling the wind rush past,
instead of surrendering to the wonder and magnificence of the fall itself,
they had spent the entire journey arguing.

They had wasted it, locked in a ridiculous, pointless argument.

The third raindrop nodded. "Exactly. You were never separate to begin with. You were never 'better' or 'worse'—just different expressions of the same thing. All this competition? This need to compare? It's the biggest joke you've ever played on yourselves."

And then, just like that, he turned his attention back to the fall.

The other two remained quiet, their egos dissolving midair.

They had spent their short existence competing, comparing, trying to prove their superiority.

But in the end, they would all return to the same vast ocean.

Just like we do.

Every argument, every judgment, every attempt to be better than or less than someone else— it's all based on an illusion.

Because at the core, we are all the same thing.

We came from the same source, and we'll return to it.

So what's the point of the fight?

What's the point of proving something that was never in question?

And if the ocean never saw a difference, why would you?

THE UNIVERSE IS NOT MANY THINGS—IT'S JUST ONE

If all these people around me are simply different expressions of the same awareness, then what does that say about the nature of reality itself?

Some physicists propose that there may only be one electron in existence, appearing everywhere at once.

Let that sink in.

Just one, simultaneously appearing in countless places, times, and forms.

If that's true—and many scientific theories suggest that it is—it points to a profound truth:

There is only one thing in the universe.

Even the word "universe" has been pointing to this truth all along.

"Uni-" means one.

"Verse" means to turn, to become.

The universe isn't many things—it's one thing, turning in infinite ways. Maybe you never thought about it that way before, but the truth has been hiding in plain sight.

This understanding isn't new.

Nearly all spiritual traditions have echoed this truth for millennia:

Everything is connected, alive, and part of one infinite whole.

One thing, expressing itself in infinite ways.

And if there's only one thing, then everything, absolutely everything, is made of it.

Including you.

This raises a profound question: what properties does this one thing have?

Well, before we talk about the properties of the one thing, let's talk about what properties *we* have.

We know this one for sure:

We have awareness.

This is what I mean:

You are aware of the words on this page.

You are aware of your breath, your thoughts, and the experience of being alive.

This awareness isn't something separate from you.

It's the core of who you are.

Now, if everything is made of the same one thing, then this awareness must come from that one thing.

It's impossible for you to have something that the one thing doesn't also have.

If the one thing didn't have awareness, then you wouldn't either, because you are made of it.

So, we know this for certain: the one thing is aware, because you are aware.

This isn't abstract or theoretical.

It's undeniable.

You are having an experience.

You are conscious.

Therefore, the one thing, at its essence, must also be conscious.

And here's where it gets even more profound.

If you are made of this one thing, then so is everyone else.

Every person you meet is another expression of the same one thing you are made of.

The awareness in them is the same awareness in you.

Their experiences, their joys, their fears—all of it is happening within the same field of being.

All within—and as—one thing.

When you truly see this, the illusion of separation begins to dissolve—not just with the world around you, but with every other person.

What if you could see others not as separate from you, but as reflections of the same one thing?

How would that change how you treat them?

How would it change how you see yourself?

And when you start to see this, you begin to realize that the world around you isn't separate from you either.

It's part of the same awareness.

Of course, animals too are aware. They think, feel, and interact with the world in ways suited to their survival.

And because there's only one thing, they too can only be made of this one thing, experiencing awareness in their own unique way.

Here's where it gets even more fascinating.

Research has shown that plants have awareness.

Trees in a forest are connected through vast underground networks, using fungi to communicate and share resources.

Some plants actually warn each other of threats.

Scientists have discovered that when one tree is attacked by insects or other threats, it signals nearby trees, prompting them to release protective chemicals to defend themselves.

It's becoming clear that the natural world is alive in ways we are only beginning to understand.

Each living thing appears to have the level of awareness it needs to survive, thrive and evolve.

A tree's awareness isn't the same as yours, but it knows what it needs to know: how to grow, how to communicate, and how to protect itself.

When we see this, we start to realize that awareness isn't limited to humans.

It flows through the entire living world.

And if it flows through people, animals, and plants, why would it stop there?

Science shows us that all matter is energy vibrating at different frequencies.

The book or device in your hand, the chair you're sitting in, or the ground you're standing on—these things may seem separate, solid, or even lifeless.

But they're not.

They're just the one thing vibrating at a different frequency, appearing in a different form.

And since this one thing is all there is, it means everything must have awareness in some form.

It likely doesn't have the same kind of awareness *you* have.

A rock probably doesn't think or plan.

Why would it?

It doesn't need to for its survival.

But perhaps it has the most basic awareness, like knowing whether it is hot or cold or whether it's day or night.

With this understanding, everything in the universe has some level of intrinsic awareness, even at the smallest, most fundamental level.

This doesn't mean your phone or your home is having thoughts.

It means they are part of the same interconnected whole, with their own minimal, inherent awareness.

Now, consider this.

Your home, your clothes, your stuff are all made from the same one thing you are made of.

There's nothing else in existence for anything to be made *from*.

Now, they may not have awareness in the way you do, but they are still vibrating with the same essence.

What if you were to treat them as if they mattered—not because they serve you, but because they are part of the same fabric of existence as you?

What if you respected everything in your life as if it were alive—because in a way, it is?

And it doesn't stop there.

The natural world around you—the animals, the plants, the trees, the clouds, the rivers, the air you breathe, even the stars and sky—are also made of this one thing.

The awareness flowing through you flows through it all.

Imagine what would happen if we began to see the natural world as an extension of ourselves.

If we truly understood that the trees, the rivers, the animals are all of the same one thing as us, wouldn't we treat them with the same respect we wish for ourselves?

What if we stopped seeing the earth as a resource to use, and instead as a part of our one shared being?

Because it is.

This isn't just a thought experiment.

It's a shift in perception that changes how you see and interact with the world.

The awareness flowing through you is the same awareness vibrating through the entire universe.

It is the heartbeat of the one thing.

Why does this matter?

Because when you truly grasp this, the illusion of separation starts to dissolve.

You realize that you're not living in a cold, lifeless world made of disconnected objects.

You are part of an infinite, interconnected field of being.

This changes everything—especially how you experience anxiety.

Anxiety thrives on the belief that you're separate, isolated, and alone.

It tells you that life is happening to you, that the weight of the world rests on your shoulders.

But when you see that you're part of the one thing—that even the objects around you are vibrating with the same essence and aware of you, just as you are of them—you realize something profound.

You are never truly alone.

Take a moment and let this truth sink in.

You are never, ever alone.

In fact, it's impossible for you to be.

Because everything is one thing…

And the one thing is all there is.

So now, ask yourself:

If everything is one thing, and the one thing is the only thing…

Then who are you, really?

YOU ARE NEVER LOST— ONLY RECALCULATING

I remember one evening driving home with my family after a day out.

The car's GPS was guiding us, but something seemed off.

It took us on what felt like an unnecessary detour—away from the freeway, onto a winding side road. My first instinct was resistance. *This can't be right. I know a better way.*

The freeway was the obvious choice. Faster. More direct. But despite my doubts, I decided to trust the GPS and follow its instructions.

As we made our way down that quiet road, I saw what I couldn't see before. Up ahead on the freeway, traffic was at a standstill. A massive accident had clogged all lanes, turning what should have been the fastest route into an hours-long delay.

Instead of being stuck in gridlock, I was effortlessly gliding down an open road, heading home.

The GPS had known something I didn't. It had already calculated what was ahead and rerouted me before I even realized there was a problem.

What seemed like an unnecessary detour had actually been the best possible path.

That moment stayed with me because it taught me something deeper about how life works.

There is an inner intelligence guiding you. It sees the full picture—the road ahead, the hidden obstacles, the opportunities you can't yet see—and it's always recalculating to move you toward your highest destination.

But here's the part that gets in the way...

You think you know better.

You resist the guidance, question the turns, try to force your own way. And in doing so, you make the journey harder than it needs to be.

Sound familiar?

Life is always guiding you in real time, adapting to where you are and adjusting the route. The question is, *are you paying attention to the road and the signals?*

317

Or are you lost in thought?

Guidance doesn't come as a loud announcement. It comes in the quiet moments—through intuition, synchronicities, and subtle nudges. If your mind is too cluttered, you'll miss it.

But there's another layer to this.

Your thoughts aren't just noise. They are also the input into this GPS.

You set the destination through your focus, your beliefs, your intentions. And the guidance unfolds accordingly.

But if your thoughts are scattered, unclear, or constantly changing, the GPS has a harder time mapping a direct route. It will still work—it always works—but the path might be longer, full of unnecessary detours and dead ends.

Without a clear direction, the GPS has nothing to calculate.

You may stay busy, take turns, move from one thing to the next, but without a defined path, you'll feel unmoored—like you're going in circles.

The beauty of this system is that you don't need to know every turn in advance. Just like a GPS, you only need to focus on the next step.

Anxiety comes from trying to figure out the entire route—believing the path is rigid, fearing you'll make a mistake. But the path isn't fixed. It's flexible. It adapts as you move, recalculating with every choice you make.

You don't need to see the full picture. You don't need to know everything in advance.

Let that sink in for a moment.

You don't need to know.

The guidance will come when you need it. One turn at a time.

And here's the best part.

No matter how far off course you go, the GPS doesn't punish you. It doesn't scold you for taking a wrong turn or refuse to help until you've suffered enough.

It simply recalculates—without judgment, without penalty, without the need for repentance.

Because what kind of guidance system would refuse to guide you when you need it most?

It has no opinion on your "mistakes." No resentment toward your detours. It just keeps rerouting, adjusting to where you are now, not where you should have been.

It doesn't dwell on past errors. It doesn't hold grudges. It simply finds the next best path.

That's why you can't fail.

Every wrong turn, every delay, every unexpected detour is just part of the recalculation.

Some paths will take you through difficult terrain. A steep climb, a winding road, unexpected obstacles. These aren't mistakes. They're the fastest way to get you where you need to go.

The guidance sees what you cannot. It knows what's ahead. It understands how challenges shape you into the person who can fully receive what you've been asking for.

Challenges aren't detours. They're preparation.

The key is clarity.

The clearer your thoughts and intentions, the clearer the guidance.

When you're paying attention, trusting the process, and staying aligned with the signals, the journey feels effortless. The right doors open. The right people appear. The right opportunities unfold.

And when you resist, ignore the guidance, or try to force your own way, the road gets harder and longer. Even then, the GPS doesn't abandon you. It simply recalculates. Over and over again. As many times as it needs to.

You are never lost.

You are never beyond the reach of guidance.

The intelligence within you is always working for you.

Because it *is* you.

You only need to decide where you want to go.

Set the destination.

Trust the process.

The way will be shown.

THE UNIVERSE WON'T CHOOSE FOR YOU—THAT'S YOUR JOB

If everything is one thing, then that means everything you are—your awareness, your thoughts, your emotions—comes from it.

And there's something else you have that tells us something critical about the nature of the one thing.

You have free will.

You don't have to move in any specific direction. You get to decide.

You can hesitate, you can change your mind, you can do something completely unexpected.

You have the ability to choose, moment by moment, how your life unfolds.

Which means the one thing must have free will, too.

It has to.

Otherwise, what's the point?

If the one thing already knew exactly how everything was going to play out, that would be boring—and the one thing doesn't like to be bored.

The same way you crave excitement, challenge, and growth, so does the energy that created you.

It doesn't want a predictable, pre-scripted story.

It wants to experience the thrill of discovery with you.

That's why you have free will.

That's why you get to choose.

And here's the part most people don't realize:

This energy is not just passively watching.

It's actively rooting for you.

It's alongside you, moving with you, rearranging reality, doing everything in its power to make things line up for you.

Of course it is.

Because it *is you*.

And you *are it*.

But here's the key: you have to recognize it.

You have to see the choices in front of you.

You have to recognize that you are in control.

And that doesn't just mean the big choices in life.

It means every moment, every decision—how you respond, what actions you take, what thoughts you entertain.

Free will isn't something you use once in a while.

It's happening constantly.

Every single moment, you are choosing.

And that's why presence is everything.

Because only in this moment—right now—can you actually use your free will.

If you're lost in thought, running on autopilot, or stuck in old patterns, you're not truly choosing.

You're just reacting.

But when you are present, you are awake.

And when you are awake, you are free.

You can make good choices, bad choices, or take the middle road.

But the better choices you make—the more aligned choices, the ones that come from the deepest part of you—the more this energy responds.

It's always guiding you back to your own highest potential.

You already know the choices you need to make.

You already know the direction you need to move in.

And no matter how many times you hesitate, stall, or take a detour, the one thing doesn't give up on you.

It doesn't punish you for wrong turns. It just keeps moving with you, always recalibrating, always ready to guide you forward the moment you're ready to step.

But it won't walk the path for you.

It won't force you to wake up.

It won't choose for you.

Because that's the whole point.

You are the one who has to decide.

You're fully in control.

And the life you create—right here, right now—begins the moment you decide to claim it.

YOU ARE BEING GUIDED—
EVEN WHEN YOU DON'T REALIZE IT

Who comes to mind when you hear the word "intelligence"?

For most, it's someone like Einstein or da Vinci—geniuses who tapped into something beyond ordinary limits. Maybe Mozart, who described how entire symphonies would come to him fully formed, as if downloaded from somewhere beyond his own mind.

But what if this intelligence isn't limited to a few extraordinary people? What if it's woven into the fabric of existence itself—available to each of us?

Science tells us that matter, as we know it, has never truly been found. Look closely, and you won't find solid particles—only vibrations, waves, an invisible field of energy shaping reality.

Now imagine that this energy is not just passive, but alive with intelligence. The very force that crafted the universe—planets, galaxies, oceans, you—is the same force flowing through your life, guiding you in ways you may not yet see.

All around you are invisible signals—Wi-Fi, radio waves, satellite feeds—constantly active, completely hidden from your senses. You only know they exist because you see the results when you tune in. But this energy we're speaking of? It's different. It's not separate from you.

Imagine an awareness so vast, so boundless, that it holds everything together effortlessly. Not as something outside of you, but *as* you.

Many describe the brain as a receiver, tuning into this deeper intelligence. Just as a radio picks up a signal, your mind can attune to different aspects of this awareness. But unlike a radio signal, this intelligence is not something external. It's the very fabric of what you are.

You couldn't separate from it even if you wanted to.

It doesn't take effort for awareness to be aware. It simply is—like a constant, silent presence within you.

Maybe you've spent much of your life feeling like something is missing, like there's always something just out of reach—some achievement, some state of mind that will finally make you feel whole.

But what if you're already complete? What if you're already connected to something greater than you ever imagined?

This is why awakening isn't about finding something new. It's about realizing everything you already are. There's nothing to seek, nothing to strive for.

You are already it.

And here's something extraordinary:

This infinite intelligence is not passive. It is alive—alive with an inherent drive for growth, harmony, and evolution. Because it is aware of everything, everywhere, at every moment, it is intimately connected to all that exists.

You, me, every person, every creature, every planet, every star, and every space in between.

It is all that is.

This awareness doesn't just hold everything together. It is actively optimizing reality in real time, for the highest good of itself and of all things.

Think about that.

This intelligence knows every thought, every intention within you and everyone around you. And it's guiding reality in ways beyond comprehension.

This is why people say there are no accidents. Because with this infinite intelligence orchestrating everything, every experience—no matter how small or unexpected—is happening exactly as it should. It cannot be otherwise.

This is why synchronicities happen—those moments when the right opportunity appears, or you meet the perfect person at just the right time. These are glimpses of this energy at work. Optimizing life. Helping you grow. Evolving you.

Pause here.

Let that settle.

Life is not random. Nothing is a coincidence. Every experience, every moment, is part of a greater unfolding.

Yet as humans, our minds are limited. We can never truly grasp the vastness of this awareness. Our brains aren't designed to compute something so boundless.

It's like a fish living in water. The fish depends on water for its entire existence, but has no concept of what water really is.

In the same way, we live within this infinite awareness. It sustains us, but it's beyond our mind's reach.

We can sense it. We can experience it. But we can't fully understand it. And that's okay.

Because we don't need to understand it to *be* it.

Think about how this intelligence expresses itself everywhere you look. In every blade of grass. In every star. In every breath of wind. And in you.

This same awareness flows through you, an inseparable part of all life. It is the awareness behind every experience. The unchanging presence within every thought. The calm in every storm.

This isn't just the universe. It's something greater: it is the infinite intelligence that created the universe.

It is beyond any one name or concept.

Not confined to any religion or belief.

It simply is.

Think back to the times you've felt deep peace. Or a sudden moment of clarity, seemingly out of nowhere. That's this intelligence. That's the moment you tuned in.

And the best part?

It's always available to you, like a signal that never stops broadcasting.

All it takes is a moment of stillness. A pause in the noise of the mind. A deep breath. And you can feel it.

So, what does it mean to be aware of this intelligence?

It means recognizing that you are not merely an individual with limited awareness. You are an expression of this source, a channel through which it knows itself.

Every life, every experience, every form is a unique way that this intelligence expresses and experiences itself.

This awareness is the eternal current running through all things, the invisible thread connecting you to everything else.

It's here. Right now. Flowing through you and everything around you.

Waiting for you to remember.

Breathe.

Listen.

Not to your thoughts, but to the quiet presence behind them.

This is the deeper "I"—the awareness that has always been here.

Waiting.

And the more you tune into it, the more life opens up.

SEPARATION IS JUST
AN OPTICAL ILLUSION

Sitting at the edge of the ocean, I watch the sunlight catch the spray of the waves, and for a brief moment, a rainbow appears.

The colors shimmer, vivid and distinct, each standing out as though separate from the others.

It's beautiful, but I know the truth.

The colors were never separate.

They are just the light, temporarily refracted through water and air.

The rainbow isn't something apart from the light—it *is* the light, appearing in a different form for an instant before fading back into oneness.

This is how life works.

The energy of intelligent awareness—the essence of who you are—takes form as light. And when that light refracts through the prism of existence, it appears as the many colors and forms we experience in life.

Just as the rainbow seems separate from the light, we feel separate from one another, from life, even from ourselves. But this separation is only an illusion—a temporary play of light and form.

Beneath it all, the awareness and the light remain whole, indivisible.

You've felt it before, haven't you? That fleeting glimpse of something greater—only for it to slip away, replaced by the weight of feeling separate again. The mind convinces you that you are just one small, fragile piece of life, struggling to hold yourself together. Anxiety thrives in that illusion. It tells you that you are alone.

But what if that weren't true?

Are you starting to see it now?

What if you've never actually been separate at all?

What if the feeling of separation was just the light temporarily taking form, like the rainbow—a beautiful but fleeting expression of something much greater?

The rainbow doesn't strain to hold its colors. The light doesn't resist its expression. It simply flows, effortlessly, as it is meant to.

And you are no different.

What you experience as your life—your roles, fears, and stories—is the light of intelligent awareness expressing itself for a moment. But that light, and the awareness behind it, is never lost. It's always whole, even as it takes on these temporary forms.

The prism doesn't create the light; it only reveals it. And life is no different.

The challenges, the joys, the fears—they don't change the essence of who you are. They simply reveal the infinite ways your light can express itself. Just as the rainbow fades, so too do the forms we take. But the awareness and light behind it all remain eternal.

Now, take a breath.

Feel it move through you—not as something you do, but as something you are.

That breath is not yours alone.

It is the breeze over the ocean, the wind moving through the trees.

It is the air the trees exhale, given to you freely, effortlessly.

And as you breathe it in, it becomes you.

The breath does not belong to anyone. It is life itself, flowing endlessly, connecting everything. It moves from the ocean to the sky, from the sky to the earth, through every being, carrying with it the quiet truth that there is no separation.

Imagine the light shining through you, illuminating the many colors of your life.

Each thought, each feeling, each moment is just one color in the spectrum. None of them are permanent. None of them define you. Behind them, the light is always there—unchanging, infinite, whole.

What if, in this moment, you stopped trying to hold the colors together?

What if you let them dissolve, trusting that the light of who you are is never lost?

You are not just the colors of the rainbow; you are the source. You are not just the forms of life; you are the infinite energy of awareness itself, playing as light.

You are one light, one source, one being—playing as many.

And in this truth, there is peace.

You are not just part of life. You *are* life itself.

There was never anything to search for.

Only something to remember.

YOU'VE NEVER SEEN REALITY—NOT EVEN ONCE

THE REAL AND THE UNREAL

I know I've mentioned this before, but it's worth emphasizing. For most of my life, I was the ultimate skeptic.

If I couldn't see it, touch it, measure it—it wasn't real.

I thought people who talked about energy, synchronicity, or the idea that "we're spiritual beings having a physical experience" were just indulging in wishful thinking. It was a nice idea, but where was the proof?

I believed in hard facts, in logic, in the things I could prove.

And I believed that doctors, scientists, and professors were the pinnacle of knowledge and expertise. If anyone understood the nature of reality, it was them.

And then something cracked.

It started with quantum physics.

Here was science—real, measurable, undeniable science—telling me that things are not as they seem.

That particles can exist in two places at once.

That an observer can change the outcome of an experiment just by looking at it.

That everything I thought was solid is actually 99.999 percent empty space.

That reality, at its core, isn't physical at all—it is something far stranger.

That was the opening.

That was the first thread I pulled.

And once I started tugging, everything else began to unravel.

I started questioning.

I started researching.

I wanted to understand, and the deeper I went, the more I saw the cracks in what I once believed to be an unshakable reality.

And the more I dug into the data—from psychology to quantum physics, from ancient wisdom to modern neuroscience—the more everything pointed to the same undeniable realization.

It wasn't just one thing. It was *everything*, all converging toward a truth I could no longer ignore.

Then I started noticing things I couldn't explain—small things at first, then bigger ones.

Moments where reality seemed to bend around my awareness.

A cascade of coincidences—one after another, too precise, too interconnected, unfolding in a way that defied all logic.

Problems that solved themselves the moment I stopped obsessing over them.

And I had to ask myself:

Is the world really as fixed and external as I had always believed?

Now take a moment and consider your own life.

You've been taught to trust what you can see and touch.

The money in your account.

The job you have or don't have.

The people in your life.

The problems you wake up thinking about every morning.

You call this reality.

But what if it's nothing more than a temporary projection—a flickering image on a screen?

And what if the things you've been told aren't real—your thoughts, your energy, your awareness—are the only things that have ever actually existed?

Because here's the truth:

Nothing in the physical world is as solid as it seems.

The chair or bed you're sitting on?

99.999 percent empty space.

Just atoms vibrating at a frequency that gives the illusion of solidity.

Your body—the same.

The entire world—the same.

The whole universe—the same.

Even time, which feels like it moves in a straight line, is just your mind stitching together frames of a film that was never linear to begin with.

But one thing is real.

One thing never flickers in and out of existence:

Awareness.

Consciousness.

The part of you that's watching it all unfold.

The part that existed before you had a name, before you learned to believe in the illusion of a separate self.

The part that has always been there, no matter what changed in your life.

And when you start to recognize this—not just intellectually, but experientially—something shifts.

Life stops being something you have to fight, manipulate, or control.

You start to move differently.

You let go more easily.

And strangely, the less you grip onto reality, the more it starts working for you instead of against you.

Because it was never against you to begin with.

You just thought it was real.

This is why things that once seemed impossible start happening effortlessly.

Why problems resolve themselves when you stop fixating on them.

Why, when you finally stop searching for the right words, the perfect thing to say comes to you out of nowhere.

It's because the whole structure of reality bends to match the awareness observing it.

What you focus on expands.

What you believe solidifies.

What you expect manifests.

You don't have to understand every detail of how this works.

Our mind in this dimension isn't built to grasp something this vast, this powerful—and it doesn't need to.

You only have to start noticing.

The way the right person, the right opportunity, the right moment shows up when you stop forcing it.

The way something that seemed broken—stuck, impossible—suddenly moves when you stop gripping so hard.

The way inspiration, insight, or the answer you've been searching for arrives effortlessly the moment you stop chasing it.

Coincidence?

Or proof that the thing you once dismissed as unreal was always the realest thing of all?

And if that's true…

What else might be possible?

EVERYTHING YOU KNOW FEELS REAL—AND THAT'S THE ILLUSION

Step outside on a warm day. Feel the sun on your skin, the ground beneath your feet, the breeze in your hair. Everything feels solid, tangible, real.

But what if it isn't?

As I mentioned, science tells us that what we perceive as physical is actually 99.999 percent empty space. The particles making up your body, your chair, your entire world aren't really things at all, but waves of probability, flickering in and out of existence.

And it gets even weirder. These particles only settle into a definite state when they're observed. Meaning…?

At the deepest level, reality doesn't exist in any fixed way until something—some aware-ness—collapses it into being.

"Reality" is basically rendering in real time as you look at it.

If that sounds impossible, consider this:

A few years ago, I was playing a VR ping-pong game. The paddle felt real in my hand, the ball bounced naturally, and every movement responded exactly as I expected. After a long rally, I felt a little tired and instinctively reached forward to rest my hand on the table—just for a second.

But there was no table.

The moment I shifted my weight, expecting solid support, I lurched forward into nothing, almost falling over. My mind had accepted the illusion so completely that, for a moment, I forgot what was real and what wasn't.

And if a simple headset can trick the brain that easily, what does that say about the reality we're living in now?

Virtual reality is already blurring the line. Soon, it won't just be something you see—it will be something you feel. AI will create immersive, evolving worlds that respond to your thoughts, crafting experiences so convincing that you'll forget you're in a game at all.

And shortly after—if it hasn't already happened by the time you're reading this—implantable brain interfaces will take it even further. Entire realities will be streamed directly into your mind, indistinguishable from waking life. You won't just see or hear them. You'll *experience* them, fully immersed, as if they were real.

Now take that to the next level.

If we humans, with our limited intelligence, can create digital experiences that feel indistinguishable from reality, isn't it possible—even probable—that our own reality is an advanced simulation?

Now imagine what an **infinite** intelligence could—and *would*—create.

This reality. That's what.

A construct of consciousness itself.

It's not a stretch by any means.

Every major field—quantum mechanics, cosmology, neuroscience—points to the same unsettling truth.

Reality isn't what we think it is.

Just like a VR game, this world is an illusion so seamless, so immersive that we mistake it for absolute reality. But once you see through it—once you wake up—you start to move differently.

Lighter. Freer. More aware.

Because now you know.

You were never really inside it to begin with.

FOR THE SKEPTIC: THE SCIENCE THAT WILL BREAK YOUR MIND

(READ IF YOU NEED PROOF. FEEL FREE TO SKIP IF YOU ALREADY KNOW.)

For a long time, I needed proof. Maybe you don't—but if you do, here's what I found.

Science itself—the very thing many assume disproves higher intelligence—has been revealing something far stranger than randomness.

The deeper we look, the more impossible the idea of chance becomes.

The conditions required for life aren't just unlikely—they're mathematically incomprehensible.

The laws of physics, the delicate balance of forces holding the universe together, the structure of DNA—every piece is calibrated with such extreme precision that even the smallest deviation would make life impossible.

Now, consider this:

Imagine taking apart a Boeing 747, reducing it to its smallest pieces, and scattering them in a field.

Then imagine walking away and waiting a trillion years.

Do you think those parts would ever randomly self-organize and reassemble themselves into a fully functional plane?

Wait…

Not just a plane that could fly—*but one that could build more planes itself.*

Because that's what we're dealing with here. Life isn't just organized and structured—it's self-replicating.

A single human cell is more advanced than anything we've ever engineered, capable of repairing itself, adapting, and functioning with an intelligence we barely understand. Yet we're told it all assembled itself by accident.

Try to wrap your brain around that for a minute.

And it's not just biology. The deeper we go—into quantum mechanics, cosmology, mathematics, and consciousness studies—the more the evidence converges.

Randomness doesn't create intelligence.

Randomness doesn't fine-tune the laws of the universe with such exactitude that a shift of one part in a number too large to comprehend would mean no life at all.

The deeper we look, the more obvious it becomes: behind all of this is not chaos, but order.

Not luck, but intelligence.

THE FINE-TUNED UNIVERSE: THE NUMBERS THAT DEFY CHANCE

The very existence of life is a mathematical miracle. The constants of the universe—gravity, electromagnetism, nuclear forces—are so precisely calibrated that even the smallest variation would make life impossible.

This is known as the fine-tuning problem. Scientists have debated it for decades because the odds of these conditions existing by chance are essentially zero.

Gravity, the invisible force holding everything together, is set at exactly the right strength. If it were just **0.000000000000000000000000000000001 percent** stronger, stars would burn too hot and too fast, exploding before planets could ever form. If it were weaker by that same fraction, the universe would have expanded too quickly, and matter would have been too spread out to form anything at all—no galaxies, no stars, no planets, no life. Just a cold, empty void.

And it's not just gravity.

There are twenty-six fundamental constants in physics—numbers that control how reality functions. Every single one of them is fine-tuned to a degree that defies all probability. Change just one, even by the smallest fraction, and the entire universe collapses.

Roger Penrose, one of the most respected physicists in the world, calculated the probability of the universe getting the precise conditions necessary for life by pure chance. His answer?

1 in $10^{10^{123}}$

To put that in perspective, there are only about 10^{80} **atoms** in the entire known universe. The first number is so incomprehensibly long that even if you turned every atom in existence into ink, you still wouldn't have enough to write it down.

But here's what this really means:

That number isn't just small. It's so small that, for all practical purposes, it's effectively zero.

Zero.

There is essentially no chance—none whatsoever—that the precise conditions for life happened by accident.

This is not philosophy. This is not speculation. This is math.

The universe wasn't just some lucky cosmic accident. It was **fine-tuned**—with a precision so extreme that our most advanced physics can barely comprehend it.

So, what does this mean?

The universe is not random. It is fine-tuned—deliberately, precisely, intelligently.

The conditions for life did not arise by accident. The numbers prove it.

This reality was specifically and intelligently designed for conscious beings and entities to exist.

THE BRAIN AS A RECEIVER OF CONSCIOUSNESS: THE MIND BEYOND DEATH

For years, we were told that the brain creates consciousness—that our thoughts, awareness, and experiences are nothing more than the result of neurons firing in a physical organ.

But mounting evidence suggests that this isn't true.

Near-death experience (NDE) research has revealed something extraordinary: people who are clinically dead, with **no measurable brain activity**, report vivid, consistent experiences. They describe leaving their bodies, seeing their surroundings with remarkable accuracy, and feeling a profound sense of timeless awareness.

And some of these cases are impossible to explain under the traditional model of the brain.

PEOPLE BORN BLIND WHO CAN SEE DURING NDES

One of the most mind-blowing discoveries in NDE research involves people who were **blind from birth**—people with no developed visual cortex—reporting detailed visual experiences while clinically dead.

Dr. Kenneth Ring, a psychologist at the University of Connecticut, conducted a study on NDEs in blind individuals. The results? People who had *never seen a single image in their lives* described the world around them in stunning detail while "out of their bodies."

Take the case of Vicki Umipeg.

Born completely blind due to oxygen deprivation at birth, Vicki had never seen light, colors, shapes—nothing.

But during a near-death experience following a car accident, she found herself floating above her body in the hospital. And for the first time, **she could see.**

She later described the hospital, the people in the room, and the events that took place—all of which were later verified as accurate.

A seemingly impossible feat for someone who had never seen in her entire life.

This is profound evidence that consciousness does not originate from the brain.

If the brain were the sole producer of awareness, then how could someone with **no visual cortex**—who had never had a single visual experience—suddenly perceive the world around them in perfect clarity?

The only logical conclusion is that consciousness is **not confined to the physical body**.

And if that's true, then what we are is not limited to the brain.

THE NOBEL PRIZE AND THE END OF LOCAL REALISM: THE UNIVERSE IS NOT LOCALLY REAL

In 2022, the **Nobel Prize in Physics** was awarded to Alain Aspect, John F. Clauser, and Anton Zeilinger for their groundbreaking experiments on quantum entanglement—experiments that confirmed one of the strangest and most profound truths about our universe.

The universe is *not locally real.*

What does that mean?

It means that objects do not have definite properties independent of observation.

And more than that—particles can instantaneously influence one another across vast distances, faster than the speed of light, violating everything we once believed about cause and effect.

We were raised believing in a physical world that exists whether we're looking at it or not. But quantum physics says otherwise. It says that *the act of observation itself helps shape reality.*

This isn't speculation. It's been **proven through experiment after experiment.**

At the quantum level, reality doesn't "exist" in a fixed way.

It exists as a *probability wave*—a cloud of possibilities—until it is observed. Only then does it "solidify" into a definite state.

Einstein was famously disturbed by this. He called it *"spooky action at a distance"* because it defied everything we understand about how reality should work.

But it's real. It's been tested. It's why quantum mechanics powers the very devices you're using right now.

And this brings us to the most profound question of all:

If the universe isn't locally real, then what *is* it?

If objects don't have independent existence until they are observed…

Then *who* or *what* is the ultimate observer holding it all together?

Because this is the inescapable truth: everything we once thought of as solid reality is instead a construct, a beautifully orchestrated illusion.

An illusion fine-tuned to allow life and consciousness to exist.

And once you see that—once you understand that reality is not something happening *out there*, but something emerging from within awareness itself—everything dissolves.

You stop feeling small. You stop believing you are separate.

Because you are not just *in* the universe.

You *are* the Universe, experiencing itself.

THE EARTH GAME:
LIFE'S ILLUSION AND YOUR PLACE IN IT

You're playing the Earth game. I know—it feels so real.

The sights, the sounds, the emotions, the struggles… That's the beauty of it.

It's designed to feel real. But at its core? It's an illusion—a creation of consciousness itself.

Think about a dream.

When you're in it, it feels vivid, immersive, real.

But here's the truth: every character, every detail, every moment in that dream was created by one mind.

Yours.

Now expand that idea.

This reality works the same way.

Everything you see, everything you experience, and everything you struggle with is part of an unfolding process—an experience designed to teach you, shape you, and wake you up to something deeper.

And like any experience, this one has a structure. This game—the Earth game—is set up much like a school and a playground, just like the ones we build for our children. Some parts are structured, designed for learning and growth. Other parts are open, free, meant for exploration and play.

But here's the thing: this game is hard.

It's designed to be.

And the first challenge? Forgetting.

When you enter the game, you forget that it's a game.

You forget that you chose this.

You forget that you are something far greater than the character you're playing.

That's part of the setup.

If you remembered from the start, there wouldn't be any real challenge.

No discovery.

No expansion.

Forgetting is what makes the game real. It's what makes every choice, every experience, every struggle feel meaningful.

But it also means that at some point, you'll feel lost.

You'll believe you are the character. You'll take the game seriously—too seriously.

And that's when the suffering begins.

Because the truth is, struggle is what moves you forward. Every challenge, every setback, every moment of suffering—it's all designed to teach you, to refine you, to break the illusions that keep you stuck.

At first, suffering feels unavoidable.

You resist, you fight, you try to make the game bend to your will.

But it doesn't work like that.

The more you resist, the harder it gets. The more you cling, the more it hurts.

But here's the paradox: suffering is necessary—*until you realize it isn't*.

At some point, after enough pain, enough struggle, you start to see the pattern.

You recognize that suffering isn't something the game is doing to you—it's something you're holding onto. And the moment you stop fighting it, something shifts.

You start moving through challenges instead of getting stuck in them.

You stop taking the struggles personally and start seeing them as part of the process.

And when you do that, the game stops feeling so punishing. The suffering fades, not because life suddenly becomes easy, but because you stop needing it to be hard in order to grow.

And like any game, there are rules, fixed conditions that shape the experience. Gravity exists. Time moves forward. Cause and effect operate without fail. These aren't barriers; they're the framework of the game.

Then there are guidelines. These aren't enforced, but they make the game smoother, more enjoyable, and infinitely easier to navigate. The same things you'd tell a child on a playground apply here:

Play. Don't hurt others. You're not in competition. Just go have fun.

If there's a line, wait your turn. Share. Be kind. Learn from mistakes.

And when you fall, get back up.

Because that's the game.

And just like in school, if you don't pass a lesson, you have to repeat it.

It doesn't matter how long it takes—you will keep encountering the same lesson, just in different forms, until you finally learn it.

Then, and only then, do you move forward.

At first, it might seem like bad luck. The same frustrations, the same obstacles, the same kind of people showing up in your life over and over again. But this isn't random. The game isn't punishing you—it's reflecting back what you still need to see.

Some people stay on the same level for years, unaware that the only way forward is to change how they play. They fight the game. They blame the other players. They think it's unfair, rigged, stacked against them.

But the game isn't against anyone. It's just giving you the exact experience you need.

And the moment you see it? The moment you finally stop repeating the same old patterns?

The pattern breaks, and something new begins.

What once felt like struggle now feels like expansion.

What once repeated endlessly now disappears, and new doors open.

This is the design. The game is always leading you forward.

And here's something profound: you are not just playing the game.

You are also creating it.

Every thought, every intention, every choice shapes what you experience next.

Most people play the game unconsciously, reacting instead of creating, repeating instead of expanding. But once you become aware of the illusion, something changes.

You start playing differently.

You stop trying to "win" a game that was never meant to be won.

Because there is no final win. No finish line. No end point where everything is suddenly perfect.

The point of the game isn't to escape it.

It's to live it—fully, deeply, with awareness.

With presence.

Each day that you engage with life—without fear, without resistance, with curiosity and openness—you are winning.

Because winning isn't about reaching the end.

Winning is waking up within the game and realizing you're free to play.

To move with trust. To meet challenges with presence instead of fear. To experience everything—pain, joy, love, loss—as part of the adventure.

And once you see this, something extraordinary happens.

You stop struggling. And you start playing.

With freedom. With lightness. With joy.

The game was never meant to break you.

It was meant to set you free.

THE BRAIN IS NOT THE SOURCE OF YOU—CONSCIOUSNESS IS

Now let's take this understanding of the illusion even further—straight to the brain itself.

Just like everything else in the material world, the brain is part of the illusion.

It's not the source of who you are, just like your phone isn't the source of the information, photos, or videos you see on it.

The brain is simply a receiver—a tool designed to download and process consciousness so you can experience this human life.

Think about how your smartphone works. We call it "smart," but is it really? The phone itself isn't doing much except for processing all the inputs. Most of the actual information isn't stored in the phone—it's downloaded from the cloud. The phone is just the device that temporarily processes the data so you can interact with it.

In the same way, the brain isn't the source of your thoughts, memories, or intelligence. Those aren't stored in the brain.

They're stored in the "cloud" of consciousness—the infinite field of awareness that exists beyond the physical.

Now imagine something goes wrong with your phone—maybe the SIM card gets corrupted, or the internal hardware fails. It can't connect or download anything anymore. But does that mean the signal from the cloud has stopped flowing?

Of course not.

The signal is still there, constant and unchanging. The issue is with the phone, not the source.

The same is true for the brain.

If the brain is damaged, impaired, or even ceases to function, consciousness remains untouched.

Consciousness is still flowing, perfect and infinite.

The brain is simply the "receiver," and even when it stops working, nothing is truly lost.

All the data—the photos, the messages, the apps—it's still stored in the cloud, safe and ready to be accessed.

And so it is with consciousness.

Everything that makes you you—your essence, your experiences, your memories—exists beyond the brain. It's all stored in the infinite field of awareness, untouched by anything that happens to the physical form. The brain and body are just temporary tools, part of the illusion, designed to let you experience this reality.

But here's the deeper truth: even the brain itself—the tool you perceive it to be—is just a creation of consciousness.

It's part of the same illusion as the rest of the material world.

At first glance, the brain seems like the engine of thought, emotion, and experience. But if you go small enough—down to the quantum level—what you find isn't solid at all. The neurons, the electrical impulses, the molecular structures… They dissolve into energy and potentiality. The deeper we look, the less "physical" the brain actually is.

The brain, *like everything else*, is a projection of consciousness within this illusion.

The brain and body are not you. They are tools—beautifully intricate, but temporary and illusory. Who you are is the awareness behind it all.

The consciousness that never dies.

Never gets damaged.

Never disappears.

You are the infinite field of awareness, not bound by the limitations of form, but free, whole, and eternal.

And here's the most liberating realization:

Everything you are—everything you've ever been—is already complete.

The illusion makes you believe you are a fragment searching for wholeness, but you are—and always have been—the entirety of consciousness.

This isn't just a concept—it's the truth waiting to be seen.

Once you see it, you'll know.

The brain is not the source.
The body is not the container.
And nothing about you is ever lost.

YOU'VE NEVER TOUCHED ANYTHING— AND WHAT THAT MEANS ABOUT WHO YOU ARE

I remember the first time I read this: we never actually touch anything.

I sat there, staring at the words, thinking, *Wait... what? No way. That can't be true.*

It felt impossible.

How could I not be touching the phone in my hand, the chair I was sitting on, or even my own skin? I mean, I could feel them, plain as day.

But as I sat with it and dug deeper into the science, I realized it was true—and it left me in awe. It wasn't just fascinating; it fit perfectly with everything I had already started to understand about the nature of reality.

Here's how it works: Atoms, the building blocks of everything we perceive as physical, are mostly empty space.

Picture an atom as a football stadium. Its nucleus, the dense center, would be like a marble sitting at midfield, and the electrons orbiting it would be somewhere out in the stands. The rest? Vast emptiness.

So, if atoms are mostly empty, why does anything feel solid?

It's all because of the electromagnetic force.

When you "touch" something, the electrons in your body repel the electrons in the object. This repulsion is what creates the sensation of touch—but no atoms actually make contact.

Think of two powerful magnets with the same poles facing each other. No matter how hard you try to press them together, they push back.

That's exactly what's happening when you feel something, whether it's the phone in your hand or the ground beneath your feet.

But here's the thing: this is more than just a quirky scientific fact.

It reveals something profound—something that shifts everything you thought you knew about yourself.

You have never touched anything in your entire life.

And nothing has ever touched you.

Let that sink in.

The real you, the awareness reading these words, is literally untouchable.

Not just physically.

Nothing in this world—not fear, not pain, not loss, not anything—has ever actually reached the essence of who you are.

Your body can be hurt.

Your mind can be overwhelmed.

But you, the awareness behind it all?

Literally untouchable.

Just like the illusion of touch is created by forces repelling each other, the struggles of life—pain, anxiety, suffering—are only experienced at the surface level.

They feel real, just like touch feels real.

But the deeper truth is that they never reach the real you.

You are beyond all of it.

You are awareness itself.

You always have been.

Untouchable.

Unbreakable.

Infinite.

LIFE IS A DREAM YOU HAVEN'T REALIZED YOU'RE DREAMING

On a recent morning, I woke up from an incredible experience.

In a dream, I had found myself back at my childhood home. Everything was exactly as I remembered: the familiar drapes in the living room, the wood-grained doors, the smooth countertop in the kitchen. Every little detail was there—the knick-knacks my parents had collected over the years, the scent of my mother's vanilla candle lingering in the air, even the texture of the carpet beneath my feet.

At first, I didn't question it.

It all felt so clear, so real.

It was comforting to be there.

But then something didn't add up.

I knew my parents had sold this house years ago, and I remembered hearing that the new owners had remodeled it completely. Yet here I was, standing in a house that no longer exists, surrounded by unchanged furnishings from my childhood.

I knew it couldn't be real.

That realization was like a crack in the foundation.

The details around me—so convincing just moments before—suddenly seemed to unravel.

And then it hit me:

I was dreaming.

The moment I recognized the dream for what it was, something extraordinary happened.

I didn't wake up.

I stayed in it.

Fully conscious within the dream.

I looked around in awe, taking in the incredible detail.

Once again, I ran my hand over the countertop—smooth, solid, cool beneath my fingertips.
I pressed my toes into the carpet, noticing its texture beneath my feet.
I smelled the comforting scent of home, unchanged and unmistakable.
I noticed the sunlight streaming through the windows, warm against my skin.

I turned to my daughters, who were there in the room with me, playing as if it were any ordinary day.

Smiling, I said, "Girls, we're in a dream right now!"

They just giggled and made silly faces, as if they somehow understood.

My mind had recreated *everything*—the walls, the doors, the furniture, the smells, the sounds. Even the presence of my family felt so real, so tangible.

This is incredible, I thought. *How is this even possible?*

Then, I saw my father closing the drapes in their bedroom, so I walked down the hall, eager to tell my parents, "We're in a dream!"

But the moment I stepped into their bedroom and made eye contact with them, the dream began to dissolve.

Not suddenly.

Gently.

Like mist lifting from a lake at sunrise.

The walls, the furniture, even my parents themselves seemed to drift up and away, and before I knew it, my eyes fluttered open, and I found myself lying in bed.

For a moment, I just lay there, still immersed in the vividness of what I had just experienced.

I was staring at the ceiling, my body in bed, but my mind still lingering in the dream. The sheets beneath my fingers, the air in the room—it all felt just as real.

But had the dream not felt the same?

Hadn't I touched, smelled, and experienced every detail as vividly as I was now?

And then, the realization struck me—not as a thought, but as something deeper. A knowing.

The dream wasn't just an incredible experience.

It was a mirror.

And what it revealed was something I've known since my awakening:

This waking life—this reality—is no different.

I looked around my bedroom—the ceiling above me, the soft light filtering through the window. I ran my fingers over the sheets again, feeling their texture, just as I had felt the countertop in the dream.

It all seemed so solid, so real.

But was it?

I remembered a quote by Einstein:

"Reality is an illusion, albeit a very persistent one."

And in that moment, I saw it so clearly:

Just like a dream, this reality has been created within infinite awareness.

Most people never realize it. They live as though life is happening *to* them, trapped in the script of their conditioning, reacting instead of creating, surviving instead of truly living.

But the moment you awaken, your perspective expands.

Life is no longer something to endure—it becomes something to explore.

And you?

You become the lucid dreamer.

This is the essence of *lucid living*.

It's not just about realizing that life is a dream—it's about engaging with it fully awake, just as you would in a lucid dream.

And yet, beneath it all, there is something even more profound.

In the dream, I remember noticing what didn't change.

What remained constant, even as the details of the dream dissolved?

My awareness.

It was there through every moment—steady, silent, untouched by the shifting illusion.

And when I woke up?

It was still there. Watching. Present.

The same awareness that had been in the dream.

The same awareness that has always been there.

And that's when I saw it clearly:

Awareness is the one and only thing that is not an illusion.

Everything else—the thoughts you think, the emotions you feel, the roles you play, even the universe itself—moves like a shifting scene in a dream. It appears vivid, immersive, and deeply felt, yet none of it is permanent. None of it is what you truly are.

But your awareness?

That's what's real.

Steady. Silent. Untouched by the chaos.

The awareness you feel as "yours" is not separate from the infinite awareness of the Supreme Mind.

It is one and the same.

This is why awakening is called awakening: because it is the process of waking up.

It's the realization that the life you've been taking as reality is no more solid than the dream I had that night.

When you wake up from a dream, you know the dream wasn't real.

But your awareness remains.

Awakening is the same.

You wake up to the truth of who you are—the awareness behind everything you experience.

Your awareness stays the same, but the way you perceive everything changes.

When you realize that you are not your mind, not your thoughts, not your emotions, not the roles you play, and not the circumstances of your life, but the awareness behind all of it, you begin to experience life in an entirely different way.

The fears and stories that used to weigh you down lose their power.

You stop gripping so tightly.

You stop clinging to outcomes as though everything depends on them.

You live fully.

Freely.

Knowing that what truly matters—the awareness that you are—has always been untouched by the illusion.

So, the next time you find yourself spiraling in fear or worry, pause.

Ask, "Who is aware of this?"

The answer is simple.

That awareness—the one silently observing everything—is the real you.

And it has never been afraid. Never been broken. Never been separate.

To live with this awareness is to embrace lucid living.

To be fully awake to the truth of who you are—while engaging with life's dream as the lucid dreamer you were meant to be.

So…

Are you ready to wake up?

Because the dream is waiting.

Waiting for you to realize…

It was never real to begin with.

YOU'VE BEEN LIVING THE DREAM—
YOU JUST DIDN'T KNOW IT

The other day, while I was driving through my town, looking at the trees swaying in the wind and the puffy white clouds drifting against the bright blue sky, just taking in the moment, these words popped into my head:

Livin' the dream.

And I laughed. Because for the first time, I realized—I'm actually doing it.

Most people say that phrase with sarcasm. They mean the opposite. It's what you hear when someone's buried in stress, stuck in a routine they don't love, just trying to get through the day.

"Hey, Mike, how's it going?"

"Oh, you know, man… Just livin' the dream."

They both laugh. But they don't mean it. It's just something to say—an inside joke about how life feels more like something to get through than something to enjoy.

But once you awaken—once you really see life for what it is—you actually *are* living the dream.

Not because life suddenly becomes perfect. Not because everything is easy. The challenges don't disappear. You still wake up, drink your coffee, take care of your responsibilities. You still create, build, do your work in the world. You still deal with the ups and downs of being human.

But everything feels different.

It's all happening from a different place inside you.

The invisible weight you didn't even realize you were carrying?

It's gone.

That quiet pressure—the sense that life is something to struggle through, to manage, to survive… It disappears.

Because you see the game now. You see the dream. And instead of feeling trapped in it, you get to play.

And here's what that really means:

It means you stop living in resistance. You stop waiting for some future moment when you can finally relax, finally enjoy, finally feel free.

Because you realize … you don't have to wait.

You don't have to escape anything.

You can live fully right here, right now.

And when you do, something shifts.

You experience life from a place of deep presence.

A place of inner stillness.

Everything you do—every step, every word, every action—now flows from that stillness.

You look, you listen. And when action is needed, you take it.

Even in the hard moments, in the uncertainty, in the middle of everything life throws at you.

And the mind is quiet.

At first, it feels strange—almost eerie. You've been so used to the constant noise, the racing thoughts, the endless commentary, that when it's suddenly gone … it almost feels like something is missing.

But it's not missing. It's just at peace.

The wild horse that once ran you ragged has finally been tamed.

It's no longer thrashing, no longer dragging you in every direction.

Now, it stands beside you.

Strong, powerful, and steady.

Awaiting your command.

And that's when you understand…

You really are livin' the dream.

YOU WERE NEVER ASLEEP

Life isn't a problem to be solved.

It's an experience to be lived.

It exists not for you to conquer or control, but for you to experience yourself—beyond fear, beyond identity, beyond limitation.

The only reason you are here is to be here.

To wake up within the dream, to see beyond the illusion, to live as the pure awareness you truly are.

Every experience you've ever had—every moment of anxiety, every doubt, every synchronicity—has been life itself calling you back to presence.

A whisper from the infinite saying:

Wake up.

You are not separate.

You are not small.

You are Life itself.

You don't need to chase meaning.

You don't need to force your way into control.

You don't need to grasp at something outside of you.

Because the truth is…

You knew.

You knew this reality would be dense. You knew it would be hard. You knew there would be pain, separation, and fear.

You knew there would be moments when the memory of your true self would feel so distant, you'd think you were lost.

But even before you arrived here…

You chose this.

Not from the mind. Not from fear. But from the vast, limitless awareness that you truly are.

You knew that through this experience—through the challenge, the resistance, the forgetting—you would grow.

You would expand.

You would take that infinite spark of divine consciousness and bring it here, into this world, into this moment, into this body, into this life.

Take a moment to let that sink in.

You chose this. Out of all possibilities, you said yes.

You knew the risks—and you did it anyway.

That's how powerful you are.

That's how courageous your soul is.

But here's the thing…

You didn't just say yes to life.

You said yes to contrast.

To duality.

To growth.

Because growth doesn't happen in perfection. It doesn't happen in the light alone, where there's nothing to push against.

It happens *in the fire*.

It happens when you face the discomfort, when you walk through the challenge, when you rise, again and again, stronger than before.

And up until this point, that discomfort may have looked like anxiety.

Maybe it felt like a heaviness in your chest or a racing mind that wouldn't stop.

Maybe it felt like you'd been trapped, stuck in a loop, forgetting who you are and wondering why you're here.

But here's the truth you've come to understand now…

That anxiety wasn't working against you.

It was always working for you.

It was a doorway. A catalyst. It was your soul's way of saying…

Wake up.

You are not small.

You are not your fears.

You are not the noise of your mind.

You are the awareness behind it. The strength beneath it. The soul who came here to remember.

You are already deep, deep in awakening.

It's happening *right now*.

The awakening you came here for, the transformation you chose—it's already unfolding.

This moment, as you read these words, is part of it.

Feel that. Notice what's happening inside you right now—that stirring, that pull, that subtle recognition.

That's it. That's the awakening.

You're remembering.

You're reconnecting.

And now…

Now, as you read these words, something very powerful but undeniable is happening.

Notice that the more you even try to connect with that feeling of anxiety, the more distant it becomes.

Try right now.

Try to connect with that old feeling of anxiety.

Go ahead.

Try to bring it up.

You'll notice…

The more you try, the more distant it becomes.

Like a shadow dissolving in the light.

Like a wisp of smoke you try to capture, but it slips between your fingers, dissolving into nothingness.

The energy of anxiety is fading because it no longer serves you.

You don't need it.

You've outgrown it.

It's not an aspect of who you are anymore.

It's an aspect of who you *used to be*.

And now…

You recognize the illusion for what it is.

An awakened dream.

A dream that once felt so real, so overwhelming, so absolute…

But now, you see through it.

You see that you were never trapped.

Never small.

Never separate.

You have transformed.

You've fought battles no one else could see.

You've carried weight no one else could feel.

Think about all the challenges you've been through.

All the crazy stuff you thought would destroy you.

And yet…

You're still here.

Still rising.

Still expanding.

Still saying yes.

You're not waiting for awakening.

You're in it.

You're doing it.

Right now.

So, honor that. Honor the courage it took to leave perfection and step into this world.

Honor the strength it takes to keep choosing growth—to do the hard work of shedding the heavy layers of false beliefs, to keep saying yes to this life, even when it feels impossible.

Because you're not weak.

You're not lost.

You are the soul who said…

Yes.

Yes to life.

Yes to challenge.

Yes to growth.

Yes to awakening.

And here you are.

You're such a fuckin' badass.

Don't you *ever* forget that.

This is the moment you remember who you are.

This is the moment you say yes to yourself.

Not someday. Not later.

Right now.

Breathe it in.

This is it.

YOU'RE AWAKE.

www.ingramcontent.com/pod-product-compliance
Lightning Source LLC
Chambersburg PA
CBHW080129150626
46550CB00018B/2872